Praise for
Moments of the Spirit:

Dov Peretz Elkins is one of the most spiritual people I know. His creative work in education and nourishing human beings is known throughout the world. He has made another useful contribution through this marvelous collection of spiritual quotations. His work continues to be chicken soup for my soul.

—Jack Canfield, coauthor, *Chicken Soup For the Soul*

Emerson said, "Next to the originator of a good sentence is the first quoter of it." Rabbi Dr. Dov Peretz Elkins has a genius for quoting very good sentences indeed. Every *bon mot* in this collection is a gem of wisdom or wit, yet not a one is stale. Elkins might be the "first quoter" and he's surely the finest quoter.

—Rabbi Stephen Listfield

ALSO BY DOV PERETZ ELKINS

Chicken Soup for the Jewish Soul

A Shabbat Reader

Moments of Transcendence

Jewish Guided Imagery

Forty Days of Transformation

Meditations for the Days of Awe

Shepherd of Jerusalem

A Tradition Reborn: Sermons and Essays on Liberal Judaism

Humanizing Jewish Life: Judaism and the Human Potential Movement

Prescription for a Long and Happy Life

My Seventy-Two Friends: Encounters with Refuseniks in the USSR

God's Warriors: Dramatic Adventures of Rabbis in Uniform

Clarifying Jewish Values

Jewish Consciousness Raising

Experiential Programs for Jewish Groups

Teaching People to Love Themselves

Glad To Be Me: Building Self-Esteem in Yourself and Others

Twelve Pathways to Feeling Better About Yourself

CHILDREN'S BOOK
Seven Delightful Stories for Every Day (ages 3 to 6)

MOMENTS
of the SPIRIT

MOMENTS
of the SPIRIT

Quotations to Inspire,
Inform and Involve

Jan 2011

To Beth,

love
uncle Denny

Compiled by Dov Peretz Elkins

Growth Associates Publishers
Princeton, New Jersey

©2003 Dov Peretz Elkins

For information regarding permission to reprint material from this book please mail, fax or email your request in writing to Growth Associates Publishers, at the address below.

ISBN 0-918834-24-4
Library of Congress Control Number: 2003102047

Printed in the United States of America.
All rights reserved.

This book was composed in MetaPlus and Adobe Caslon and designed by Maia Coven Reim.

For a complete catalog of books contact:
Growth Associates Publishers
212 Stuart Road East
Princeton, NJ 08540-1946
609-497-7375
Fax: 609-497-0325
E-mail: GrowthAssociates@earthlink.net
www.DPElkins.com

DEDICATION

Dedicated to three special people—our grandchildren
Who give their grandparents endless spiritual moments

Ari Jack Levin Elkins

Mollie Jo Stadlin

Leila Sol Adatto

With unbounded love

CONTENTS

CONTENTS

x

CONTENTS

PREFACE

A note regarding gender

A large number of the quotations in this book use the male gender. One could easily get the impression that the editor of the book ignores the modern trend to write in gender-sensitive style. Were it not for the fact that the wisdom contained herein was written in the pre-modern age, I am certain that the totality of the quoted matter would use words like "human" instead of "man," "humanity" instead of "mankind," etc. However, since an editor does not have the right change or modify the words of great writers, thinkers and teachers—by law or by moral right—I have reluctantly permitted myself to present these thoughts in their original, and ask the reader's patient and compassionate understanding, and request that wherever such phrases as "man" and "mankind" appear, that the reader merely make a mental substitution with words that would be used in the 21st century. —*Editor*

Appreciation

Janice Berg's assistance with several African and African-American spiritual quotations is greatly appreciated.

Maia Coven Reim has worked closely with me in designing this book, as she has on several of my previous publications, with her usual professionalism, artistic flair, and exceptional cooperation.

I am grateful for all the help I have received from the above, and feel blessed by the embarrassment of riches in the large library of reading I have been privileged to enjoy over many decades.

Dov Peretz Elkins
Erev Pesah, 5763
April, 2003

I have always imagined that paradise will be
a kind of library.
Jorge Luis Borges, writer (1899-1986)

Isn't it funny the way some combinations of words
can give you "almost apart from their meaning"
a thrill like music?
—*C.S. Lewis (1898-1963)*

ACCEPTANCE

When a person feels that he is truly accepted by another, as he is, then he is free to move from there and to begin to think about how he wants to change, how he wants to grow, how he can become different, how he might become more of what he is capable of being.

—THOMAS GORDON

Healing for the whole person must ... be based on balance and synthesis of opposites in the psyche, not the repression, denial, or projection of what one does not like. Mental health depends on self-acceptance at least as much as on self-improvement.

—FRANCES VAUGHAN

We want to be accepted just as we are, but at the same time we want the other person to win the right to our acceptance of him.

—HOWARD THURMAN

Too many of us have a need to be accepted no matter what the cost.

—SHIRLEY CHISHOLM

I learned early that loss and pain and death are a part of the fabric of a richly textured life, and that pain can sometimes underscore and intensify a deep and loving relationship.

—MIRIAM DECOSTA-WILLIS

ACCOUNTABILITY

Know these things—from whence you come ... and to whom you are to give account.

—TALMUD

Sunlight is the most powerful disinfectant.

—LOUIS BRANDEIS

Daniel Webster was once asked what was the greatest thought that had passed through his marvelous brain. He answered, "My accountability to God."

—ANONYMOUS

Be responsible for our actions, and take responsible actions.

—HAKI MADHUBUTI

Your job is to help somebody.

—THE DELANY SISTERS

Some people want to take curtain calls without being part of the performance.

—ALTON MADDOX

I cannot walk upon your legs, or you upon mine. I cannot breathe for you, or you for me; I must breathe for myself, and you for yourself.

—FREDERICK DOUGLASS

Remember, wherever you are and whatever you do, someone always sees you.

—MARIAN ANDERSON

ACTION

There should be less talk; a preaching point is not a meeting point. What do you do then? Take a broom and clean someone's house. That says enough.

—MOTHER TERESA

Lose this day loitering—'twill be the same story
Tomorrow—and the next more dilatory;
Each indecision brings its own delays,
And days are lost lamenting o'er lost days.
Are you in earnest? seize this very minute—
Boldness has genius, power and magic in it,
Only engage, and then the mind grows heated—
Begin it, and then the work will be completed!

—JOHANN WOLFGANG VON GOETHE

Thought and analysis are powerless to pierce the great mystery that hovers over the world and over our existence, but knowledge of the great truths only appears in action and labor.

—ALBERT SCHWEITZER

When I rest, I rust.

—GERMAN PROVERB

A tree that reaches from your embrace grows from one small seed.
A structure over nine stories high begins with a handful of earth.
A journey of a thousand miles starts with a single step.

—TAO DE CHING

A centipede was asked which foot it puts down first, and it became paralyzed, unable to walk.

—*ANONYMOUS*

Leave your home and go out into the wicked world. It is easy to be a saint in such surroundings as your household, where you are shielded against temptation. But get yourself to places in which your virtue will be challenged at every step by the sirens that lurk everywhere. If you can maintain your integrity there, you will have shown yourself to be a true saint.

—*THE DUBNO MAGGID*

Every man is born into the world to do something unique and something distinctive and if she or she does not do it, it will never be done.

—*BENJAMIN E. MAYS*

Up you mighty race, you can accomplish what you will!

— *MARCUS GARVEY*

When do any of us do enough?

—*BARBARA JORDAN*

Men must not only know, they must act.

—*W.E.B. DU BOIS*

God never appears to you in person but always in action.

—*GANDHI*

I don't base my actions on popularity. If you're in a position of leadership, you can't wait to determine how it's going to affect you in terms of good or bad. You have to lead and do what you think is good.

—*L. DOUGLAS WILDER*

One who can do nothing, does nothing.

—*SENAGALESE PROVERB*

Words are nothing but words; power lies in deeds. Be a person of action.

—*MALI GRIOT MAMADOU KOUYATE*

God gives nothing to those who keep their arms closed.

—*MALIAN PROVERB*

Throughout history it has been the inaction of those who could have acted, the indifference of those who should have known better, the silence of the voice of justice when it mattered most, that has made it possible for evil to triumph.

—*HAILE SELASSIE*

In Germany, they first came for the communists, and I didn't speak up because I wasn't a communist.

Then they came for the Jews, and I didn't speak up because I wasn't a Jew.

Then they came for the trade unionists, and I didn't speak up because I wasn't a trade unionist.

Then they came for the Catholics and I didn't speak up because I wasn't a Catholic.

Then they came for me—and by that time there was nobody left to speak up.

—REV. MARTIN NIEMOLLER

ADVERSITY

A person who cannot move and lead a somewhat normal life because she is pinned under a boulder has more time to think about her hopes than someone who is not trapped that way.

—ANONYMOUS

If we had no winter, the spring would not be so pleasant; if we did not sometimes taste of adversity, prosperity would not be so welcome.

—ANNE BRADSTREET

There is no education like adversity.

—BENJAMIN DISRAELI

There are times in everyone's life when something constructive is born out of adversity. There are times when things seem so bad that you've got to grab your fate by the shoulders and shake it. Setbacks are a natural part of life, and you've got to be careful how you respond to them. When times get tough, there's no choice except to take a deep breath, carry on, and do the best you can.

—LEE IACOCCA

Real difficulties can be overcome; it is only the imaginary ones that are unconquerable.

—BENJAMIN FRANKLIN

In the midst of winter, I finally learned that there was in me an invincible summer.

—ALBERT CAMUS

There are things which can help a person under any circumstances of life: A person's closeness to his family, tradition and faith, as well as love, literature, science, and one's sense of humor. These things, when brought down to a level of utter simplicity, help to enlighten and purify man's actions as well as the motivation behind his actions.

—NATAN (ANATOLY) SHARANSKY

Some say that when you cannot go forward, you must pass under, but the Musarniks [devotes to a movement to promote ethics] say, "What you cannot go through you must rise above."

—NOTA ZVI HIRSCH FINKEL

Adversity makes the man, prosperity the monster.

—VICTOR HUGO

The one who most truly can be accounted brave is one who most knows the meaning of what is sweet in life and what is terrible, then goes out undeterred to meet what is to come.

—SOCRATES

Struggle is strengthening. Battling with evil gives us the power to battle evil even more.

—OSSIE DAVIS

Thinking your way through a problem is better than wishing your way through.

—COLEMAN YOUNG

I have born thirteen children and seen them all sold into slavery, and when I cried out with all my mother's grief none but Jesus heard.

—SOJOURNER TRUTH

There may be obstacles, but keep going because the struggle is continuous.

—RACHEL ROBINSON

The pain of life may teach each of us to understand life and in our understanding of life, to love life.

—HOWARD THURMAN

ADVICE

Some folks welcome advice so long as it doesn't interfere with their previous plans.

—ANONYMOUS

Listen and learn from people who have already been where you want to go. Benefit from their mistakes instead of repeating them. Read good books... because they open up new worlds of understanding.

— BEN CARSON

If you are hiding, don't light a fire.

—ASHANTI PROVERB

One thing alone I charge you. As you live, believe in life!

—W.E.B. DU BOIS

Advice is like snow; the softer it falls, the longer it dwells upon, and the deeper it sinks into the mind.

—SAMUEL TAYLOR COLERIDGE

Fundamentally, the therapist is a teacher of need—satisfying, conflict-resolving communication.

—HOWARD CLINEBELL

AFFIRMATION

God wove a web of loveliness
Of clouds and stars and birds,
But made not anything at all,
So beautiful as words.

—ANNA HEMPSTEAD BRANCH

The measure of mental health is the disposition to find good everywhere.

—RALPH WALDO EMERSON

I can live for two months on one good compliment.

— MARK TWAIN

Beware of people who slap you on the back—they probably want you to cough up something.

—ANONYMOUS

Speak ill of no man, but speak all the good you know of everybody.
—*BENJAMIN FRANKLIN*

The deepest principle in human nature is the craving to be appreciated.
—*WILLIAM JAMES*

The realm of silence is large enough beyond the grave.
—*GEORGE ELIOT*

As long as one can admire and love, then one is young forever.
—*PABLO CASSALS*

Whenever you tell good news, Elijah the Prophet is with you.
—*NACHUM OF CHERNOBIL*

Every human being is endowed by God with two eyes. With one he is expected to look at his virtues, his excellence, his desirable qualities. With the other eye, he is to turn inward to see his own shortcomings in order to correct them.
—*RABBI ISRAEL SALANTER*

Of the dead, speak only good.
—*DIOGENES LAERTIUS*

God created humans to admire the splendor of the world. Every author, be he ever so great, needs praise; every author, regardless of who he is, desires the praise of his work.
—*HEINRICH HEINE*

How beautiful upon the mountains are the feet of the messenger who announces peace, who brings good news, who announces salvation.
—*BIBLE (ISAIAH 52:7)*

Never give anyone a dollar's worth of blame without a dime's worth of praise.
—*COLONEL L.P. HUNT*

Anticipate the good so you can enjoy it.
—*CONGOLESE PROVERB*

Out of the sighs of one generation are kneaded the hopes of the next.
—*JOAQUIM MACHADO DE ASSIS*

My soul has grown deep like the rivers.
—*LANGSTON HUGHES*

I must slide down like a great dipper of stars and lift men up.
—*LUCILLE CLIFTON*

Believe the best about people; and if you're wrong, you've only made a mistake on the side of love.
—*ROBERT SCHULLER*

A hammer sometimes misses its mark—a bouquet never.
—*MONTA CRANE*

By emphasizing that which is good in people and in the world, and by bringing the positive to the fore, the evil is superceded by the good, until it eventually disappears.
—*RABBI MENACHEM SCHNEERSON*

If you wish your merit to be known, acknowledge that of others.
—*ANONYMOUS*

The music that can deepest reach, and cure all ill, is cordial speech.
—*RAPLH WALDO EMERSON*

Pleasant words are a honeycomb,
Sweet to the soul and healing to the bones.
—*BIBLE (PROVERBS 16:24)*

One kind word can warm up three winter months.
—*JAPANESE PROVERB*

The supreme happiness in life is the conviction that we are loved.
—*VICTOR HUGO*

ALTRUISM

The will to live is animal, the will to let live is human, the will to help others is divine.
—*ANONYMOUS*

If you don't look out for others, who will look out for you?
—*WHOOPI GOLDBERG*

Everybody can be great because anybody can serve.

—DR. MARTIN LUTHER KING, JR.

During an earthquake, the owner of a hilltop farm looked down to see a mighty tidal wave in formation. He knew that all his neighbors toiling in the low fields would be submerged within minutes if something were not done. Quickly the farmer set fire to his rice fields and loudly rang his bell. When his neighbors below heard the bell and looked up to see the flames, they rushed up to help him. When they reached the top of the hill, they saw the farms where they had been working only moments before engulfed by the massive tidal wave.

—LAFCADIO HEARN

Service is the price you pay for room on this earth.

—SHIRLEY CHISHOLM

AMBIVALENCE

Ambivalence is when your luxurious yacht is sinking with your enemy on it.

—ANONYMOUS

AMERICA

I think the true discovery of America is before us. I think the true fulfillment of our spirits, of our people, of our mighty and immortal land, is yet to come. I think the true discovery of our own democracy is still before us ... and that this glorious assurance is not our living hope, but our dream to be accomplished.

—THOMAS WOLFE

I sought for the greatness of America in her commodious harbors and her ample rivers, and it was not there. I sought for the greatness of America in her rich mines and her vast world of commerce, and it was not there. I sought for the greatness of America in her democratic Congress and her matchless Constitution, and it was not there. Not until I went into the churches of America and heard her pulpits flame with righteousness did I understand the secret of her genius and power. America is great because America is good; and if America ceases to be good, America will cease to be great.

—ALEXIS DE TOCQUEVILLE

What have I or those I represent to do with your national independence? I am not included within the pale of this glorious anniversary. Your high independence only reveals the immeasurable distance between us. The blessings which you this day rejoice are not enjoyed in common. This Fourth of July is yours, not mine. You may rejoice; I must mourn.

—*FREDERICK DOUGLAS*

America will destroy herself and revert to barbarism if she continues to cultivate things of the flesh and reject the higher virtues.

—*NANNIE BURROUGHS*

I see America, not in the setting sun of a black night of despair ahead of us.

I see America in the crimson light of a rising sun, fresh from the burning, creative hand of God.

I see great days ahead, great days possible to men and women of will and vision.

—*CARL SANDBURG*

We shall nobly save or meanly lose the last, best hope of earth.

—*ABRAHAM LINCOLN*

They came to our shores a lone shelterless few,
They drank of our cup, and they e'er found us true.
But the serpent we cherished and warmed at our breast,
Has coiled round our vitals; let time tell the rest.

—*MIAMI INDIAN*

As an American citizen I feel it born in my nature to share in the fullest measure all that is American. I sympathize in all my hopes, aspirations, and fruitions of my country. In a word, I am an American citizen, I have a heritage in each and every provision incorporated in the Constitution of my country.

—*T. THOMAS FORTUNE*

The meaning of America is the possibilities of the common man.

—*W.E.B. DU BOIS*

I love America more than any other country in the world, and, exactly for this reason, I insist on the right to criticize her perpetually.

— *JAMES BALDWIN*

America is essentially a dream, a dream as yet unfulfilled. It is a dream of a land where men of all races, of all nationalities and all creeds can live together as brothers.

—*MARTIN LUTHER KING, JR.*

America has abandoned the strong woman of spirituality and is shacking up with the harlot of materialism.

—*REV. JOSEPH LOWERY*

America is the greatest nation in history. Measure it however you like. We are a mere five percent of the world's population, but produce thirty percent of the goods and services. In science, mathematics, and medicine, we walk away with most of the Nobel Prizes. In the Olympics, our amateurs defeat the state-supported athletic elite of other nations. And with America doing eighty-five percent of all world giving, you'd think we invented charity.

—*WALTER E. WILLIAMS*

America is moral guerrillas who simply decide to do what appears to be right heedless of the immediate consequences.

—*MARIAN WRIGHT EDELMAN*

ANGER

Do not make friends with a person who is given to anger.

—*THE BIBLE*

Speak when you are angry and you will make the best speech you will ever regret.

—*AMBROSE BIERCE*

When the kettle boils, it spills hot water down its side.

—*MIDRASH*

Anger is an acid that can do more harm to the vessel in which it is stored than to anything on which it is poured.

—*ANONYMOUS*

When dealing with one's passions, one's child, and one's spouse, one should push them away with one's left hand and draw them near with one's right.

—*TALMUD*

The Buddha compared holding on to anger to grasping a hot coal with the intent of throwing it at someone else. You, of course, are the one who gets burned.

—JOAN BORYSENKO

A wit is an angry man in search of a victim.

— OSCAR WILDE

Since I have tamed my anger, I keep it in my pocket. When I need it, I take it out.

— RABBI PINHAS OF KORETZ

Anger has a real biological cost, but only for subjects with high hostility.

—REDFORD WILLIAMS

Give a person a dollar and he will bless you with six blessings; but if you tranquilize an angry person with soft words, he will bless you with eleven blessings.

—TALMUD

Don't be afraid to be as angry or as loving as you can, because when you feel nothing, it's just death.

—LENA HORNE

Defile not your souls by quarrelsomeness and petulance. I have seen the white become black, the low brought still lower, families driven into exile, princes deposed from their high estate, great cities laid in ruins, assemblies dispersed, the pious humiliated, the honorable held lightly and despised, all on account of quarrelsomeness. Glory in forbearance, for in that is true strength and victory.

—MOSES MAIMONIDES

At 50, one learns that anger is overrated. It is false to say older people are kinder, but the smart ones are. As we age, we realize that none of us will be here in 100 years, so it is not necessary to do each other in: The "problem" will take care of itself.

—KAREN DECROW

Anybody can become angry—that is easy; but to be angry with the right person, and to the right degree, and at the right time, and for the right purpose, and in the right way—that is not within everybody's power and is not easy.

—ARISTOTLE

All that we are is the result of what we think. How then can one escape being filled with hatred, if the mind is constantly repeating: "He misused me, he hit me, he defeated me, he robbed me?" Hatred can never put an end to hatred; hate is conquered only by love.

—BUDDHA

Anger begins in folly and ends in repentance.

—ROBERT BOHN

When a man angers you, he conquers you.

—TONI MORRISON

Anger is like the blade of a sword. Very difficult to hold for long without harming oneself.

—CHARLES JOHNSON

Muffle your rage. Get smart instead of muscular.

—ROY WILKINS

ANIMALS

Once when Reb Zusya was traveling cross-country collecting money to ransom prisoners, he came on a room in an inn in which there was a large cage with all kinds of birds. Sensing how the birds wanted to fly through the spaces of the world again, Zusya opened the cage and freed these prisoners too. When the angry innkeeper returned and took him to task, Zusya cited the verse from the Psalms, "His tender mercies are over all His works." The innkeeper beat Zusya until his hand got tired and threw him out of the house, but Zusya went on his way serenely. Zusya's whole life was a web of need and anguish, yet he accepted his suffering with such love that he did not recognize it as suffering.

—MAURICE FRIEDMAN

ANTI-SEMITISM

Anti-Semitism is contagious. The racist, the bigot, the fanatic begins by hating Jews but does not stop with Jews. This much we have learned from history: When Jews are attacked, the entire human community ought to feel unsafe.

—ELIE WIESEL

When a Jew is beaten up, it is humanity that is falling to the ground.

—FRANZ KAFKA

I have a crazy theory about anti-Semitism—that non-Jews have never forgiven the Jews for introducing moral and ethical concerns into the realms of religion. Before Judaism, man could have his religion and his immorality in the same package, but the Jews said that their worship of God had to include a respect for man—this was a terrific albatross. The Christian religion bought this from the Jewish Rabbi Christ and some Christians are angry that the Jews, through Christ, imposed this terrific burden upon them.

— *KENNETH CLARK*

You can't insure the Jewish will to live by fear of death. You can't insure a Jewish future by fear of anti-Semitism.

—*HAROLD SCHULWEIS*

The most vivid impression to be gained from a reading of medieval allusions to the Jew is of hatred so vast and abysmal, so intense that it leaves one gasping for comprehension.

— *JOSHUA TRACHTENBERG*

They can't forgive us for giving the moral law, the Torah, which is diametrically opposed to their philosophy of life.

—*MAURICE SAMUEL*

The world is now feeling what Jews have always felt. A recent film about nuclear destruction made it clear that where the Jews have been in the past, the whole world now is today. The Jews have always lived at the edge of uncertainty; now it's the whole world that lives there. The Jews have always been in danger; now the whole world is in danger. The Jews have always depended on the whim of some ruler or other anywhere in the world; now the whole world depends on the whim of some ruler or other anywhere in the world.

—*ELIE WIESEL*

It's a free world; you don't have to like Jews, but if you don't I suggest that you boycott certain Jewish products like the Wasserman Test for syphilis; digitalis, discovered by Dr. Nuslin; insulin, discovered by Dr. Minofsky; chlorohydrate for convulsions, discovered by Dr. Lifreich; the Shick Test for diphtheria; vitamins discovered by Dr. Funk; streptomycin, discovered by Dr. Z. Woronan; the polio pill by Dr. A. Sabin and the polio vaccine by Dr. Jonas Salk.... You want to be mad? Be mad! But I'm telling you, you ain't going to feel so good!

—*SAM LEVENSON*

If you ever forget you're a Jew ... [an anti-Semite] will remind you.

—*BERNARD MALAMUD*

Hath not a Jew eyes? Hath not a Jew hands, organs, dimensions, senses, affections, passions? Fed with the same food, hurt with the same weapons.... If you prick us, do we not bleed? If you tickle us, do we not laugh? If you poison us, do we not die?

—*WILLIAM SHAKESPEARE (The Merchant of Venice)*

The only place the extreme right and the extreme left join hands is around the throat of the Jew.

—*DAVID POLISH*

Dictators are anti-Semitic because they know or sense that liberty is Semitic in origin and character.

— *ABBA HILLEL SILVER*

Were I of Jew blood, I do not think I could ever forgive the Christians; the ghettoes would get in my nostrils like mustard or lit gunpowder.

—*ROBERT LOUIS STEVENSON*

Discrimination is the common element between the anti-Semite and the anti-Zionist. The former says that every man is equal except the Jew; the latter says the every nation is equal except Israel.

—*ABBA EBAN*

The destructive workings of Judaism in the bodies of other nations can at bottom only be ascribed to the perpetual effort to undermine the importance of personality throughout the nations who are their hosts, and to subvert the will of the multitude.

—*ADOLF HITLER*

I would call anti-Semitism a poor man's snobbery.

—*JEAN PAUL SARTRE*

If my theory [of relativity] is correct, the Germans will call me a German and the French will say I'm a Jew; if I'm wrong, the French will call me a German, and the Germans will call me a Jew.

—*ALBERT EINSTEIN*

Strange inconsistency! to persecute in the name of religion those who had given the religion.

—*MADISON PETERS*

Oh, monstrous doctrine! O, what infernal counsel! Contrary to prophets, hostile to apostles, practically subversive to all piety and grace!—a sacrilegious harlot of a doctrine, impregnated with the very spirit of falsehood, conceiving anguish, and bringing forth iniquity!

—*ST. BERNARD OF CLAIRVAUX*

From our very beginning in Egypt, we were hated. And all during our history, we have been hated because, as a people, we remember.... [What is the source of anti-Semitism?] Too rich, too poor. Jews are capitalists. Communists. Too anti-establishment. Too mainstream.... As long as there are people whose pleasure it is to be anti-Semitic, our response must be to become more Jewish, to become better Jews, more aware of our obligations and our destiny.

—ELIE WIESEL

Anti-Semitism is a disease of Europe and white Christianity. And Afro-American victims of the fiery cross must not be dragged into the vortex of anti-Semitism.

—CLAUDE MCKAY

One of the more unprofitable strategies we could ever adopt is to join in history's oldest and most shameful witch hunt, anti-Semitism.

—BAYARD RUSTIN

ANXIETY

The reason why worry kills more people than work is that more people worry than work.

—ROBERT FROST

The reason why our public life is so disordered and our private life so hampered by anxiety is because we will not be still and know God.

—A. MAUDE ROYDEN

In these times of uncertainty, we are often prone to succumb to anxiety. But we can turn to the Word of God and find the power to overcome it—and get on with the business of trusting in the Lord and abiding in His peace.

—TONYA BOLDEN

APATHY

If you look at the stars and yawn,
If you see suffering and don't cry out,
If you don't praise and you don't revile,
Then I created you in vain, says God.

—AHARON ZEITLIN

People take what is happening almost for granted. They read about thousands of people being destroyed, and then they turn to the stock tables as if nothing had really happened. People take the attitude, "If it happens to other people, it's not going to happen to me." In that way, I would say that civilization has hardened men's hearts more than it has softened them.... You become less sensitive to other people's anguish if you hear about it all the time. "You see it every day, you have to make peace with it." That is how modern man feels.

—ISAAC BASHEVIS SINGER

When Satan wants to attack religion, he afflicts it with a yawn.

—CHAIM GREENBERG

The opposite of love is not hate, but indifference in times of evil. Indifference to evil is evil. Neutrality always helps the killer, not the victim.

—ELIE WIESEL

[Most people] read of injustice, feel outrage, have their dinner, and go to sleep!

—VOLTAIRE

It may be that the greatest tragedy of this period of social transition is not the glaring noisiness of the so-called "bad people," but the appalling silence of the so-called "good people."

—MARTIN LUTHER KING, JR.

Truth is not only violated by falsehood; it may be equally outraged by silence.

—HENRI FREDERIC AMIEL

The most important thing I learned in my life and under those tragic circumstances [in Nazi Germany] is that bigotry and hatred are not the most urgent problems. The most urgent, the most disgraceful, the most shameful and the most tragic problem is silence.

—JOACHIM PRINZ

It was not a large and active group of anti-Semites that made possible Hitler's persecution of Jews, but a small group which was permitted to act by an indifferent public.

—RICHARD GELWICK

What hurts the victim most is not the cruelty of the oppressor, but the silence of the bystander.

—ELIE WIESEL

There is an evil which most of us condone and are even guilty of: indifference to evil. We remain neutral, impartial, and not easily moved by the wrongs done to other people. Indifference to evil is more insidious than evil itself, more dangerous.... To do justice is what God demands of every man: it is the supreme commandment, and one that cannot be fulfilled vicariously.

—ABRAHAM JOSHUA HESCHEL

The worst sin toward our fellow creatures is not to hate them, but to be indifferent to them. That is the essence of inhumanity.

—GEORGE BERNARD SHAW

ARROGANCE

There is no room for God in one who is full of oneself.

—ANONYMOUS

"Persons can meet, but mountains never." When one considers oneself just a human being, pure and simple, and the other does so too, they can meet. But if the one considers oneself a lofty mountain, and the other thinks the same, then they cannot meet.

—RABBI ZEVI YEHUDA

ART

Once you love an art enough that you can be taken up in it, you are able to experience an echo of the great creative act that mysteriously had given life to us all. It may be the closest any of us can get to God.

—KENT NERBURN

Good art is nothing but a replica of the perfection of God and a reflection of God's art.

—MICHELANGELO

Oh, how great and glorious art is! It shows more devotion than a friend, it is more faithful than a mistress, more consoling than a confessor.

—ALEXANDER DUMAS

Art is a refining and evocative translation of the materials of the world.

—GWENDOLYN BROOKS

It seems to me that the best art is political and you ought to be able to make it unquestionably political and irrevocably beautiful at the same time.

—TONI MORRISON

All art makes us more powerfully whom we wish to become.

—AUDREY LOURDE

Art is not simply works of art. It is the spirit that knows beauty, that has music in its soul and the color of sunsets in its handkerchief, that can dance on a flaming world and make the world dance too.

—W.E.B. DU BOIS

Art is confrontational in that it challenges someone's way to thinking.

—DANNY GLOVER

Art is animated by invisible forces that rule the universe.

—LEOPOLD SENGHOR

Because a genuine artist, no matter what he says he believes, must feel in his blood the ultimate enmity between art and orthodoxy.

—CHINUA ACHEBE

An artist is a sort of emotional or spiritual historian. His role is to make you realize the doom and glory of knowing who you are and what you are. He has to tell, because nobody else can tell, what it is like to be alive.

—JAMES BALDWIN

It is important that the artist identify with the self-reliance, hope and courage of the people about him, for art must always go where energy is.

—ROMARE BEARDON

If we had a better sense of art and a stronger sense of history, we wouldn't have to accept the idea that entertainers are artists.

—WYNTON MARSALIS

ASCETICISM

The holy law imposes not asceticism. It demands that we grant each mental and physical faculty its due.

—YEHUDAH HALEVY

Asceticism is the denial of the will to live.

—ARTHUR SCHOPENHAUER

A student came to a teacher and claimed that he was qualified to be a rabbi. The teacher asked him, "What are your qualifications?" He responded, "I have disciplined my body so that I can sleep on the ground, eat grass, and be whipped three times a day." The teacher responded, "See yonder ass. It sleeps on the ground, eats the grass, and is whipped no less than three times a day. Up to the present you may qualify to be an ass, but certainly not a rabbi.

—*HASIDIC TALE*

ASSERTIVENESS

True peace can only be the result of assertion of rights. Nice doesn't mean meek.

—*BENJAMIN BLECH*

When one sins against another, the injured party should not hate the offender and keep silent.... It is the duty to inform the offender and say, "Why did you do this to me? Why did you sin against me in this matter?"

—*MOSES MAIMONIDES*

Make yourselves sheep and the wolves will eat you!

—*BENJAMIN FRANKLIN*

My greatest ambition is to secure a speaking part in my own life.

—*ASHLEIGH BRILLIANT*

ASSIMILATION

We may, should, imitate gentile ways that are good and just; we must not imitate foreign ways that are ignoble and immoral.

—*TALMUD*

Why conceal the fact that you are a Jew? Be a real Jew, obeying the law of justice and love, and you will be respected. Be just, truthful, and loving to all, as the Torah teaches. Give food to the hungry and clothes to the naked; comfort those who mourn and care for the sick; give counsel and help to all in sorrow and need.

—*SAMSON RAPHAEL HIRSCH*

The Jews in Germany were more German than the Germans.

—*GEORGE BERNARD SHAW*

Why sprinkle blood of lamb on the doorposts of Israel during the plague of the first born? Obviously God knew anyway which house was Jewish. The lamb was an Egyptian god, and it took courage to announce defiantly that they believed in God and not in Egyptian paganism. Only if the Jews were courageous enough to announce their Judaism publicly were they fit for redemption.

—ABRAHAM COHEN

There is a difference between assimilating and being assimilated. To assimilate means to absorb things from outside while keeping one's own identity. To be assimilated means to let oneself be absorbed by the outside world. I can eat all the roast beef I want without turning into an ox, because I have a mechanism in me that absorbs everything that is good and nourishing in the roast beef and makes it part of me.

—SOLOMON SCHECHTER

ASSUMPTIONS

Consciousness-raising consists of turning assumptions into questions.

—GEORGE LEONARD

ATHEISM

In Frankfurt I met a watch that did not believe in watchmakers.

—HEINRICH HEINE

A Jewish atheist knows full well what the God in whom he doesn't believe expects of him.

—LEONARD FEIN

Ethical atheists are like cut flowers. They look beautiful, they have a nice scent for a while, but they are moved from their roots and are dying.

—JOSHUA LIEBMAN

Atheism leads not to badness but only to an incurable sadness and loneliness.

—W. P. MONTAGUE

The atheist is a man who has no invisible means of support.

—LORD TWEEDSMUIR

ATTITUDE

God asks no man whether he will accept life. That is not the choice. You must take it. The only question is how.

—HENRY WARD BEECHER

There is nothing either good or bad, but thinking makes it so.

—WILLIAM SHAKESPEARE

The most handicapped person in the world is a negative thinker.

—HELEN KELLER

We are not victims of the world we see. We are victims of the way we see the world.

—SHIRLEY MACLAINE

Life is 10% what you make it, and 90% how you take it.

—ANONYMOUS

The mind is its own place, and in itself can make a heaven of hell, and a hell of heaven.

—JOHN MILTON

Your success and happiness lie in you.... Resolve to keep happy, and your joy and you shall form an invincible host against difficulties.

—HELEN KELLER

One who says it cannot be done should not interrupt one who is doing it.

—CHINESE PROVERB

A happy person is not a person in a certain set of circumstances, but rather a person with a certain set of attitudes.

—HUGH DOWNS

To be upset over what you don't have ... is to waste what you do have.

—KEN KEYES, JR.

It is one of life's laws that as soon as one door closes, another opens. But the tragedy is that we look at the closed door and disregard the open one.

—ANDRE GIDE

Make the most of the best, and the least of the worst.

—ROBERT LOUIS STEVENSON

Most folks are about as happy as they make up their minds to be.
—*ABRAHAM LINCOLN*

Everything can be taken from a man but one thing: the last of the human freedoms—to choose one's own attitude in any given set of circumstances, to choose one's own way.
—*VIKTOR FRANKL*

We see things not as they are, but as we are.
—*BENJAMIN FRANKLIN*

If you are pained by any external thing, it is not this thing that disturbs you, but your own judgment about it. And it is in your power to wipe out this judgment now.
—*MARCUS AURELIUS*

The greatest discovery of any generation is that human beings can alter their lives by altering their attitudes of mind.
—*ALBERT SCHWEITZER*

Funny is an attitude.
—*FLIP WILSON*

When you get negative thoughts, use that as inspiration to empower your positive self.
—*ROLANDA WATTS*

The right mental attitude is more important than knowledge.
—*DENNIS KIMBRO*

Find the good. It's all around you. Find it, showcase it. You'll start believing in it.
—*JESSE OWENS*

AUTHENTICITY

What counts is sincerity and honesty. If you can fake these, you've got it made.
—*GEORGE BURNS*

The word "individual" can trace its source to the word "individe," which means "undivided." An individual is a man who does not split himself by presenting one face to an applauding public and a completely contrary countenance to his inner being.
—*SAUL TEPLITZ*

A wise student whose lips and heart violate the work of the mouth is not worthy to be called a wise student.

—*TALMUD*

The root of all conflict between me and my fellow human is that I do not say what I mean and I do not do what I say.

—*MARTIN BUBER*

No one will fool you as much as you will fool yourself.

—*YIDDISH SAYING*

More often than not we don't want to know ourselves, don't want to depend on ourselves, don't want to live with ourselves. By middle life most of us are accomplished fugitives from ourselves.

—*JOHN GARDNER*

A favorite form of social entertainment for European aristocrats was the masked ball. Guests came in costume, most prominently with a face mask. At midnight, off came the masks, leaving the guests revealed in their own identities. The Latin word "persona" comes from the word for "mask," as if to say that if you would truly be a person, you must wear a mask. Do our masks ever come off? Do we have a midnight hour when we have the courage to stand barefaced in front of our loved ones and ourselves?

—*RABBI SIDNEY GREENBERG*

Only if one knows oneself, has no illusions about oneself, and understands every existing thing in relation to oneself, will one find true peace of mind.

—*MOSES MAIMONIDES*

AUTHORITY

Those who conduct an argument by appealing to authority are not using their intelligence; they are just using their memory.

—*LEONARDO DA VINCI*

Authority is the source of knowledge, but our own reason remains the norm by which all authority must be judged.

—*JOHANNES SCOTUS ERIGENA*

AWAKE

In biblical days prophets were astir while the world was asleep; today the world is astir while church and synagogue are busy with trivialities.

—*ABRAHAM JOSHUA HESCHEL*

In the ordinary waking state ... one does not see the real world.... He lives in hypnotic sleep.... "To awaken"... means to be "dehypnotized."

—P.D. OUSPENSKY

Humanity is asleep, concerned only with what is useless, living in a wrong world.

—SANAI OF AFGHANISTAN

We do not want to attain truth. We do not want anyone to break our dream.

—SWAMI VIVEKANANDA

Our conscious thinking has all the characteristics of a dream. The representation it gives us of the world is illusory.... In [a higher awareness state], consciousness is awakened in a way which is no longer exclusive or attached.... It is liberated from usual hypnosis.

—HUBERT BENOIT

Disciples of Buddha said to him one day, "Are you a god?" He answered, "No, I am not a god." They asked, "Are you an angel?" He answered, "No, I am not an angel." They asked, "Are you a prophet?" He answered, "I am not a prophet." "Then," they pressed, "What are you?" Buddha replied, "I am awake."

—BUDDHIST TEACHING

AWARENESS

If the doors of perception were cleansed, everything would appear as it is, infinite.

—WILLIAM BLAKE

Do not look back in anger, or forward in fear, but around in awareness.

—JAMES THURBER

The real voyage of discovery consists not in seeking new landscapes, but in having new eyes.

—MARCEL PROUST

Earth is crammed with Heaven.
And every common bush afire with God.
But only he who sees
Takes off his shoes.

—ELIZABETH BARRETT BROWNING

Sometimes you can see a whole lot just by looking.

—YOGI BERRA

AWE

We teach children how to measure, how to weigh. We fail to teach them how to revere, how to sense wonder and awe. The sense of the sublime, the sight of the inward greatness of the human soul and something which is potentially given to all men, is now a rare gift.

—ABRAHAM JOSHUA HESCHEL

God does not die when we cease to believe in a personal deity, but we die on the day when our lives cease to be illuminated by steady radiance, renewed daily, of a wonder, the source of which is beyond all reason.

—DAG HAMMERSKJOLD

We don't have to strive to make beauty in our lives, or look far to find it. When the mind is still, we can see a magnificence in even the most ordinary things —the vividness of a sunset, the warmth of a smile, the simplicity of serving a cup of tea. We can see new life and new growth. Each thing is different from all others, each moment is unique. And we can see decay and passing. This is the natural course of things and has its own exquisite kind of clarity.

— JOSEPH GOLDSTEIN & JACK KORNFIELD

For me, everything is still mysterious, even the most natural things. When I throw a stone and it falls back to the earth I know that it's gravity, but isn't that a great mystery? Just because you've seen a thing ten times should it stop being mysterious? A writer gave me once a short story about a man with a chopped-off head who could still talk. I said to him, "Isn't it marvelous enough that a man with a head can talk?

—ISAAC BASHEVIS SINGER

The world will not starve for want of wonders, but only for want of wonder.

—G.K. CHESTERTON

Awe enables us to perceive in the world intimations of the divine, to sense in small things the beginning of infinite significance, to sense the ultimate in the common and the simple, to feel in the rush of the passing the stillness of the eternal.

— ABRAHAM JOSHUA HESCHEL

The invariable mark of wisdom is to see the miraculous in the common.

—EDWARD ERICSON

The most beautiful thing we can experience is the mysterious. It is the source of all true art and science. He to whom this emotion is a stranger, who can no longer pause to wonder and stand rapt in awe, is as good as dead—his eyes are closed.

—ALBERT EINSTEIN

To be alive, to be able to see, to walk, to have houses, music, paintings ... it's all a miracle. I have adopted the technique of living life from miracle to miracle.

—ARTUR RUBINSTEIN

It is a wholesome and necessary thing for us to turn again to the Earth and in the contemplation of her beauties to know the sense of wonder and humility.

—RACHEL CARSON

Love all God's creation, the whole and every grain of sand in it. Love every leaf, every ray of God's light. Love the animals, love the plants, love everything. If you love everything, you will perceive the divine mystery in things. Once you perceive it, you will begin to comprehend it better every day. And you will come at last to love the whole world with an all-embracing love.

—FYODOR DOSTOYEVSKY

If the stars were to shine once every 1000 years, they would evoke awe —we'd be awestruck. Since they shine daily, we ignore them. What's granted easily is taken for granted.

—RALPH WALDO EMERSON

Intelligence is not so much the capacity to learn as the capacity to wonder.

—OLIVER WENDELL HOLMES

Education begins in wonder and ends in wisdom.

—JOHN DEWEY

The scale of Hubble's images is so enormous and so incredible that it makes human events, even who wins the World Series, seem to be of no importance by comparison. Nobody says, "I've found God by looking at Hubble images." But it can be a religious experience when you look at the awe and beauty of creation.

—JOHN BAHCALL

Our life is a faint tracing on the surface of a mystery.

—ANNIE DILLARD

BAR/BAT MITZVAH

I have long admired the Hebrew ceremony of the Bar Mitzvah, which is the symbolic and public drawing of a new contract, or a statement of mutual expectations. At the end of the thirteenth year, the Jewish boy becomes a Jewish man, assuming responsibility and religious duty. He does not do so without preparation. This moment has been a goal long established, and he is prepared for the acceptance of responsibility by rigorous training and discipline as prescribed by Hebrew law. It is unfortunate that a similar event cannot take place in the life of every teen-ager.

—THOMAS HARRIS

Probably even at Mount Sinai, some smart aleck father or son said, "My boy doesn't have time to show up for the preliminaries. He has to play in a tennis tournament, but he'll be there when the Ten Commandments are handed down." And I can imagine God saying, "You want to play tennis? They've got the best courts in the world in Egypt."

—RABBI DAVID POLISH

The Bar Mitzvah ceremony is significant because it confirms the young man in his growing identity at a most appropriate time and in a setting of the greatest possible significance.... This ritual has far greater significance than is apparent on the surface. Bar Mitzvah is a *rite de passage*. It allows a young man to formalize his passage from childhood to adolescence.... Not only does the ceremony formalize the child's entry into manhood, it also is the occasion of the parents' entry into middle age. Parents are as much in need of a *rite de passage* as are children. They often "enjoy" Bar Mitzvah more than their children.

—RICHARD RUBINSTEIN

But there are also problems: children who come to the brink of tears because of the pressure "to perform"; rabbis who find themselves in the position of asking unruly teenage guests to leave services; and parents who have to empty out their savings accounts so that their son's or daughter's b'nai mitzvah celebration matches the style of their neighbors, even as it deviates radically from the spirit of Jewish tradition.

—RABBI JEFFREY SCHEIN

BEAUTY

We all share beauty. It strikes us indiscriminately.... There is no end to beauty for the person who is aware. Even the cracks between the sidewalk contain geometric patterns of amazing beauty. If we take pictures of them and blow up the photographs, we realize we walk on beauty every day, even when things seem ugly around us.

—MATTHEW FOX

I was never a beauty. There was a time when I was sorry about that, when I was old enough to understand the importance of it and I overheard people referring to it. Looking in any mirror, I realized it was something that I was never going to have. Then I found what I wanted to do in life and being called pretty no longer had any importance. It was only much later that I realized that not being beautiful was a blessing in disguise. It forced me to develop my inner resources. I came to realize that women who cannot lean on their beauty and need to make something on their own have the advantage.

—GOLDA MEIR

Beauty is like the digit zero. Alone, it is nothing, but if other numbers — the values of good character — are placed in front of it, it increases their value ten-fold.

—RABBI AVRAHAM PAM

The little girl who saw a rainbow for the first time said, "What's it advertising?" So has our society become blinded to the beauties of nature by its preoccupation with utilitarian values.

—ANTHONY FRIES PERRINO

Commend not a man for his beauty; neither abhor a man for his outward appearance.

—BEN SIRA

You are beautiful; but learn to work, for you cannot eat your beauty.

—CONGOLESE PROVERB

Pretty can only get prettier, but beauty compounds itself.

—"DUKE" ELLINGTON

Who is rich? One who is beautiful in deeds.

—TALMUD

BELIEF

To the believer, there are no questions. To the non-believer, there are no answers.

—RABBI ISRAEL MEIR HA-KOHEN

A belief is something that I hold. A conviction is something that holds me.

—ANONYMOUS

Believe nothing because a so-called wise man said it.
Believe nothing because a belief is generally held.
Believe nothing because it is written in ancient books.
Believe nothing because it is said to be of divine origin.
Believe nothing because someone else believes it.
Believe only what you yourself judge to be true.

—BUDDHA

As a person thinks, so is that person.

—BIBLE (PROVERBS 23:7)

There are two ways to be fooled: One is to believe what isn't so; the other is to refuse to believe what is so. It is not clear that there are any limits to the human mind other than those we believe in.

—WILLIS HARMAN

What you think you are is a belief to be undone.

—A COURSE IN MIRACLES

The belief system ... can transform expectations into physiological change. Nothing is more wondrous about the fifteen billion neurons in the human brain than their ability to convert thoughts, hopes, ideas and attitudes into chemical substances. Everything begins therefore with belief. What we believe is the most powerful option of all.

—NORMAN COUSINS

When civilizations fail, it is almost always man who has failed—not in his body, not in his fundamental equipment and capabilities, but in his will, spirit and mental habits.... Men and civilization live by their beliefs and die when their beliefs pass over into doubt.

—PHILLIP LEE RALPH

Be careful what you believe to be true, because so long as you believe it, then for you it is true. But your beliefs about reality, your "attributions of reality" or your "ontic projections," profoundly influence your life. Of especial importance for healthy personality are those beliefs about limits, about your weaknesses and lack of aptitude. If you believe you cannot do without food for three days, go on a five day fast. Challenge your own beliefs, especially about yourself and others, because what you believe to be true about self and others functions more as persuasion than as description.

—SIDNEY JOURARD

Those who believe they can do something and those who believe they can't are both right.

—HENRY FORD

If people can be persuaded to believe absurdities, they can be persuaded to commit atrocities.

—VOLTAIRE

To be a great champion you must believe you are the best. If you're not, pretend you are.

—MUHAMMAD ALI

BIBLE

For 2000 years the Jewish People preserved the Book, even as the Book preserved the People.

—DAVID BEN GURION

I do not read the Bible not because I don't understand it, but because I do understand it.

—MARK TWAIN

What a sculptor does to a block of marble, the Bible does to our finest intuitions.

—ABRAHAM JOSHUA HESCHEL

Why do we find new meaning in the Bible each time we come back to its chapters, while we seldom find new meaning by rereading a novel? Perhaps it is because, like the old paintings of the great masters, the Scriptures "soak up" something from all the people who have interacted with them over the ages.

—ELIE WIESEL

A man was once packing his suitcase for a trip, and he said to his wife, "I have nearly finished packing. All I have to put in are a guide book, a lamp, a mirror, some fine poetry, and a few biographies." "You will never put all that into your bag," his wife objected. "Oh, yes I can," he said, and he put his Bible into the corner of his suitcase.

—*SAUL TEPLITZ*

The Bible is mankind's greatest privilege. It is so far off and so direct, categorical in its demands and full of compassion in its understanding of the human situation. No other book so loves and respects the life of man. No loftier songs about his true plight and glory, about his agony and joys, misery and hope, have ever been expressed, and nowhere has man's need for guidance and the certainty of his ultimate redemption been so keenly conceived. It has the words that startle the guilty and the promise that upholds the forlorn. And he who seeks a language in which to utter his deepest concern, to pray, will find it in the Bible.

—*ABRAHAM JOSHUA HESCHEL*

The Bible is more famous than known.

—*VOLTAIRE*

Seek out the book of the Lord, and read.

—*BIBLE (ISAIAH 34:16)*

On becoming more acquainted with the world of the Bible, I began to understand so much more of what I had been taught, and of what I had learned about life and about the people in mine.

—*DUKE ELLINGTON*

BIGNESS

It's the little things in life that make you happy—but only after you learn that you can't get your hands on the big ones.

—*ANONYMOUS*

It's amazing how much of our lives is determined not by big decisions, but by little ones that pile up on us.

—*RICHARD DEVOSS*

No one ever stubbed a toe against a mountain. It's the little temptations that bring us down.

—*ISAAC LOEB PERETZ*

Behold, the ultimate religion of our seemingly rational age—the myth of the machine—bigger and bigger, more and more, farther and farther, faster and faster become ends in themselves as expressions of godlike power. The going was the goal—a defensible doctrine for colliding atoms or falling bodies, but not for men.

—*LEWIS MUMFORD*

So often we get the frightening feeling that we really don't count; and that in the greater scheme of things, we really don't matter. Many of us protest in despair, "My influence is like a drop in the bucket." But that tiny drop can be very important. One drop of water, falling into a bucket of acid, can cause an explosion. One drop of germ culture may change the contents of the bucket in a few hours. A small speck of yeast introduced into the dough will leaven the entire mixture. One drop of disinfectant may neutralize a whole bucket of poisonous material. "A drop in the bucket" is not at all unimportant. It depends on what the drop is, and the result it achieves.

—*SAUL TEPLITZ*

Piety, especially Jewish piety, respects the little—the little person, the little matter, the little task, the little duty. Through the little, religion meets the greatness that lies behind.

—*RABBI LEO BAECK*

Before one attains greatness, one must descend to lowliness.

—*RABBI NAHMAN OF BRATZLAV*

I am done with Great things and Big things, with Great institutions and Big success, and I am for those tiny invisible molecular forces that work from individual to individual, creeping through the crannies of the world like so many soft rootlets, or like the capillary oozing of water, but which, give them time, will rend the hardest monuments of men's pride.

—*WILLIAM JAMES*

There is exalted greatness in everything small.

—*RABBI AVRAHAM YITZHAK KOOK*

Events of great consequences often spring from trifling circumstances.

—*RALPH WALDO EMERSON*

It is insufficiently considered how much of human life passes in little incidents.

—*SAMUEL JOHNSON*

God has chosen little nations as the vessels by which He carries His choicest wines to the lips of humanity to rejoice their hearts, to exalt their vision, to strengthen their faith.
—DAVID LLOYD GEORGE

I long to accomplish a great and noble task, but it is my chief duty and joy to accomplish humble tasks as though they were great and noble ... for the world is moved along, not by only the mighty shoves of its heroes, but also by the aggregate of tiny pushes of each honest worker.
—HELEN KELLER

If you think you are too small to be effective, you have never been in the dark with a mosquito.
—ANONYMOUS

BLESSINGS

The word "b'rakhah" [blessing] means increase. When we say God is blessed, or "Blessed are You, O God," we are asking that God increase the Divine presence in the world.
—RABBI CHAIM OF VOLOZHIN

May you live to see your world fulfilled, may your destiny be for the world still to come and may you trust in generations past and yet to be. May your heart be filled with intuition and your words be filled with insight. May songs of praise ever be upon your tongue, and your vision be on a straight path before you. May your eyes shine with the light of holy words and your face reflect the brightness of the Heavens. May your lips ever speak wisdom and your fulfillment be in righteousness. Even as you yearn to hear the words of the Holy Blessed One.
—TALMUD

May the road rise to meet you.
May the wind always be at your back.
May the sunshine warm upon your face,
The rains fall soft upon your fields,
And until we meet again—
May God hold you in the palm of His hand.
—IRISH BENEDICTION

BODY

One should always regard oneself as if the Holy One dwelled within the body, for it is written, "The Holy One is within you." Therefore one should not mutilate one's body.

—*TALMUD*

The well-being of the soul could be obtained only after that of the body had been secured.

—*MOSES MAIMONIDES*

A small hole in the body turns into a large hole in the soul.

—*THE MAGGID OF MEZERITCH*

All creatures that are formed of heaven, both their soul and body are heavenly; and all creatures that are formed of earth, both their soul and body are earthbound, with the exception of humans, whose soul is from heaven and whose body is from earth.

—*SEYMOUR ROSSEL*

A man's body is his bridge to and model of the world; therefore, as a man is in his body so will he be in the world.

—*SAM KEEN*

Careful attention to the way one's body feels as one lives his life can also be useful for growth and well-being. One's body can function as did the canaries that miners used to take into the depths of a mine, where oxygen depletion was a grave danger to life. If the canary stopped singing, the miners would know that the air was becoming unfit for humans, and they would improve ventilation or get out.

—*SIDNEY JOURARD*

It is God's gift that we should eat and drink, and enjoy the pleasures of our toil.

—*BIBLE (ECCLESIASTES 3:13)*

The body often seems to have more insight than the soul, and one thinks frequently far better with the back and belly than with the head.

—*HEINRICH HEINE*

What a marvelous machine it is, the human body. A chemical laboratory, a power-house. Every movement, voluntary or involuntary, full of secrets and marvels!

—*THEODOR HERZL*

The general purpose of the Torah is twofold: the well-being of the soul and well-being of the body. The well-being of the soul is ranked first, but the well-being of the body comes first.

— *MOSES MAIMONIDES*

Rabbi Huna once asked of his son Rabbah why he did not attend the lectures of Rabbi Hisda, who was noted for his wit. The son replied, "When I go to him, he speaks of mundane matters; he tells about certain natural functions of the digestive organs and how one should behave in regard to them." His father replied, "He occupies himself with the life of God's creatures and you call that a mundane matter? All the more reason you should go to him."

— *TALMUD*

Truly, Western civilization's neglect of the body is nothing less than scandalous, for it has made a rich universe of energy, action, and information practically invisible. The body may also be thought of as an extension of the outer environment, for outside stimuli are processed, filtered, changed by it before they reach consciousness. Inner and outer are composed alike of matter and energy and possibilities. Seeing each as extensions of the other helps us perceive essential unity where multitudes of theoreticians have debated fruitlessly over modes of separateness.

— *GEORGE LEONARD*

BOOKS

Make books your companions; let your bookshelves be your gardens. Bask in their beauty, gather their fruit, pluck their roses, take their spices and myrrh. And when your soul is weary, change from garden to garden.

— *JUDAH IBN TIBBON*

Those who burn books will in the end burn people.

— *HEINRICH HEINE*

For one thousand years our enemies have been trying to kill us [Jews] every day. And we have been trying to live every day. And every day we manage it somehow. Do you know why? Because we never gave up on our books, never, never, never!

— *ANDRE SCHWARTZBART*

If we encounter a man of rare intellect, we should ask him what books he reads.

— *RALPH WALDO EMERSON*

To me, one of the noblest images of human history is that of the newly arrived immigrant mother, unable to speak a word of English, who hastened to her branch library and held up one, two, three fingers—the number signaling the number of children for whom she wanted library cards.

—LEO ROSTEN

Outside of a dog, a book is a man's best friend. Inside of a dog, it's too hard to read.

—GROUCHO MARX

Other people have wars. We have books on God's wars—books about how God acts in our lives. This is the Jewish sword and shield—faith in God, knowledge of God's actions—books about God are our wars.

—RABBI MEIR SHAPIRO

There are more treasures in books than all the treasures in "Treasure Island," and you can enjoy them every day.

—WALT DISNEY

Those who don't read good books have no advantage over those who can't.

—MARK TWAIN

I never saw my grandfather without a book.... My father had books in his grocery store.... "You have nothing to do?" he admonished me. "Take a book into your hands...." As a child I would spend my meager allowance on books.... I would buy more books than I could afford, but my credit was good. Many books were left unpaid.... A certain event occurred and our lives were interrupted. When I left for that place, I had in my knapsack more books than food.

—ELIE WIESEL

It's not you that's reading the book; it's the book that's reading you.

—HANS CHRISTIAN ANDERSON

A book is the most delightful companion.... An inanimate thing yet it talks.... It stimulates your latent talents. There is in the world no friend more faithful and attentive, no teacher more proficient.... It will join you in solitude, accompany you in exile, serve as a candle in the dark, and entertain you in your loneliness. It will do you good and ask no favor in return.

—MOSHE IBN EZRA

The theory of books is noble. The scholar of the first age received into him the world around; brooded thereon; gave it the new arrangement of his own mind; and uttered it again. It came into him life; it went out from him truth. It came to him short-lived actions; it went out from him immortal thoughts. It came to him business; it went from him poetry. It was dead fact; now, it is quick thought. It can stand, and it can go. It now endures, it now flies, it now inspires. Precisely in proportion to the depth of the mind from which it issued, so high does it soar, so long does it sing.

—*RALPH WALDO EMERSON*

Of all the things which man can do or make here below, by far the most momentous, wonderful and worthy are the things we call books.

—*THOMAS CARLYLE*

Read good books ... because they open up new worlds of understanding.

— *BEN CARSON*

A good book is a garden carried in the pocket.

— *AFRICAN PROVERB*

Other than [my father], I relied on books. During [the] time of my withdrawal in junior high I had my own private world, and my most prized possession was my library card from the Oakland Public Library.

—*BILL RUSSELL*

While other students were out playing I would often slip into my seat during recess and read a book.

—*TOM BRADLEY*

BOREDOM

Boredom is the feeling that everything is a waste of time; serenity, that nothing is.

—*THOMAS SZASZ*

A terrible thing happened again last night—nothing.

—*PHYLLIS DILLER*

Boredom ... is the shriek of unused capacities.

—*SAUL BELLOW*

BRAIN

There are one hundred million neurons, or nerve cells, in the brain, and in a single human brain the number of possible interconnections between these cells is greater than the number of atoms in the universe.... The brain is uniquely complicated and mysterious, unlike anything man has ever made. To carry the workload of its one hundred million cells would call for a computer the size of Texas.

—ROBERT ORNSTEIN

BREVITY

The Gettysburg Address has 266 words. The Ten Commandments has 297 words. The Declaration of Independence has 300 words. And a recent federal order on the price of cabbage has 26,911 words. There has to be a message here somewhere.

—ANONYMOUS

BUSINESS

When I was a child my mother used to make breakfast for me. She would make me eggs, and I can recall how, if she ever found a blood spot on an egg, she would recoil ... because the law is that you are not allowed to eat an egg that has a blood spot on it. One of the Hasidic teachers said, "Sometimes there is a bloodspot on a dollar." We should recoil from a drop of blood on a dollar, just as we do from a drop of blood in an egg.

—ABRAHAM JOSHUA HESCHEL

The test of the worth of a man's religion is to do business with him.

—JOHN SPALDING

CALLING

We never self-actualize in a vacuum, but always in relation to people and circumstances around us.... Self-actualization involves a "calling" to service from the external, day-to-day world, not only a yearning from within.

—EDWARD HOFFMAN

What you need to do is think of work as "vocation." This word may seem stilted in its tone, but it has a wisdom within it. It comes from the Latin word for calling, which comes from the word for voice. In those meanings it touches on what work really should be. It should be something that calls to you as something you want to do, and it should be something that gives voice to who you are and what you want to say to the world. So a true vocation calls to you to perform it and it allows your life to speak.

—*KENT NERBURN*

The essential task of the human being is to learn what is his calling in this world.

—*"THE PATH OF THE RIGHTEOUS"*

This is the true joy in life, the being used for a purpose recognized by yourself as a mighty one.... I want to be thoroughly used up when I die, for the harder I work the more I live. I rejoice in life for its own sake. Life is no "brief candle" to me. It is a sort of splendid torch which I have got hold of for the moment, and I want to make it burn as brightly as possible before handing it on to future generations.

—*GEORGE BERNARD SHAW*

The world needs each and every human being because every person has the mission to make something perfect in this world. That mission is unique to the individual, who must fulfill his or her own personal destiny.

—*DAVID S. ARIEL*

CAPITAL PUNISHMENT

If you are kind to the cruel, you will eventually become cruel to the kind.

—*MIDRASH*

Capital punishment has to be understood from an entirely new point of view. Race and class are important ingredients in the process that puts you in death row in the first place and determines if you go to the (electric) chair.

—*JOHN CONYERS*

CARING

Caring is biological. One thing you get from caring for others is you're not lonely. And the more connected you are to life, the healthier you are.

—JAMES LYNCH, M.D.

I care about all people, especially those most vulnerable in our society, like children, and seniors, and the disabled.

—DAVID DINKINS

CENSORSHIP

Knowledge, like the sky, is never private property. No teacher has a right to withhold it from anyone who asks for it.

—RABBI ABRAHAM JOSHUA HESCHEL

CENTERING

Yoga is a matter of calming and centering your mind and body, so that the least little thing gives you pleasure. When your body and mind are jangled and disturbed, you're always louder than your internal noise. But when you calm down physically and mentally, even a small plant can give you joy.

—YOGI DESAI

Drink the water of your own well.

—BIBLE (PROVERBS 5:15)

> The sun to warm me,
> The sea to center me,
> The wind to set me free.

—ANONYMOUS

CHALLENGES

I thank God for my handicaps, for, through them, I have found myself, my work, and my God.

—HELEN KELLER

Every problem contains a gift. Sometimes we seek problems for the gifts they contain.

—*RICHARD BACH*

In a critical time in one of the wars waged by Napoleon, the drummer boy was ordered by the commander to beat a retreat. The boy declared, "Sir, I know not how, but I can beat a charge! I beat a charge at Lodi, at the Pyramids, and Mount Tabor. May I beat a charge here?" And over the dead and wounded, he led the way to victory.

—*SAUL TEPLITZ*

We learn the rope of life by untying its knots.

—*JEAN TOOMER*

We are challenged to see that the barriers of yesterday—the barriers built by prejudice, fear and indifference which are now crumbling—are not replaced by new barriers of apathy, of underdeveloped skills, of lack of training. If this happens, our gains will be but temporary, our victories hollow.

—*WHITNEY YOUNG*

The challenge is in the moment, the time is always now.

—*JAMES BALDWIN*

Now my life is really starting. Fighting injustice, fighting racism, fighting crime, fighting illiteracy, fighting poverty.

—*MUHAMMAD ALI*

The challenge facing us is to equip ourselves that we will be able to take our place wherever we are in the affairs of men.

—*BARBARA JORDAN*

CHANGE

It is far easier to precipitate change than to control it.... It is much easier to unravel a tradition than to knit a new one.

—*MORDECAI M. KAPLAN*

I detest all change,
And most a change in aught I loved long since.

—*ROBERT BROWNING*

The dogmas of a quiet past are inadequate to the stormy present.... As our case is new, so we must think anew and act anew. We must disenthrall ourselves.

—ABRAHAM LINCOLN

Change comes as an enemy only to those who have lost the art of accepting it as a friend.

—TAGORE

We need new ideas to preserve old ideals.

—ANONYMOUS

A challenge to legitimacy is probably the most powerful force for change to be found in history. To the empowering principle that the people can withhold legitimacy, and thus change the world, we now add another—by deliberately changing the internal image of reality, people can change the world.

—WILLIS HARMAN

Mere conservation without change cannot conserve, while mere change without conservation is a passage from nothing to nothing.

—ALFRED NORTH WHITEHEAD

Be not the first by whom the new are tried,
Nor yet the last to lay the old aside.

—ALEXANDER POPE

Progress is like whiskey. A little of it is a good thing; too much, and it starts to come up on you.

—LYNDON JOHNSON

I am not an advocate for frequent changes in laws and constitutions, but laws and institutions must go hand in hand with the progress of the human mind. As that becomes more developed, more enlightened, as new discoveries are made, new truths discovered and manners and opinions change, with the change of circumstances, institutions must advance also to keep pace with the times. We might as well require a man to still wear the coat which fitted him when a boy as civilized society to remain ever under the regimen of their barbarous ancestors.

—THOMAS JEFFERSON

Consider the turtle. He makes progress only when he sticks his neck out.

—JAMES CONANT

The new comes not out of the old but out of the death of the old.

—*PAUL TILLICH*

No one really likes the new. We are afraid of it. Even in slight things the experience of the new is rarely without some stirring of foreboding. We have to adjust ourselves, and every radical adjustment is a crisis in self-esteem: we undergo a test, we have to prove ourselves.

—*ERIC HOFFER*

Taking a new step, uttering a new word, is what people fear most.

—*FYODOR DOSTOYEVSKY*

Change is essential to man. Change is life itself. But change rampant, change unguided and unrestrained, accelerated change overwhelming not only man's physical defenses but his decisional processes—such change is the enemy of life.

—*ALVIN TOFFLER*

The true task is to design a society capable of continuous change, continuous renewal, continuous responsiveness to human need.

—*JOHN GARDNER*

There is nothing permanent except change.

—*HERACLITUS*

Not everything that is faced can be changed. But nothing can be changed until it is faced.

—*JAMES BALDWIN*

There is nothing more difficult to take in hand, more perilous to conduct, or more uncertain in its success, than to take the lead in the introduction of a new order or things.

—*NICOLO MACHIAVELLI*

That which man will not change for the better, time will change for the worse.

—*BENJAMIN FRANKLIN*

The past is our cradle, not our prison.... The past is for inspiration, not imitation.

—*ISRAEL ZAN GWILL*

The historic fact [is] that we are living through the closing chapters of the established and traditional way of life. We are in the early beginnings of a struggle, which will probably last for generations, to remake our civilization. It is not a good time for politicians. It is a time for prophets and leaders and explorers and inventors and pioneers, and for those who are willing to plant trees for their children to sit under.

—WALTER LIPPMAN

Only one who has mastered a tradition has a right to attempt to add to it or to rebel against it.

—CHAIM POTOK

In a world buffeted by change, the only way to conserve is to innovate. The only stability possible is stability in motion.

—JACOB STEIN

The past should be altered by the present as much as the present is directed by the past.

—T.S. ELIOT

The danger is that people may mistake what is basically a change of vocabulary for a change in behavior, practices, and attitudes.

—WHITNEY YOUNG

World-changing is a hazardous pursuit. The lives of men who would dare to change the world and challenge the Gods of Power and the Status Quo are never smooth, indeed are always fraught with great danger.

—JOHN KILLENS

We must change in order to survive.

—PEARL BAILEY

I just want to be a change agent. I want to do my part in helping people to change their negative attitudes about us as a people. And hopefully, if we have any negative attitudes about ourselves, I want to help change those, too.

—CAMILLE COSBY

CHARACTER

As a splendid palace deserted by its inmates looks like a ruin, so does a man without character, all his material belongings notwithstanding.

—GANDHI

Just as a river becomes crooked by following the line of least resistance, so do we humans. Real character is what one does when no one is around. Too often we tend to ignore principle for profit, conviction for convenience, and excellence for expediency.

—SAUL TEPLITZ

Culture avails nothing unless it ennobles and strengthens character. Too often it gives rise to self-complacency. Who has not seen the scholar's thin-lipped smile when he corrects a misquotation and the connoisseur's pained look when someone praises a picture he does not care for?

—W. SOMERSET MAUGHAM

To be a mensch has nothing to do with success, wealth, status. A judge can be a zhlob. A millionaire can be a momzer. A professor can be a schlemiel, a doctor a klutz, a lawyer a bulvon. The key to being a mensch is nothing less than—character, rectitude, dignity, a sense of what is right, responsible, decorous. Many a poor man, many an ignorant man, is a mensch.

—LEO ROSTEN

A person of character is a person of wealth.

—EGYPTIAN PROVERB

Character, not circumstances, makes the man.

—BOOKER T. WASHINGTON

There is something in every one of you that waits and listens for the sound of the genuine in yourself. It is the only true guide you'll ever have. And if you cannot hear it, you will all of your life spend your days on the ends of strings that somebody else pulls.

—HOWARD THURMAN

Actions do build attitudes, and attitudes, of course, build character. You have to watch what you are doing.

—MARIE DUTTON BROWN

CHARITY

Blessed are they who give without remembering and take without forgetting.

—ANONYMOUS

The wife of Rabbi Naftali of Ropshitz said to him, "Your prayer was lengthy today. Have you succeeded in bringing about that the rich should be more generous in their gifts to the poor?" The Rabbi replied, "Half of my prayer I have accomplished. The poor are willing to accept them."

—HASIDIC TALE

Not he who has much is rich, but he who gives much.

—ERICH FROMM

We make a living by what we get, but we make a life by what we give.

—WINSTON CHURCHILL

Give in any way you can, of whatever you possess. To give is to love. To withhold is to whither. Care less for your harvest than for how it is shared, and your life will have meaning and your heart will have peace.

—KENT NERBURN

True service is not merely concerned with temporary relief for the individuals one is helping, but rather is based on the ability of the server to step into the shoes of those people, understand their situation, lead them to believe in themselves, and help them to stand on their own feet.

—PIERO FERRUCCI

You can give without loving, but you can't love without giving.

—ANONYMOUS

My bounty is as endless as the sea.... The more I give, the more I have to give.

—SHAKESPEARE

The longest road in the world is the one that leads from your pocket.

—YIDDISH SAYING

When it comes to giving, some people stop at nothing.

—ANONYMOUS

There is more pleasure in giving than in taking, for all taking is submission and all giving is mastery.

—WILL DURANT

Beware of people who slap you on the back. They probably want you to cough up something.

—ANONYMOUS

There are ten strong things in the world: Rock, but iron cleaves it. Iron, but fire softens it. Fire, but water quenches it. Water, but clouds bear it. Clouds, but wind scatters them. Wind, but the body withstands it. The body, but fright crushes it. Fright, but wine banishes it. Wine, but sleep works it off. Death is stronger than all, and charity saves from it.

—THE TALMUD

If help is given to us let us accept it, but let us not sit down and say nothing can be done until the rest of the world out of the goodness of its heart is willing to grant us charity.

—ARTHUR LEWIS

CHILDREN

We each have the kind of children we deserve.

—RABBI NAHMAN OF BRATSLAV

There are only two lasting bequests we can leave our children: one is roots, the other is wings.

—ANONYMOUS

Even if you found yourself in some prison, whose walls let in none of the world's sounds—wouldn't you still have your childhood, that jewel beyond all price, that treasure house of memories?

—RAINER MARIA RILKE

On the one hand the parent is urged to begin educating his child early in life to moral and spiritual values; for the impressions of childhood are imprinted deeply on the psyche and have a much stronger effect, even in old age, than later impressions. On the other hand, a child should be educated "according to his way." For all of us have our own mental ability, talents and propensities which can be recognized and should be respected. Then a child's education will be a lasting one.

—RABBI MEIR LEIBUSH MALBIM

Do everything right, all the time, and the child will prosper. It's as simple as that, except for fate, luck, heredity, chance, the astrological sign under which the child was born, his order of birth, his encounter with evil, the girl who jilts him in spite of his excellent qualities, the war that is being fought when he is a young man, the drugs he may try once or too many times, the friends he makes, how he scores on tests, how well he endures kidding about his shortcomings, how ambitious he becomes, how far he falls behind, circumstantial evidence, ironic perspective, danger when it is least expected, difficulty in triumphing over circumstance, people with hidden agendas, and animals with rabies.

—ANN BEATTIE

> If you want to touch the past, touch a rock.
> If you want to touch the present, touch a flower.
> If you want to touch the future, touch a child.

—ANONYMOUS

In many cases, it is the parents who make it impossible for the young to obey the [commandment to honor thy mother and father]. My message to parents is: Every day ask yourselves the question, "What is there about me that deserves the reverence of my child?"

—RABBI ABRAHAM JOSHUA HESCHEL

> Hold your child's hand so that she can walk,
> Let go so that she can run.
> Cheer so that she can fly.

—ANONYMOUS

When I was a kid, they told me to do what my parents wanted. When I became a parent, they told me to do what my kids wanted. When do I get to do what I want?

—SAM LEVENSON

Give your children unconditional love, a love that is not dependent on report cards, clean hands, or popularity. Give your children a sense of your whole-hearted acceptance, acceptance of their human frailties as well as their abilities and virtues. Give your children your permission to grow up to make their own lives independent of you. Give them a sense of truth; make them aware of themselves as citizens of a universe in which there are many obstacles as well as fulfillments. Bestow upon your child the blessings of your faith. These are the laws of honoring your son and your daughter as children are committed to honor their parents.

—RABBI JOSHUA LOTH LIEBERMAN

Children are the messages we send to a future we will not see.

—*NEIL POSTMAN*

What a parent says to his child is not heard by the world, but it is felt by posterity.

—*JEAN PAUL RICHTER*

When God asked for collateral from Moses for the gift of the Torah, Moses offered Abraham, Isaac, and Jacob to underwrite the note. God refused. Moses suggested the prophets. God replied, "Insufficient collateral." Only when Moses said, "Our children will be our guarantors," did God accept Moses' terms and give him the Torah.

—*MIDRASH*

There are so many fathers who have children but so few children who have fathers.

—*ADLAI STEVENSON*

Your son or daughter at five is your master, at ten your slave, at fifteen your double, and after that your friend or foe, depending on his or her upbringing.

—*ASIAN PROVERB*

A child needs love most when he is most unlovable.

—*PHOEBE ANDERSON*

Never threaten a child; either punish him or forgive him.

—*YIDDISH SAYING*

Your children are not your children.
They are the sons and daughters of Life's longing for itself.
They come through you but not from you,
And though they are with you, yet they belong not to you.
You may give them your love but not your thoughts,
For they have their own thoughts....
You may strive to be like them, but seek not to make them like you.
For life goes not backward nor tarries with yesterday.

—*KHALIL GIBRAN*

How sharper than a serpent's tooth it is to have a thankless child!

—*WILLIAM SHAKESPEARE*

Our children are in trouble because we adults are in trouble.

—*CAMILLE YARBOROUGH*

It is the duty of children to wait on elders and not the elders to wait on children.

—*KENYAN PROVERB*

You are the product of the love and affection of your parents, and throughout your life you have drawn strength and hope from that love and security.

—*NELSON MANDELA*

CHOSEN PEOPLE

For a long time Jews have so passionately thought of themselves as chosen, that they have indeed become chosen. They have a special role in history and in the world because they gave themselves that role. Perhaps that is the core of their history!

—*PAUL JOHNSON*

The Lord said ... "I have chosen [Abraham] so that he may charge his children and his household after him to keep the way of the Lord by doing righteousness and justice."

—*BIBLE (GENESIS 18:19)*

CHRISTIANITY

Not Herod, not Caiaphas, not Pilate, not even Judas ever contributed to fasten upon Jesus Christ the reproach of blandness; that final indignity was left for pious hands to inflict. To make of his story something that could neither startle, nor shock, nor excite, nor inspire a living soul is to crucify the Son of Man afresh and put him to an open shame.... Let me tell you, good Christian people, an honest writer would be ashamed to treat a nursery tale as you have treated the greatest drama in history.

—*DOROTHY SAYERS*

Heaven and earth I call to witness that whether it be Gentile or Jew, man or woman, slave or handmaid, according to the deeds one does, will the holy spirit rest on him.

—*TALMUD*

That great Christian body which expresses itself in opposition to card playing, athletics, sports, and promiscuous dancing, protested against saloons, inveighed against tobacco, wholly ignored the seven million colored people whose plea was for a word of sympathy and support.

—*IDA B. WELLS BARNETT*

Some fear being a Christian. I fear not being one.

—*BRENDA PRICE*

We were good Christians, and God never let us down.

—*ANNIE ELIZABETH DELLANY*

It is difficult to see all the religions in the world and then come back to Christianity thinking it has all the answers.

—*ARTHUR ASHE*

CHRISTIAN/MOSLEM-JEWISH RELATIONS

We realize now that many, many centuries of blindness have dimmed our eyes, so that we no longer see the beauty of Thy Chosen People and no longer recognize in their faces the features of our first-born brother. We realize that our brows are branded with the mark of Cain. Centuries long has Abel lain in blood and tears, because we had forgotten Thy love. Forgive us the curse which we unjustly laid on the name of the Jews. Forgive us that, with our curse, we crucified Thee a second time.

—*POPE JOHN XXIII*

We are separated from the Jews because we are not completely Christian.

—*VLADIMIR SOLOVYEV*

The foundation of all religion is one,
and God's is the East and the West;
and wherever ye turn, there is God's face.

—*KORAN*

CIVIL DISOBEDIENCE

The Roman emperor Caligula once sought to install an idol of his own image in the Holy Temple of Judea. 10,000 people stood in the way of his officer, Petronius, and said they would have to be killed before such an outrage could occur. This act of civil disobedience, in keeping with the Talmudic law to accept death rather than idolatry, so moved Petronius that he risked his life and refused to implement the Roman emperor's order.

—JOSEPHUS

Every person of humane convictions must decide on the protest that best suits his convictions, but we must all protest.

—MARTIN LUTHER KING, JR.

COMMENTARY

A poem may appear to mean very different things to different readers, and all of these meanings may be different from what the author thought he meant. For instance, the author may have been writing about some peculiar personal experience, which he saw quite unrelated to anything outside; yet for the reader the poem may become the expression of a general situation, as well as some private expression of his own.... There may be much more in a poem than the author was aware of.

—T.S. ELIOT

A word is not a crystal, transparent and unchanging, it is the skin of living thought and changes from day to day as does the air around us.

—OLIVER WENDELL HOLMES

"Is not my word like fire, says the Lord, and like a hammer which breaks the rock into pieces?" (Jeremiah 23:29). Just as a hammer strikes the anvil and kindles clouds of sparks, so does Scripture yield many meanings, as it is said, "Once did God speak, but two things have I heard." (Psalms 62:11)

—TALMUD, TRACTATE SANHEDRIN

COMMITMENT

If I thought at the end of the year that all I did was make a living, I'd regard it as a pretty incomplete year.

—PAUL O'DWYER

One person with a belief is a social power equal to ninety-nine who have only an interest.

—JOHN STUART MILL

My grandfather once told me that there are two kinds of people: those who do the work and those who take the credit. He told me to try to be in the first group; there was less competition there.

—INDIRA GANDHI

The Bible teaches us that life without commitment is not worth living, that thinking without roots will bear flowers but no fruit. Our commitment is to God, and our roots are in the prophetic events of Israel.

—RABBI ABRAHAM JOSHUA HESCHEL

I once said "yes" and that "yes" changed my entire life.

—DAG HAMMERSJOLD

The greatest use of life is to spend it on something that will outlast it.

—WILLIAM JAMES

We must create new models for adults who can teach their children not what to learn, but how to learn, and not what they should be committed to, but the value of commitment.

—MARGARET MEAD

Every calling is great when greatly pursued.

—OLIVER WENDELL HOLMES

Humanity's sole salvation lies in everyone making everything their business.

—ALEXANDER SOLZHENITSYN

To act is to be committed, and to be committed is to be in danger.

—JAMES BALDWIN

Commitment means that it is possible for a man to yield the nerve center of his consent to a purpose or cause, a movement or an ideal, which may be more important to him than whether he lives of dies.

—HOWARD THURMAN

It is time we rolled up our sleeves and put ourselves at the top of our commitment list.

—MARIAN WRIGHT EDELMAN

COMMUNICATION

Lord, what an organ is human speech when played on by a master.

—MARK TWAIN

Communication can be a wall or a window.

—ANONYMOUS

The reality of the other person is not in what he reveals to you, but in what he cannot reveal to you. Therefore, if you would understand him, listen not to what he says, but rather to what he does not say.

—KAHLIL GIBRAN

The objective of our discussion is not that my words may triumph over yours, or that yours may gain victory over mine, but that between us we may discover the perfect truth.

—SOCRATES

It is the disease of not listening, the malady of not marking, that I am troubled withal.

—WILLIAM SHAKESPEARE

God gave us two ears and one mouth so that we might learn to listen twice as much as we talk.

—DIOGENES

To the man of our age, nothing is as familiar and nothing as trite as words. Of all things, they are the cheapest, most abused, and least regarded.... We all live in them, feel in them, think in them, but, failing to uphold their independent dignity, to respect their power and weight, they turn, elusive, a mouthful of dust.... There can be no prayer without a sense for the dignity of words, a degree of deference to what they stand for.

—RABBI ABRAHAM JOSHUA HESCHEL

Communication and reconciliation introduces harmony into another's life by sensing and honoring the need to be cared for and understood.

—HOWARD THURMAN

In order to have a conversation with someone you must reveal yourself.

—JAMES BALDWIN

COMMUNITY

There is, among the people we have come to know, a powerful, perhaps desperate, longing for community, a longing that is apparently not adequately addressed by any of the relevant institutions in most people's lives.... Large numbers of people never experience the warmth, the shared emotion, the sense of support, which community provides.

—LEONARD FEIN

In community, there is shared memory, unity of purpose, mutual commitment, reciprocal responsibility, and common destiny. In community, there is powerful energy that heightens awareness, supports unfolding consciousness, strengthens cosmic connection, enhances prayer, deepens meditation, and affirms transcendent experience. In community there is sharing of tragedy amid triumph—joy enhanced, sorrow eased. In community, there is support for personal healing—the pain and sufferings of physical disease and emotional trauma tempered and soothed. In community there is encouragement and energy for global healing—the task of transforming and perfecting the world advocated and empowered.

—RABBI WAYNE DOSICK

In and through community lies the salvation of the world.

—M. SCOTT PECK

A human being is like a letter of the alphabet: to produce a word one must combine with another.

—BENJAMIN MANDELSTAMM

The whole of the holy life is association with good and noble friends, with noble practices, and with noble ways of living.

—BUDDHA

Independence? That's middle-class blasphemy. We are all dependent on one another, every soul of us on earth.

—*GEORGE BERNARD SHAW*

Let them only band together and they will redeem one another.

—*MIDRASH*

I looked for my soul
But my soul I could not see
I looked for my God
But my God eluded me
I looked for a friend
And there I found all three.

—*WILLIAM BLAKE*

A man is a bundle of relations, a knot of roots whose flower and fruitage is the world.

—*RALPH WALDO EMERSON*

True community does not come into being because people have feelings for each other, but rather on two accounts: all of them have to stand in a living, reciprocal relationship to a single living center, and they have to stand in a living, reciprocal relationship to one another.

—*MARTIN BUBER*

The quest for community will not be denied, for it springs from some of the powerful needs of human nature—need for a clear sense of cultural purpose, membership, status, and continuity. Without these, no amount of mere material welfare will serve to arrest the developing sense of alienation in our society.

—*ROBERT NISBET*

In some ways modern society binds the individual too tightly, but in other ways it holds him too loosely—and the latter causes as much pain as the former. He feels constrained by the conformity required in a highly organized society, but he also feels lost and without moorings. And both feelings may be traced to the same cause: the disappearance of the natural human community and its replacement by formula controls that irk and give no sense of security.

—*JOHN GARDNER*

A man is bound up with his fellows even without knowing it. When a friend dies, a piece of our soul dies with him.

—*ELIEZER STEINMAN*

One who withdraws from the ways of the community, even though that one does not commit himself any transgression, but merely separates oneself from the congregation of Israel, and does not perform the commandments in their midst, and does not enter into their sorrow, nor fast on their fast days, nor feast on their feast days, such a one has no share in the hereafter.

—*MOSES MAIMONIDES*

Behold how good and how pleasant it is for friends to be together.

— *BIBLE (PSALMS 133:1)*

Community cannot feed for long on itself, it can only flourish with the coming of others from beyond, their unknown and undiscovered brothers.

—*HOWARD THURMAN*

COMPASSION

What is the difference between kindness and compassion? Kindness gives to another. Compassion knows no "other".

—*TZVI FREEMAN*

Heaven's gate is shut to him who comes alone,
Save thou a soul and it will save thine own.

—*ANONYMOUS*

Reverence for life does not allow the scholar to live for his science alone, even if he is very useful to the community in so doing. It does not permit the artist to exist only for his art, even if he gives inspiration to many by its means. It refuses to let the businessman imagine that he fulfills all legitimate demands in the course of his business activities. It demands from all that they should sacrifice a portion of their own lives for others.

—*ALBERT SCHWEITZER*

Compassion ... is the eternal mercy of the Lord toward the folly and misery of man.

—*RABBI SAMUEL DRESNER*

Can I see another's woe,
And not be in sorrow too?
Can I see another's grief?
And not seek for kind relief?
Can I see a falling tear,
And not feel my sorrow's share?
Can a father see his child
Weep, nor be with sorrow fill'd?
Can a mother sit and hear
An infant groan, an infant fear?
No, No! never can it be!
Never, never can it be!

—WILLIAM BLAKE

Two important things are to have a genuine interest in people and to be kind to them. Kindness, I've discovered, is everything in life.

—ISAAC BASHEVIS SINGER

A man who works with his hands is a laborer; a man who works with his hands and brain is a craftsman; but a man who works with his hands and his brain and his heart is an artist.

—LOUIS NIZER

Religion is not what man does with his solitariness, but rather what man does with God's concern for all men.

—RABBI ABRAHAM JOSHUA HESCHEL

Sympathy is never wasted except when you give it to yourself.

—ANONYMOUS

Earthly power doth show likest God's
When mercy seasons justice.

—WILLIAM SHAKESPEARE

Even God prays. What does God pray? "May it be My will that My mercy may subdue My wrath, and may My attribute of mercy prevail over My attribute of justice, so that I may deal with My children with the quality of mercy and enter on their behalf within the line of strict justice."

—TALMUD

COMPETITION

You don't have to blow out the other fellow's light to let your own shine.

—BERNARD BARUCH

We live generally in a competitive world. Competition arouses our combativeness, our pugnacity. It pits us against our neighbor. It becomes a contest, an Olympic game. You have seen pictures of athletes who did not come in first. The camera has caught the grief and disappointment that are engraved upon their faces. There must also be resentment in their hearts against those who came in first. Within all of us, however, there is also unexpressed and unevoked kindliness. I have seen people in emergencies display so much tenderness that I said to myself, "It must have been there all the time; it required an extraordinary situation to elicit it."

—RABBI MORRIS ADLER

COMPROMISE

A reconciliation without an explanation that error lay on both sides is not a true reconciliation.

—TALMUD

A bad compromise is better than a good battle.

—RUSSIAN PROVERB

To compromise is to give each other something for the mutual benefit of both. It is a way of building bridges between different worldviews that allows communication and enrichment while preserving the integrity of both partners.

—JOAN BORYSENKO

The hardest thing to give is in.

—ANONYMOUS

The Torah resembles two paths—one of fire, the other of snow. If one inclines too much to one, he will die by fire; if one inclines too much to the other, he will die of cold. What shall he do? Let him walk in the middle. This is the choice of the Golden Mean.

—MOSES MAIMONIDES

CONFIDENCE

["Then sang Moses...." Exodus 15] How could Moses sing? He was a stutterer. He could sing because his people had faith in him. Thus he had faith in himself.

—ELIE WIESEL

The mind is a powerful thing. From the tip of my toes to the last hair on my head, I had complete confidence.

—JOE LOUIS

If you don't have confidence, you'll always find a way not to win.

—CARL LEWIS

CONFLICT

The man who strikes first admits that his ideas have given out.

—CHINESE PROVERB

The Holy One will ignore those who stubbornly reject proof that they are mistaken.

—RABBI NAHMAN OF BRATSLAV

The cause of all quarrels is the desire to quarrel.

—ELIEZER STEINMAN

If you want to get along, you have to go along.

—ANONYMOUS

You can only hope to find a lasting resolution to a conflict if you have learned to see the other objectively, but, at the same time, to experience the difficulties subjectively.

—DAG HAMMARSKJOLD

Heaven came into being when God made peace between fire and water. If God can create harmony between such elemental opposites, then surely we can resolve our often trifling differences and help to create peace on earth.

—HEBREW PROVERB

Peace in a community is a sign that the community is without a person of great intellect. For if there were such a one, then some would agree and some would argue. But when a person of great intellect is missing, there is peace but no intellect.

—RABBI NAHMAN OF BRATSLAV

Like the course of the heavenly bodies, harmony in national life is a resultant of the struggle between contending forces. In frank expression of conflicting opinion lies the greatest promise of wisdom in governmental action; and in suppression lies ordinarily the greatest peril.

—LOUIS BRANDEIS

When two people agree on everything, it just proves that one of them is dispensable.

—OSCAR WILDE

Conflict is the gadfly of thought. It stirs us to observation and memory. It instigates us to invention. It shocks us out of sheep-like passivity, and sets us at noting and contriving.... Conflict is a *sine qua non* of reflection and ingenuity.

—JOHN DEWEY

In great contests, each party claims to act in accordance with the will of God. Both may be, and one must be, wrong. God cannot be for and against the same thing at the same time.

—ABRAHAM LINCOLN

In truth, each person has a unique opinion; everyone who is engaged in a dispute must acknowledge that his companion also has a unique point of view. One should not stay rigidly attached to one's own idea, but search for truth. In this way, God will help their eyes see clearly, and peace will come from conflict.

—RABBI YEHUDAH ARYEH LEIB ALTER

A clash of doctrines is not a disaster—it is an opportunity.

—ALFRED NORTH WHITEHEAD

CONFORMITY

When people are free to do as they please, they usually are pleased to imitate each other.

—ANONYMOUS

CONSCIENCE

By favor of the gods, I have, since my childhood, been attended by a semi-divine being whose voice from time to time dissuades me from some undertaking, but never directs me what I am to do.... The prophetic voice has been heard by me throughout my life; it is certainly more trustworthy than omens from the flight of entrails of birds. I call it God or daemon.... The voice has never been wrong.

—SOCRATES

Conscience is a small three-cornered object in the heart that stands still when we are good, but turns around when we are bad. If we continue to do evil, the corners wear off and our conscience doesn't hurt us anymore.

—NATIVE AMERICAN LEGEND

The more faithfully you listen to the voice within you, the better you will hear what is sounding outside.

—DAG HAMMERSKJOLD

A very few men serve the State with their consciences, and they are commonly treated as enemies by it.

—HENRY DAVID THOREAU

When I come to lay down the reins of power and may have lost every other friend on earth, I pray that I shall at least have one left, and that friend shall be deep down inside me.

—ABRAHAM LINCOLN

Can people hide themselves in secret places that I shall not see them?

—BIBLE (JEREMIAH 23:24)

People should concern themselves more that they not injure others than that they not be injured.

—TALMUD

All people receive a reward from God for what they are convinced is the right thing, if this conviction has no other motive but the love of God.

—RABBI ZEDEKIAH BEN ABRAHAM

Follow the impulses of your heart.

—BIBLE (ECCLESIASTES 11:9)

Once I believed some gray and giant judge
Kept careful toll of all the deeds of men,
That with some black and lusting kind of pen,
He cautiously recorded every petty crime,
    and most all—mine!
Now I know there is no judge with righteous pen,
Who bothers keeping track of deeds and time,
For every face records what life has been about,
And sculpts a memory with every crack and line,
    and most of all—mine.

—JAMES CAVANAUGH

CONSISTENCY

Do I contradict myself? Very well then,
I contradict myself (I am large, I contain multitudes).

—WALT WHITMAN

Consistency requires you to be as ignorant today as you were a year ago.

—BERNARD BERENSON

Myself I may contradict. The truth I do not.

—MONTAIGNE

The only completely consistent people are the dead.

—ALDOUS HUXLEY

A foolish consistency is the hobgoblin of little minds, adored by little statesmen and philosophers and divines. With consistency a great soul has simply nothing to do. He may as well concern himself with his shadow on the wall.

—RALPH WALDO EMERSON

Don't be "consistent," but be simply true.

—OLIVER WENDELL HOLMES

It is also said of me that I now and then contradict myself. Yes, I improve wonderfully as time goes on.

—G.J. NATHAN

The wise man does not expect consistency or harmony ... for he sees that man is a mosaic of characteristics and qualities that only rarely achieve an internal and intrinsic harmony.

—A. MYERSON

Consistency is the last refuge of the unimaginative.

—OSCAR WILDE

CONVICTION

Most people waver between various systems of value, and hence never fully develop in the one or the other direction. They have neither great virtues nor great vices. They are ... like a coin whose stamp has been worn away; the person has no self and no identity, but is afraid to make this discovery.

—ERICH FROMM

It's easier to fight for one's principles than to live up to them.

—ALFRED ADLER

When a person goes against his values in the choices he makes, the failure is automatic.

—LORD ACTON

CORRUPTION

Everything is good when it comes from the hands of the Almighty; everything degenerates in the hands of man.

— JEAN JACQUES ROUSSEAU

It is my earnest belief that everything we see before us today is more or less polluted, diluted and devalued.

—KARL BARTH

A worm can enter a fruit only after it has begun to rot.

—S. ANSKY

The best, when corrupted, become the worst.

—LATIN PROVERB

Your silver has become dross, your wine mixed with water.

—BIBLE (ISAIAH 1:22)

Power tends to corrupt, and absolute power corrupts absolutely.

—LORD ACTON

COURAGE

Strength is not force. It is an attribute of the heart. Its opposite is not weakness and fear, but confusion, lack of clarity, and lack of sound intention. If you are able to discern the path with heart and follow it even when at the moment it seems wrong, then and only then are you strong.

—KENT NERBURN

Great spirits have always encountered violent opposition from mediocre minds.

—ALBERT EINSTEIN

Success is never final, and failure is never fatal. It's courage that counts.

—ANONYMOUS

> Life is mostly froth and bubble,
> Two things stand like stone;
> Kindness in another's trouble,
> Courage in your own.

—ADAM LINDSEY GORDON

The most sublime courage I have ever witnessed has been among that class of people too poor to know they possessed it and too humble for the world to discover it.

—HENRY WHEELER SHAW

Sometimes you have to go on living even if it kills you.

—SHOLOM ALEICHEM

Worry is the act of borrowing trouble from the future. Courage is the act of borrowing hope from the future.

—ANONYMOUS

Courage is the highest virtue that counts most. Courage to act on limited knowledge and insufficient evidence—that is all any of us has, so we must have the courage to go ahead and act on a hunch. It is the best we can do.

—ROBERT FROST

We are capable at the same time of taking risks and of estimating them beforehand. Others are brave out of ignorance. When they stop to think they begin to fear. But the one who most truly can be accounted brave is one who most knows the meaning of what is sweet in life and what is terrible, then goes out undeterred to meet what is to come.

—SOCRATES

Who is courageous? They who master their passions.

—TALMUD

Some heroes hear the sound of drums,
The heartbeat of all praise that comes
For deeds on battlefields afar,
Or reaching toward a distant star;
While others, smiling through their pain,
May never feel the paper rain
Of ticker tape, as motorcades
Maneuver them through gay parades.
Yet, somewhere silver bells are rung
For bravery that seems unsung.

—THELMA SCHREIBER

One who loses wealth loses much. One who loses a friend loses more. But one who loses courage loses all.

—MIGUEL DE CERVANTES

Lose not courage, lose not faith, go forward.

—MARCUS GARVEY

Courage is one step ahead of fear.

—COLEMAN YOUNG

One isn't necessarily born with courage, but one is born with potential. Without courage, we cannot practice any other virtue with consistency. We can't be kind, true, merciful, generous, or honest.

—MAYA ANGELOU

CREATIVITY

How to be an artist: Stay loose. Learn to watch snails. Plant impossible gardens. Make little signs that say "yes" and post them all over your house. Make friends with uncertainty.

—HENRY MILLER

Any activity becomes creative when the doer cares about doing it right, or better.

—JOHN UPDIKE

The future is uncertain ... but this uncertainty is at the very heart of human creativity.

—ILYA PRIGOGINE

The individuals by whom the great artworks of history have been brought forth are persons who leapt off the plateau of culture to make a creative act of their moment in time. Taken together, their works constitute humanity's collective leap beyond the confines of earthly life, the cumulative building of an opus that is progressively the spiritual history of mankind's future. It is thus that the reality of spirit establishes itself, building itself out of the accretion of personal experiences that form the transpersonal dimension of human existence.

—IRA PROGROFF

There is tension between creativity and fidelity. Mere fidelity can be static, lifeless. Mere creativity is likely to be restless and self-arrogating. Taken together, they represent human possibility in the face of divine repose.

—MARTIN MARTY

Ultimate creativity is maintaining a perpetual newness, a childlike openness and a curiosity in life.

—YOGI AMRIT DESAI

Poetry, like all birth and creativity, is accompanied by pain and sacrifice.

—ROBERT FROST

Most people are other people. Their thoughts are someone else's opinions, their life a mimicry, their passions quotations.

—OSCAR WILDE

Education for creativity is nothing short of education for living.

—ERICH FROMM

When I am, as it were, completely myself, entirely alone, and of good cheer ... my ideas flow best and most abundantly. Whence and how they come, I know not, nor can I force them.

—WOLFGANG AMADEUS MOZART

Far out thinking is a means to an end—to him whose elastic and vigorous thought keeps pace with the sun, the day is a perpetual morning.

—HENRY DAVID THOREAU

The great secret of all creative geniuses is that they possess the power to appropriate the beauty, wealth, the grandeur, and sublimity within their own souls, which are a part of Omnipotence, and to communicate those riches to others.

—GIACOMO PUCCINI

Ordinary education and social training seem to impoverish the capacity for free initiative and artistic imagination. We talk independence, but we enact conformity. The hunger in many people for what is called self-expression is related to this unrealized intuitive resource. Brains are washed (when they are not clogged), wills are standardized, that is to say immobilized. Someone within cries for help. There must be more to life than all these learned acts, all this highly conditioned consumption. A person wants to do something of his own, to feel his own being alive and unique. He wants out of bondage. He wants in to the promised land.

—MARY RICHARDS

Creativity is the encounter of the intensely conscious human being with his world.

—ROLLO MAY

The writer, perhaps more than any of his fellow artists, has access to the human subconscious. His words sink deep, shaping dreams, easing the pain of loneliness, banishing incantations and omens, keeping alive the memories of the race, providing intimations of immortality, nourishing great anticipations, sharpening the instinct for justice, and imparting respect for the fragility of life. These functions are essential for human evolution. Without them, civilization becomes brittle and breaks easily.

—NORMAN COUSINS

The man who follows the crowd will usually get no further than the crowd. The man who walks alone is likely to find himself in places no one has ever been before.

—ALAN ASHLEY

[Nothing] brings home to us so effectively the reality of God as the zest of living that accompanies all creative achievement. We cannot doubt the power for good in the world, when our own personalities function as part of that power.

—RABBI MORDECAI M. KAPLAN

Creative thinking is not stimulated by vicarious issues, but by personal problems.

—RABBI ABRAHAM JOSHUA HESCHEL

The Creator's continuous radiation of creative force never ceases from the world; in every instant these emanations radiate to its creations, to all the world, to all the [realms of higher consciousness] and to all the angels.

—RABBI LEVI YITZHAK OF BERDICHEV

You were born an original. Don't die a copy.

—JOHN MASON

And so our mothers and grandmothers have, more often than not anonymously, handed on the creative spark, the seed of the flower they themselves never hoped to see: or like a sealed letter they could not plainly read.

—ALICE WALKER

Potential powers of creativity are within us and we have the duty to work assiduously to discover these powers.

—MARTIN LUTHER KING, JR.

We are all creative, but by the time we are three or four years old, someone has knocked creativity out or us. Some people shut up the kids who start to tell stories. Kids dance in their cribs, but someone will insist they sit still. By the time the creative people are ten or twelve, they want to be like everyone else.

—MAYA ANGELOU

One of the strongest characteristics of genius is the power of lighting its own fire.

—JOHN W. FOSTER

CRISIS

[A crisis] is not a threat of catastrophe, but a turning point, a crucial period of increased vulnerability and heightened potential.

—ERIK ERIKSON

CRITICISM

To escape criticism—do nothing, say nothing, be nothing.

—*ELBERT HUBBARD*

It is much easier to be critical than to be correct.

—*BENJAMIN DISRAELI*

It is well to reflect on how people generally reprove people to make them change their way. It may well be that that particular way, though beset with defects, is good, in the light of one's circumstances. These very defects may shield one against more grievous defects.... It is the evil impulse that leads us to concentrate on faultfinding with everybody.

—*RABBI AVRAHAM YITZHAK KOOK*

Do not chastise scoffers lest they hate you. Chastise a wise person who will then love you.

—*TALMUD*

The criticism that hurts most is the one that echoes my own self-condemnation.

—*HUGH PRATHER*

The history and tradition of our country make it plain that the essence of the American way of life is its hospitality to criticism, protest, unpopular opinions and independent thought.... The heart of democracy is independent criticism.

—*ROBERT HUTCHINS*

When someone points a finger at someone else, such a one is pointing at least three fingers at oneself.

—*ANONYMOUS*

Only false prophets shun criticism because they do not want their real motives revealed.

—*JAMES CONE*

The greatest threat to freedom is the absence of criticism.

—*WOLE SOYINKA*

It is not a sign of weakness, but a sign of high maturity, to rise to the level of self-criticism.

—*MARTIN LUTHER KING, JR.*

CYNICISM

A cynic is a person who knows the price of everything and the value of nothing.

—OSCAR WILDE

DEATH

Rich person, poor person.... After the game, the king and the pawn go into the same box.

—ITALIAN PROVERB

Death fascinates the living. We want to know as much about it as we can. We do not want to believe that death is the end, so we explore wisdom-teachings that are thousands of years old to find a clue. Almost all traditions suggest that death is not an end but a transition. It is intriguing that the world's wisdom-teachings agree on this point. Despite a wide variety of interpretations of what happens, how it happens, or where it happens, the end result is that death is a gateway to other realities.

—DAVID COOPER

Death ... faceless enemy, fearsome monster who devours our days, confounds the philosopher, silences the poet, and reduces the mighty to offering their gold, in vain, for yet another hour.

—RABBI ABRAHAM JOSHUA HESCHEL

There is no greater testimony to one's faith than the words: "I'm ready; I'm at peace," spoken by one in life's final days. We who are younger find them difficult to understand because we ourselves are not ready—we still have so many things to do. What we cannot fully understand is that, in the fullness of time, the person of faith experiences a sense of completion that makes death the natural and easy next step.

—KENNETH STOKES

'Tis well to learn that sunny hours
May quickly change to mournful shade;
'Tis well to prize life's scattered flowers
Yet be prepared to see them fade.

—ELIZA COOK

Do not be dismayed at good-byes. A farewell is necessary before one can meet again. And meeting again after moments or lifetimes is certain for those who are friends.

— *RICHARD BACH*

I am forgotten like a dead person, out of mind and out of heart.

— *BIBLE (PSALMS 31:13)*

In our long and obsessive passion for youth, we have ... avoided direct approach to age and dying by denying them in word, in fact and — above all — in worth.... Until the last three decades, Death has been unmentionable in what is known as "polite society." We "pass away," not die. We do not tell our children about dying.

— *MARYA MANNES*

The tragedy of life is not death; rather it is what we allow to die within us while we live.

— *NORMAN COUSINS*

I am not going to die, I'm going home like a shooting star.

— *SOJOURNER TRUTH*

No one can escape death. Then why be afraid of it? In fact, death is a friend who brings deliverance from suffering.

— *GANDHI*

Last year I look death in the face and found its lineaments not unkind. But it was not my time. Yet in nature time comes soon and in the fullness of days I shall die, quietly, I trust with my face turned south and eastward; and dream or dreamless I shall death enjoy as I have life.

— *W.E.B. DUBOIS*

I imagine death to be like sleep. When death comes to you, you just pass out, just the way you passed out last night.

— *RAY CHARLES*

There is a skeleton of death that flees in the face of my will to live.

— *FREDA KAHLO*

Death is a friend of ours; and he that is not ready to entertain him is not at home.

— *FRANCIS BACON*

DEEDS

To perform deeds of holiness is to absorb the holiness of deeds.

—RABBI ABRAHAM JOSHUA HESCHEL

Be isolated, be ignored, be attacked, be in doubt, be frightened, but do not be silenced.

—BERTRAND RUSSELL

I know only two things for certain. One is that we gain nothing by walking around the difficulties and merely indulging in wishful thinking. The other is that there is always something one can do oneself. In the most modest form, this means: to study, to try to sort out different proposals, and weigh the effect of proposed solutions—even if they are only partial solutions. Otherwise there would be nothing left but to give up. And it is not worthy of human beings to give up.... The greatness of being human ... lies in not giving up, in not accepting one's own limitations.

—ALVA MYRDAL

Action is eloquence.

—WILLIAM SHAKESPEARE

The smallest good deed is better than the grandest intention.

—ANONYMOUS

There are risks and costs to a program of action. But they are far less than the long-range risks and costs of comfortable inaction.

—JOHN F. KENNEDY

The Lord gave us two ends—one to sit on and the other to think with. Success depends on which one we use the most.

—ANN LANDERS

Think like a person of action, act like a person of thought.

—HENRI BERGSON

Nobody made a greater mistake than he who did nothing because he could only do a little.

—EDMUND BURKE

It is easier to act your way into a new way of thinking, than to think your way into a new way of acting.

—ALBERT MERHABIAN

If you will it, it is not a dream.

—THEODORE HERZL

Do the thing, and you shall have the power. But they who do not the thing, have not the power.

—RALPH WALDO EMERSON

Whatever you can do, or dream you can, begin it. Boldness has genius, power and magic in it.

—JOHANN WOLFGANG VON GOETHE

Do the act and the attitude will follow.

—WILLIAM JAMES

It is personal influence that determines the size of life, not words. The abstract inconsideration of good intentions is not enough. Nor are the recurrent unilluminating bows made toward distant horizons. Nor is the burning of incense at empty shrines. What needs to be done, needs to be done here and now. Every human being is a problem in search of a solution. We must ask ourselves the question whether we are going to continue to be part of the problem, or whether we are going to make ourselves part of the solution.

—HENRY SCHUMAN

When we do nothing, we run the risk of becoming nothing.

—PAUL GOODMAN

Judge a tree by the fruit it bears, not by the bark it wears.

—ANONYMOUS

Every act of kindness is a prayer—a prayer that walks, moves, breathes and lives.

—RABBI ISRAEL SALANTER

Go put your creed into your deed.

—RALPH WALDO EMERSON

The sickness of our society is not that we have problems. The sickness is this ominous sense of impotence which renders us unable to act on our beliefs.

—BILL MOYERS

In the process of doing good to our fellow humans, we begin to think well of them! The power of the good deed extends to both the performer and the recipient alike.

—GERSHON WINER

To judge an intellectual it is not enough to examine his ideas; it is the relation between his ideas and his acts which counts.

—REGIS DEBRAY

Not what I have, but what I do is my kingdom.

—THOMAS CARLYLE

DEHUMANIZATION

A specter is stalking in our midst whom only a few see with clarity.... It is a new specter: a completely mechanized society, devoted to maximal material output and consumption, directed by computers; and in this social process, man himself is being transformed into a part of the total machine, well-fed and entertained, yet passive, unalive, and with little feeling.

—ERICH FROMM

The individual ... has been caught up in the organized machinery of Church, State, Party, Union, or Business. The result is that the individual himself gets to behave like a machine and treats every other being, animate or inanimate, as a mere object, something to be analyzed and utilized, rather than as a subject or person.

—RABBI HAROLD SCHULWEIS

DEMOCRACY

In a democracy, error by the majority may be tolerated as long as the minority is left free to correct it.

—THOMAS JEFFERSON

We must remember what intellectuals habitually forget: that people matter more than concepts and must come first. The worst of all despotisms is the heartless tyranny of ideas.

—PAUL JOHNSON

Man's capacity for justice makes democracy possible; but man's inclination to injustice makes democracy necessary.

—REINHOLD NIEBUHR

Our founding fathers ... realized what a mistake it would be to lodge power in the hands of any one group.... Indeed, in the end, all saw that they were best protected when there was no concentration of power in the society at all, when power was most completely dispersed ... in short that their lives and fortunes were all best protected in a democracy.

—CHARLES MEE, JR.

Only if the human being is capable of moral decisions and therefore of governing himself, is the dream of a free democratic society capable of fulfillment.

—A.J. MUSTE

A democratic way of life occurs when we are every day reaffirming the rights of ordinary, everyday people.

—CORNEL WEST

A democracy cannot long endure with the head of a God and the tail of a demon.

—JOSEPHINE YATES

This country can have no more democracy than it accords and guarantees to the humblest and weakest citizen.

—JAMES WELDON JOHNSON

Privilege is anathema to democracy.

—NIKKI GIOVANNI

A born democrat is a born disciplinarian. Democracy comes naturally to him who is ... willing to yield willing obedience to all laws, human or divine.

—GANDHI

Democracy is not tolerance. Democracy is a prescribed way of life erected on the premise that all men are created equal.

—CHESTER HIMES

DEPRESSION

The fundamental reason why people are far from God is because of depression. They lose their morale, they come to despise themselves because they see blemishes within themselves and the great damage which they do. In secret each one knows the soreness of his own heart and his private pain.

—RABBI NAHMAN OF BRATSLAV

There is no sadness in the presence of God.

—RABBI DAVID WOLPE

DIALOGUE

In genuine dialogue, each of the partners, even when he stands in opposition to the other, heeds, affirms, and confirms his opponent as an existing other. Only so can conflict certainly not be eliminated from the world, but be humanly arbitrated and led towards its overcoming.

—MAURICE FRIEDMAN

The motto of life is "Give and take." Everyone must be both a giver and a receiver. He who is not both is as a barren tree.

—RABBI YITZHAK EISEK

Our race develops its human qualities in essence only from face to face, from heart to heart. It can do this only in small circles which gradually grow larger in the warmth of feeling and love, and in trust and confidence.

—HERBERT READ

As iron sharpens iron, so does one person sharpen the wits of another.

—BIBLE (PROVERBS 27:17)

DIGNITY

It is better for a person to cast oneself into a fiery furnace rather than put another to shame in public.

—TALMUD

No race can prosper till it learns that there is as much dignity in tilling a field as in writing a poem.

—BOOKER T. WASHINGTON

There is a battle to be fought, there are obstacles to be overcome. There is a world struggle for human dignity to be won. Let us address ourselves seriously to the supreme tasks that lie ahead.

—KWAME NKRUMAH

Human dignity is more precious than prestige.

—*CLAUDE MCKAY*

There is no dignity without freedom. For any subjection, any coercion, dishonors the one who submits, deprives him of part of his humanity and arbitrarily turns him into an inferior being.

—*SEKOU TOURE*

DISCIPLINE

There are only two pains in life. The pain of discipline and the pain of regret. The pain of discipline weighs ounces, but the pain of regret weighs tons.

—*ANONYMOUS*

Man who man would be
Must rule the empire of himself.

—*PERCY BYSSHE SHELLEY*

Human being is boundless, but being human is respect for bounds.

—*RABBI ABRAHAM JOSHUA HESCHEL*

Let your left hand push away the child, and let your right hand draw him near.

—*TALMUD*

I am the master of my fate;
I am the captain of my soul.

—*WILLIAM ERNEST HENLEY*

Amid the turmoil of conflicting ideas in which we live, in the spheres of art, of science, and above all of politics where statesmen of towering importance can display in their savagery, fear and unreasonableness all the worst features of an undisciplined nursery, there seems to be one proposition commanding nearly universal assent. The control man has secured over nature has far outrun his control over himself. Man's unhappiness and the threats of doom overhanging him proceed from this unassailable truth. Man's chief enemy and danger is his own unruly nature and the dark forces pent up within him.

—*ERNEST JONES*

Without discipline true freedom cannot survive.

—KWAME NKRUMAH

When I decided to make the transition and become a pop performer, I had to sit down and learn pop music with the same discipline and approach that I learned classical pieces.

—ROBERTA FLACK

DISCRIMINATION

He drew a circle that shut me out—
Heretic rebel, a thing to flout.
But Love and I had the wit to win:
We drew a circle that took him in!

—EDWIN MARKHAM

The people who invented discrimination in public places to ostracize people of a different race or nationality or color or religion are the direct descendants of medieval torturers. It is the most powerful instrument in the world that may be employed to prevent rapprochement and understanding between different groups of people. It is a cancer in the universal human body and poison to the individual soul.

—CLAUDE MCKAY

DISSENT

A free society is one where it is safe to be unpopular.

—ADLAI STEVENSON

Even as you should not reject that which is good of our institutions and that accumulated wisdom we possess, we in turn must not reject those among you who dissent.

—WALTER CRONKITE

DIVORCE

When a man divorces the wife of his youth, the very altar sheds tears.

—TALMUD

It is better for four people to be happy than two people to be miserable.

—ANONYMOUS

DOUBT

We are just beginning to glimpse a stage beyond doubting, the stage when ... we became mature enough to doubt our doubts.

—RABBI DAVID WOLPE

If you begin with certainties, you end with doubt. If you begin with doubt, you end with certainties.

—FRANCIS BACON

To be genuinely thoughtful, we must be willing to sustain and protract that state of doubt which is the stimulus to thorough inquiry.

—JOHN DEWEY

> Ever insurgent let me be,
> Make me more daring than devout;
> From sleek contentment keep me free,
> And fill me with a buoyant doubt.

—LOUIS UNTERMEYER

A healthy religious climate fosters self-honesty with reference to doubts, a quality of flexibility concerning one's beliefs that leaves one open to new insights. It recognizes that there are elements of wish-fulfillment in most religions, but that healthy religion is not dominated by these elements.

—HOWARD CLINEBELL

If two people have no experience of God, the one who denies God is perhaps nearer to God than the other.

—RABBI STANLEY YEDWAB

The badge of intellect is a question mark.

—RABBI SHLOMO YITZHAKI (RASHI)

The tension between doubt and trust, between fear and faith, is of the very essence of religion.... At the margin of finite human knowledge and experience there is, and must be, mystery. But it is a divine mystery, luminous with goodness and wisdom, and strong with the power of everlasting mercy.

—R.B.Y. SCOTT

DREAMS

Go confidently in the direction of your dreams! Live the life you've imagined. As you simplify your life, the laws of the universe will be simpler.

—HENRY DAVID THOREAU

Every dream has a particle of prophecy in it.

—TALMUD

Dreams are private myths. Myths are public dreams.

—JOSEPH CAMPBELL

I [the Lord] shall pour out my spirit on all flesh, and your sons and daughters shall prophesy, your old shall dream dreams, and your young shall see visions.

—BIBLE (JOEL 3:1)

When life itself seems lunatic, who knows where madness lies? Perhaps, to be too practical is madness. To surrender dreams —this may be madness. To seek treasure where there is only trash. Too much sanity may be madness. And maddest of all, to see life as it is and not as it should be.

—DALE WASSERMAN

It isn't a calamity to die with dreams unfulfilled, but it is certainly a calamity not to dream. It is not a disaster to be unable to capture your ideal, but it is a disaster to have no ideal to capture.

—BENJAMIN E. MAYS

I have a cow in the sky, but I can't drink her milk.

—CONGOLESE PROVERB

Hold fast to dreams
For if dreams die
Life is a broken-winged bird
That cannot fly.

Hold fast to dreams
For when dreams go
Life is a barren field
Frozen with snow.

—LANGSTON HUGHES

If you have built castles in the air, your work need not be lost; that is where they should be. Now put the foundations under them.

—HENRY DAVID THOREAU

Thou hast made the flowers to bloom
And the stars to shine
Hid rare gems of richest ore
In the tunneled mine.
But chief of all Thy wondrous works
Supreme of all Thy plan
Thou hast put an upward reach
In the heart of man.

—HARRY KEMP

Most people think that I am a dreamer. Through dreams many things come true.

—MARY MCLEOD BETHUNE

Man is what his dreams are.

—BENJAMIN MAYS

Life at times could be so brutal that the only thing that made it livable were dreams.

—BUCHI EMCHETA

The only thing that will stop you from fulfilling your dreams is you.

—TOM BRADLEY

EDUCATION

The words of the wise are listened to when spoken pleasantly.

—BIBLE (ECCLESIASTES 9:17)

I learn most from you, not when you "try" to teach me ... but when you "are" what you want me to know.

—BROCK TULLY

Much have I learned from my teachers, more from my friends, but most have I learned from my students.

—TALMUD

Only the educated are free.

—ARISTOTLE

Next to the care of our own souls a right education of our children is greatest.

—JOHN BELLERS

Education is not to make people know what they do not know; but to make them behave as they do not behave.

—JOHN RUSKIN

Truth is recognized, not learned, and those who would travel the spiritual path to completion must be willing to recognize themselves in others without pretense or defenses.

—FRANCES VAUGHAN

I never let my schooling get in the way of my education.

—MARK TWAIN

Help your students become human. Your efforts must never produce learned monsters, skilled psychopaths.... Reading, writing, arithmetic are important only if they serve to make our children more human.

—HAIM GINNOTT

I see and I forget.
I hear and I remember.
I do and I understand.

—ANONYMOUS

You cannot teach a person anything. You can only help one discover it within.

—GALILEO

The burden of learning is on the person who wants to learn, not on the person who wants to teach.

—NAPOLEON HILL and W. CLEMENT STONE

There is no poverty worse than that of being excluded by ignorance, by insensibility, or by failure to master the language, from the meaningful symbols of one's culture. These forms of social deafness or blindness are truly death to the human personality.

—LEWIS MUMFORD

Knowledge without feeling is not knowledge and can lead only to public irresponsibility and indifference, and conceivably to ruin.

—ARCHIBALD MACLEISH

There is only one subject-matter for education, and that is Life in all its manifestations.

—JOHN DEWEY

The teacher's function ... is to help increase the learner's awareness of his strength and capabilities rather than judge his performance.

—GEORGE ISAAC BROWN

What nature has disposed and sealed
Is called the inborn self.
The unburying of this self
Is called the Process of Education.

—TSZE SZE

The two essential secrets of moral education [are] intimacy and activity.

—SIR HERBERT READ

We have become more concerned about the minds of our students than we have about their hearts, more concerned with their intellect than their emotions. We examine intellectual growth more than we examine growth in values. We have emphasized what students know but underemphasized a concern for what they deeply care about, their attitude toward life, their zest for living.

—EDGAR DALE

Upon the subject of education, I can only say that I view it as the most important subject which we as a people can be engaged in.

—*ABRAHAM LINCOLN*

Human survival is a continual race between education and catastrophe.

—*H.G. WELLS*

The best preacher is the human heart;
The best teacher is time;
The best book is the world;
The best friend is God.

—*SHOLOM ALEICHEM*

Education is that which remains when one has forgotten everything he learned in school.

—*ALBERT EINSTEIN*

Education is precept by precept, precept by precept, line by line, line by line, here a little, there a little.

—*BIBLE (ISAIAH 28:10)*

If you want to understand the real psychological temper of any time, you can do no better than to try to understand its art, for in the art the underlying spiritual meaning of the time is expressed directly in symbols.

—*H.H. ANDERSON*

The only way we can pay our debt to the past is to put the future in debt to us.

—*ANONYMOUS*

Moral education is impossible apart from the habitual vision of greatness.

—*ALFRED NORTH WHITEHEAD*

One's work may be finished some day, but one's education never.

—*ALEXANDRE DUMAS*

Education is a ladder.

—*MANUELITO OF THE NAVAHOS*

Educate your sons and daughters, send them to school and show them that beside the cartridge box, the ballot box, and the jury box, you have also the knowledge box.

—*FREDERICK DOUGLASS*

EFFORT

It is not because things are difficult that we do not dare; it is because we do not dare that they are difficult.

—SENECA

For a trivial goal, any hardship is great. For a great goal, any hardship is trivial.

—ANONYMOUS

If there is no struggle, there is no progress. Those who profess to favor freedom and yet deprecate agitation are men who want crops without plowing up the ground. They want rain without thunder and lightning. They want the ocean without the awful roar of its many waters. This struggle may be a moral one, or it may be a physical one, or it may be both moral and physical; but it must be a struggle. Power concedes nothing without a demand. It never did and it never will.

—FREDERICK DOUGLASS

Virtue will have naught to do with ease. It seeks a rough and thorny path.

—MICHEL MONTAIGNE

Let us not try to be the best or worse of others, but let us make the effort to be the best of ourselves.

—MARCUS GARVEY

If you want that hill, you got to bleed for it.

—NELSON PEERY

By patience and hard work, we brought order out of chaos, just as will be true of any problem if we stick to it with patience and wisdom and earnest effort.

—BOOKER T. WASHINGTON

EMOTION

The heart is deceitful above all things, and it is exceedingly weak—who can know it?

—BIBLE (JEREMIAH 17:9)

Reacting against emotions—fearing our fear, being angry about our anger, getting depressed about our sadness—is much worse than these primary feelings themselves, for it freezes them and turns us against ourselves. Befriending emotions opens us to ourselves and allows us to discover the intelligence and responsiveness contained in them.... In judging these feelings, we cut ourselves off from our aliveness; in feeling them fully, their energy becomes available to us, enlarging our sense of what life is about.

—*JOHN WELWOOD*

The wind of emotion often blows out the light of reason.

—*ANONYMOUS*

I was angry with my friend,
I told my wrath, my wrath did end.
I was angry with my foe,
I told it not, my wrath did grow.

—*WILLIAM BLAKE*

The ennobling difference between one man and another is that one feels more than another.

—*JOHN RUSKIN*

Man is a speck of reason in an ocean of emotion.

—*WILLIAM JAMES*

The meanest fear is the fear of sentimentality.

—*G.K. CHESTERTON*

Our emotions are part of our basic power. They serve two major functions in our psychic life. They monitor our basic needs, telling us of a need, a loss or a satiation. Without our emotional energy, we would not be aware of our most fundamental needs. Emotions also give us the fuel or energy to act.... This energy moves us to get what we need. When our basic needs are being violated, our anger moves us to fight or run.

—*JOHN BRADSHAW*

When the heart overflows, the eyes tear.

—*SHOLOM ALEICHEM*

I have always felt sorry for people afraid of feeling, of sentimentality, who are unable to weep with their whole heart. Because those who do not know how to weep do not know how to laugh either.

—*GOLDA MEIR*

EMPATHY

A man, to be greatly good, must imagine intensely and comprehensively; he must put himself in the place of another and of many others; the pains and pleasures of his species must become his own. The great instrument of moral good is the imagination.... Poetry strengthens that faculty which is the organ of the moral nature of man in the same manner as exercise strengthens a limb.

—PERCY BYSSHE SHELLEY

Those who have never suffered are very often insufferable.

—ROBERT GORDIS

I never ask the wounded person how he feels; I myself become the wounded person.

—WALT WHITMAN

If we could read the secret history of our enemies, we should find in each man's life sorrow and suffering enough to disarm all hostility.

—HENRY WADSWORTH LONGFELLOW

A high degree of empathy in a relationship is possibly the most potent factor in bringing about change and learning.

—CARL ROGERS

If you want to raise a man from mud and filth, you must go all the way down yourself, down into mud and filth. Then take hold of him with strong hands and pull him and yourself into the light.

—RABBI SHLOMO OF KARLIN

I have heard their cry ... for I know their pains.

—BIBLE (EXODUS 3:7)

Friendship is born at that moment when one person says to another, "What? You too! I thought I was the only one."

—C.S. LEWIS

ENTHUSIASM

To lead you need passion ... ardor, zeal, enthusiasm—this personal involvement is absolutely necessary in a good leader.

—ROBERT HORTON

When a man dies, if he can pass enthusiasm along to his children, he has left them an estate of incalculable value.

—THOMAS EDISON

Years wrinkle the skin, but to give up enthusiasm wrinkles the soul.

—SAMUEL ULLMAN

None are so old as those who have outlived enthusiasm.

—HENRY DAVID THOREAU

ENVIRONMENT

Losing a species to extinction is like tearing a page out of sacred scripture.

—CALVIN DEWITT

If we attack nature with our polluting methods of manufacturing, and if we let the quality of life fade in the name of speed and efficiency, then symptoms may arise.... Our bodies reflect or participate in the world's body, so that if we harm that outer body, our own bodies will feel the effects. Essentially there is no distinction between the world's body and the human body.

—THOMAS MOORE

We have not inherited the earth from our parents, we are borrowing it from our children.

—LESTER BROWN

Pollution, defilement, squalor are words that never would have been created had man lived conformably to nature.

—JOHN MUIR

All is from You, and it is Your gift that we have given to You. For we are sojourners with You, mere transients.... Our days on earth are like a shadow.
—BIBLE (I CHRONICLES 29:14-15)

Those who cut down good trees are reckoned among the sinners who will never see any good in their lifetime.
—RABBINIC MIDRASH, "TOSEFTA BIKKURIM"

ENVY

Today upon a bus I saw a girl with golden hair.
She seemed so gay, I envied her, and wishes that I was half so fair.
I watched her as she rose to leave, and saw her hobble down the aisle
She had one leg and wore a crutch, but as she passed—a smile.
Oh God, forgive me when I whine: I have two legs and the world is mine.
Two legs to take me where I go,
Two eyes to see the sunset's glow,
Two ears to hear all that I should know.
Oh God, forgive me when I whine;
I'm blessed indeed, the world is mine.
—SAUL TEPLITZ

There is not a passion so strongly rooted in the human heart as envy.
—RICHARD SHERIDAN

He that envies is possessed of self-made hurts.
—SHAIKH SAADI

Envy-what a plague of one's thoughts, how great a rust of the heart, to be jealous of another.
—ST. CYPRIAN

Men in general are so inclined to envy the glory of others, as so jealous of good which they have not themselves accomplished, that a man often makes himself enemies by the simple fact that he has rendered great service.
—TOUSSAINT L'OUVERTURE

ETHICS

Do not be concerned about the purity of your ideals but rather the integrity of your compromises.

—*REINHOLD NIEHBUR*

Always do right. This will gratify some people and astonish the rest.

—*MARK TWAIN*

We have spent 5,000 years as a race of rational human beings, trying to drag ourselves out of the primeval slime by searching for truth and moral absolutes. In its purest form, truth is not a polite tap on the shoulder. It is a howling reproach. What Moses brought down from Mount Sinai were not the Ten Suggestions.

—*TED KOPPEL*

We've learned to fly through the air like birds and to swim under the seas like fish. All that remains for us to learn is how to walk on the earth like men.

—*PIERRE TEILHARD DE CHARDIN*

To be profoundly dishonest, a person must have one of two qualities: either he is unscrupulously ambitious, or his in unswervingly egocentric.

—*MAYA ANGELOU*

EVIL

Evil is a necessary part of good; good rests on evil. Within evil are many heavenly sparks which a righteous person can find and raise to a level of good.

—*KABBALAH*

If only it were so simple! If only there were evil people somewhere committing evil deeds and it were necessary only to separate them from the rest of us and destroy them. But the dividing line between good and evil cuts through the heart of every human being. And who is willing to destroy his own heart?

—*ALEXANDER SOLZHENITSYN*

Where God is, tragedy is only provisional and partial.

—*WILLIAM JAMES*

The problems of this world, when viewed from a certain angle, may even be seen as a demonstration of God's concern. Divinity is seen not only in interconnectedness, but in insufficiency, in the room left for human beings to create, to explore, to err.... God [was] trusting enough to leave us room for creative achievement and horrible mistakes, a God who loved enough to leave spaces.

—RABBI DAVID WOLPE

Good can be done only with the whole soul, evil is never done with the whole soul.

—MARTIN BUBER

It is good for me that I have been afflicted for thus have I learned Your precepts.

—BIBLE (PSALMS 119:71)

> The evil that men do lives after them,
> The good is oft interr'd with their bones.

—WILLIAM SHAKESPEARE

God could have ... planned the world so as to have perfection reign everywhere. We would have been spared much trouble in such a world, but we would have been denied one precious blessing—the privilege to stand on our own feet, to grow through our own effort, to know the thrill of discovery, of vanquishing evil and advancing the good.

—RABBI BEN ZION BOKSER

And God saw that the world was good. And God was partly right.

—NEVIL COGHILL

While humans are basically good, it is easier for them to do wrong than do right. The good impulse, rooted in altruism and selfishness, is weaker than the evil impulse. The good impulse is passive, with little power or influence over human conduct. The evil impulse is a powerful source of human energy.

—DAVI D S. ARIEL

Evil knows where evil sleeps.

—NIGERIAN PROVERB

For every evil there are two remedies: time and silence.

—ALEXANDRE DUMAS, FILS

Evil enters like a needle and spreads like an oak tree.

—ETHIOPIAN PROVERB

The purpose of evil was to survive it.

—TONI MORRISON

EXISTENTIAL LIVING

Yesterday is past; tomorrow is the future. Today is a gift. That's why it's called the "present."

—ANONYMOUS

To remember the past, to live in the present, and to trust in the future.

—ABBA KOVNER

Losing our ground ... is precisely what happens when we slip and fall away from being present. It is only in the stillness and simplicity of presence—when we are aware of what we are experiencing, when we are here with it as it unfolds—that we can really appreciate our life and reconnect with the ordinary magic of being alive on this earth.

—JOHN WELWOOD

Some there are that torment themselves afresh with the memory of what is past; others again, afflict themselves with the apprehensions of evils to come. The one does not now concern us, and the other not yet. One should count each day a separate life.

—SENECA

Every moment that I am centered in the future I suffer a temporary loss of this life.

—HUGH PRATHER

God's miracles belong to those who can concentrate on one thing and limit themselves.

—BAAL SHEM TOV

Any man can fight the battles of just one day. It is not the experience of today that drives men mad-it is remorse or bitterness for something which happened yesterday and the dread of what tomorrow may bring. It is only when we add the burdens of those two awful eternities that we break down. Let us, therefore, live but one day at a time.

—RAYMOND GALE

EXPERIENCE

Training is learning the rules. Experience is learning the exceptions.

—ANONYMOUS

Wisdom comes from life experience, well-digested. It's not what comes from reading great books. When it comes to understanding life, experiential learning is the only worthwhile kind.

—ERIK ERIKSON

Religious seekers have always been reminded that they must let go of all their concepts in order to directly experience reality, from the concepts of self and other, to those of birth and death, permanence and impermanence, existence and nonexistence. If reality is described as inconceivable, the tool to directly experience reality must be a mind pure of all concepts.

—THICH NHAT HANH

Knowledge is really nothing but experience.

—ALBERT EINSTEIN

What you have inherited from your ancestors, earn over again for your-selves, or it will not be yours.

—JOHANN WOLFGANG VON GOETHE

Experience is a wonderful thing. It enables you to recognize a mistake when you make it.

—ANONYMOUS

As for the man who lacks experience and listens not, he nothing good can do, knowledge he seems to see in ignorance, profit in loss—to mischief he will go, and running in the error of his ways, chooses the opposite of what man praises.

—PTAH HOTEP

Close you eyes as I take you on the experience of my life, the experience of hearing many different sounds from many different cultures from around the world.

—STEVIE WONDER

How you perceive experience and how you handle it determine how your life turns out in the long run.

—BILL COSBY

FAITH

For there is still a vision for the appointed time. At the destined hour it will come in breathless haste, it will not fail. If it delays, wait for it; for when it comes it will be no time to linger.

—BIBLE (HABAKKUK 2:3)

Just as a small fire is extinguished by the storm whereas a large fire is enhanced by it—likewise a weak faith is weakened by predicament and catastrophes, whereas a strong faith is strengthened by them.

—VIKTOR FRANKL

Faith is the true force of life.

—LEO TOLSTOY

For the believer, there are no questions. For the unbeliever, there are no answers.

—HAFETZ HAIM

Trust that the cosmos are benign.

—JONATHAN OMER-MAN

Faith is an oasis in the heart which will never be reached by the caravan of thinking.

—KAHLIL GIBRAN

The mind can proceed only so far upon what it knows and can prove. There comes a point where the mind takes a leap—call it intuition or what you will-and comes out upon a higher plane of knowledge, but can never prove how it got there. All great discoveries have involved such a leap.

—ALBERT EINSTEIN

Faith may be defined briefly as an illogical belief in the occurrence of the improbable.

—H.L. MENCKEN

They that wait for the Lord shall renew their strength
They shall mount up with wings as eagles
They shall run, and not be weary
They shall walk and not faint.

—BIBLE (ISAIAH 40:30)

Faith is not belief in spite of the evidence, but adventure in scorn of the consequences.

—*L.P. SACKS*

I believe in the human race. I believe in the warm heart. I believe in man's integrity. I believe in the goodness of a free society. And in the largest sense, I believe that what I did was done for me—that it was my faith in God that sustained me in my fight. And that what was done for me must and will be done for others.

—*JACKIE ROBINSON*

Faith is not a blind leap into nothing but a thoughtful walk into the light we have.

—*ELTON TRUEBLOOD*

The faith of a religious person comes with the triumphant assurance of God's salvation even in the darkest period ... and ever deepening gloom.

—*WILLIAM JAMES*

Hope is hearing the melody of the future. Faith is dancing to it.

—*RUBEN ALVES*

Faith is not a cushion for me to fall back upon; it is my working energy.

—*HELEN KELLER*

It is the heart that senses God, and not the reason. That is what faith is, God perceptible to the heart and not to reason.

—*BLAISE PASCAL*

Without faith man becomes sterile, hopeless, and afraid to the very core of his being.

—*ERICH FROMM*

In the midst of lonely days and dreary nights I have heard an inner voice saying, "Lo, I will be with you."

—*MARTIN LUTHER KING, JR.*

FAMILY

From the loving example of one family a whole state becomes loving.

—*"THE GREAT LEARNING"*

In a family where there is a stress, the whole organism shifts to bring balance, stability or survival. This is the type of dynamic each of us entered into when we came into a family.

—ANONYMOUS

Whatever is great and good in the institutions and usages of mankind is an application of sentiments that have drawn their first nourishment from the soil of the family.

—FELIX ADLER

In my culture, there is no such thing as a single woman alone with children. There is no such thing as "alone" at all. There is the family.

—MIRIAM MAKEBA

If relatives help each other, what evil can hurt them?

—ETHIOPIAN PROVERB

The family is an important source of emotional support and love given in an unconditional and consistent manner.

—CAROL E. BONNER

FANATICISM

Frantic orthodoxy is never rooted in faith but in doubt. It is when we are not sure that we are doubly sure.

—REINHOLD NIEBUHR

The greatest dangers to liberty lurk in insidious encroachment by men of zeal, well-meaning but without understanding.

—LOUIS BRANDEIS

How can you answer a man who tells you that he would rather obey God than men, and who is therefore sure to deserve heaven in cutting your throat?

—VOLTAIRE

For many of us the benevolent command "to love thy neighbor as thyself" has been replaced by the more dogmatic declaration: "Love thy neighbor when he is like thyself."

—RABBI HASKEL LOOKSTEIN

Nothing great is done without fanaticism. Fanaticism is religion; and eighteenth century "philosophers" who decried the former actually overthrew the latter. Fanaticism is faith, the essence of faith, burning faith, active faith, the faith that works miracles.

—GUSTAVE FLAUBERT

Be not righteous overmuch, and do not make yourself overwise; why should you destroy yourself?

—BIBLE (ECCLESIASTES 7:16)

An idealist is one willing to suffer for his cause. A fanatic is one who wants others to suffer for his cause.

—ANONYMOUS

> The best lack all conviction
> While the worst
> Are full of passionate intensity.

—WILLIAM BUTLER YEATS

FEAR

Keep your fears to yourself, but share your courage with others.

—ROBERT LOUIS STEVENSON

I'm an old man, and I have had many troubles, but most of them never happened.

—MARK TWAIN

Our fears are always more numerous than our dangers.

—SENECA

> Make believe you're brave
> And the trip will take you far
> You may be as brave as you make believe you are.

—RICHARD RODGERS and OSCAR HAMMERSTEIN

Have no fear.

—BIBLE (DEUTERONOMY 20:1)

It is not death or hardship that is dreadful, but the fear of death and hardship.

—EPICTETUS

Fear is an uneasiness of the mind, upon the thought of future evil likely to befall us.

—JOHN LOCKE

Men are apt to idolize or fear that which they cannot understand, especially if it be a woman.

—JEAN TOOMER

Fearlessness is the first requisite of spirituality. Cowards can never be moral.

—MOHANDAS GANDHI

Fear brings out the worst thing in everybody.

—MAYA ANGELOU

I was frightened, but I figured we needed help to get us more jobs and better education.

—ROSA PARKS

He who fears is literally delivered to destruction.

—HOWARD THURMAN

Fear is a noose that binds until it strangles.

—JEAN TOOMER

Because they are afraid of us, we are afraid of them.

—RICHARD WRIGHT

There can be no courage without fear, and fear comes only from the imagination.

—PETER ABRAHAMS

To defend oneself against a fear is simply to insure that one will, one day, be conquered by it; fears must be faced.

—JAMES BALDWIN

Fear is a two-edged sword that sometimes cuts the wielder.

—JEAN TOOMER

No man lives in safety as along as his brother lives in fear.

—WILLIAM BRANCH

If you are not afraid to look back, nothing you are facing can frighten you.

—*JAMES BALDWIN*

Distrust is motivated by fear, and fear is motivated by the unknown.

—*JULIA BOYD*

FEELINGS

When tears come, I breathe deeply and rest, I know I am swimming in a hallowed stream where many have gone before. I am not alone, crazy, or having a nervous breakdown.... My heart is at work. My soul is awake.

—*MARY MARGARET FUNK*

When you pour out your heart, it feels lighter.

—*MOSES MAIMONIDES*

That tears have a purifying, rejuvenating, and light-bearing power and capability-this was known by the masters of spiritual life: the hermits, monks, and members of spiritual orders in the past. The gift of tears was highly esteemed by them.... And just as the moving waters precede the appearance of the rainbow in the primeval light so does weeping precede the rainbow of illuminating light in the soul.

—*VALENTINE TOMBERG*

Heroism feels and never reasons and is always right.

—*RALPH WALDO EMERSON*

Angels are another name for feelings.
When we love and act with kindness
We create angels of love and kindness.
When we hate and act with violence
We create angels of hatred and violence.
It is our task ... to fill our world
With angels of love—
Messengers of kindness
That link all people together as one family.

—*RABBI RAMI SHAPIRO*

We are healed of a suffering only by experiencing it to the full.

—*MARCEL PROUST*

The greater the person, the greater the passion.

—*TALMUD*

We do not change the world except as we change individuals; we do not change individuals except as we change their hearts.

—*QUAKER PROVERB*

The only way to stop experiencing something is to be totally willing to experience it.

—*GAY HENDRICKS*

Give sorrow words; the grief that does not speak
Whispers the o'er-fraught heart, and bids it break.

—*WILLIAM SHAKESPEARE*

FLEXIBILITY

In a storm, it is the bamboo, the flexible tree, that can bend with the wind and survive. The rigid tree that resists the wind falls, victim of its own insistence to control.

—*JOAN BORYSENKO*

FORCE

A little subtleness is better than a lot of force.

—*CONGOLESE PROVER*

FORGIVENESS

A retentive memory may be a good thing, but the ability to forget is the true token of greatness.

—*ELBERT HUBBARD*

Forgiveness is letting what was, be gone; what will be, come; what is now, be.

—DAVID AUGSBURGER

To understand all is to forgive all.

—FRENCH PROVERB

To be wronged is nothing unless you continue to remember it.

—CONFUCIUS

Forgiveness is not a lack of discrimination whereby we let all the criminals out of prison; it is an attitude that permits us to relate to the pain that led to their errors and recognize their need for love. Whereas judgmentalism focuses on flaws, forgiveness focuses on wholeness.

—JOAN BORYSENKO

Nothing that is worth doing can be achieved in our lifetime; therefore we must be saved by hope. Nothing which is true or beautiful or good makes complete sense in any immediate context of history; therefore we must be saved by faith. Nothing we do, however virtuous, can be accomplished alone; therefore we are saved by love. No virtuous act is quite as virtuous from the standpoint of our friend or foe as it is from our standpoint. Therefore we must be saved by the final favor of love which is forgiveness.

—REINHOLD NIEBUHR

Living life as art requires a readiness to forgive.

—MAYA ANGELOU

FREEDOM

Liberty is to be sought from within rather than from without.

—JOHN MILTON

Freedom is not free. Preserving [our] society involves commitment, risk and constant effort.... Nothing grows unless one plows, tends the soil and keeps it fertile year after year.

—EDMOND KAHN

Those who would deny freedom to others deserve it not for themselves, and, under a just God, cannot long retain it.

—ABRAHAM LINCOLN

You can never enslave somebody who knows who he is.

—ALEX HALEY

Freedom with tragedy is better than compulsory happiness.

—FYODOR DOSTOYEVSKY

Men are qualified for civil liberty in exact proportion to their disposition to put moral chains upon their own appetites. Society cannot exist unless a controlling power upon will and appetite be placed somewhere and the less of it there is within, the more there is without. It is ordained in the eternal constitution of things, that men of intemperate minds cannot be free; their passions forge their fetters.

—EDMUND BURKE

There is nothing more arduous than the apprenticeship of liberty.

—ALEXIS DE TOCQUEVILLE

We should be eternally vigilant against attempts to check the expression of opinions that we loathe and believe to be fraught with death.

—OLIVER WENDELL HOLMES

Almighty God hath created the mind free.... No man shall be compelled to frequent or support any religious worship or ministry or shall otherwise suffer on account of his religious opinions or belief, but all men shall be free to profess and by argument to maintain, their opinions in matters of religion.

—THOMAS JEFFERSON

The aim of art, the aim of life can only be to increase the sum of freedom and responsibility to be found in every man and in the world. It cannot, under any circumstances, be to reduce or suppress that freedom, even temporarily.... There is not a single true work of art that has not in the end added to the inner freedom of each person who has known and loved it.

—ALBERT CAMUS

Man is born free, but one of the first things he learns is to do as he is told, and he spends the rest of his life doing that.

—ERIC BERNE

The greatest blessing of our democracy is freedom. But in the last analysis, freedom is rooted in our ability to discipline ourselves. Freedom and responsibility are like Siamese twins: They die if they are parted.

—BERNARD BARUCH

Not free from what, but free for what?

—FRIEDRICH NIETZSCHE

If there is any principle of the Constitution that more imperatively calls for attachment than any other it is the principle of free thought—not free thought for those who agree with us but freedom for the thought that we hate.

—OLIVER WENDELL HOLMES

The peculiar evil of silencing the expression of an opinion is, that it is robbing the human race; posterity as well as the existing generation; those who dissent from the opinion, still more than those who hold it.

—JOHN STUART MILL

We do not need to fear ideas but the censorship of ideas. We do not need to fear criticism but the silencing of criticism. We do not need to fear resistance to political leaders but unquestioning acquiescence in whatever policies those leaders adopt.

—HENRY STEELE COMAGER

If liberty means anything at all, it means the right to tell people what they do not want to hear.

—GEORGE ORWELL

If a nation values anything more than freedom, it will lose its freedom; and the irony of that is that if it is comfort or money, then it will lose that too.

—SOMERSET MAUGHAM

Freedom is a state of mind: a spiritual unchoking of the wells of human power and superhuman love.

—W.E.B. DU BOIS

In every human breast God has implanted a principle which we call love of freedom; it is impatient of oppression and pants for deliverance.

—PHILLIS WHEATLEY

When I liberate others, I liberate myself.

—FANNIE LOU HAMER

A piece of freedom is no longer enough for human beings; freedom is like life. It cannot be had in installments.

—JAMES BALDWIN

Those who profess to favor freedom, and yet depreciate agitation, are men who want crops without plowing up the ground.

—FREDERICK DOUGLASS

There is no easy walk to freedom anywhere and many of us will have to pass through the valley of the shadow of death again and again before we reach the mountaintop of our desires.

—NELSON MANDELA

I can come when I please
I can go when I please
I can flit, fly, and flutter,
like the birds in the trees.

—ETHEL WATERS

Freedom is not free.

—MARTIN LUTHER KING, JR

FRIENDSHIP

Our duty is not to see through one another, but to see one another through.

—LEONARD SWEET

Go often to the house of your friend, for weeds soon choke up the unused path.

—SCANDINAVIAN PROVERB

The sweetness of friendship issues from the response to a basic need in human nature. One needs friends, companions, to supplement the intimacy of family relationships if his life is to be complete.

—RABBI BERYL COHON

So unique and important is friendship that God Himself teaches the skill to human beings and creates friendships among people.

—RABBI DAVID WOLPE

A friend may well be reckoned a masterpiece of nature.

—RALPH WALDO EMERSON

Friendship must be kept in constant repair.

—SAMUEL JOHNSON

He makes no friend who never made a foe.

—ALFRED LORD TENNYSON

A friend is one who knows your song, and sings it to you when you forget.

—ANONYMOUS

It is highly necessary for every person to have at least one sincere friend, one true companion. This friend must be so close to us that we are able to tell even that of which we are ashamed.

—RABBI SIMHAH BUNAM

Friendship is the comfort, the inexpressible comfort of feeling safe with a person having neither to weigh thoughts nor measure words, but pouring all right out just as they are, chaff and grain together, certain that a faithful friendly hand will take and sift them, keep what is worth keeping and with a breath of comfort, blow the rest away.

—GEORGE ELIOT

Be first to greet others. Invite them to your joyous occasions. Call them by complimentary names. Do not give away secrets, help others when they are in trouble. Look after their interests when they are away. Overlook their shortcomings and forgive them promptly. Criticize them when they have done wrong. Respect them always. Do not deceive them. Do not lie to them. Pray for them and wish them happiness.

—"MENORAT HA-MAOR"

Friendships have defended more borders than arms and cannon ever have.

—DWIGHT EISENHOWER

A friend is one who walks in when others walk out.

—WALTER WINCHELL

The only way to have a friend is to be one.

—RALPH WALDO EMERSON

When you know who his friend is, you know who he is.

—SENEGALESE PROVERB

The name of Bravest of the Brave,
On whom should we bestow?
On one who turns into a friend
One's greatest mortal foe.

—TALMUD

Equals make the best friends.

—AESOP

A good friendship makes you feel at ease.

—UGANDAN PROVERB

Mutual gifts cement friendship.

—IVORY COAST PROVERB

Being a friend means mastering the art of timing. There is a time for silence. A time to let go and allow people to hurl themselves into their own history. And a time to pick up the pieces when it's all over.

—GLORIA NAYLOR

FULFILLMENT

Let each become all that he was created capable of being: Expand, if possible, to his full growth; and show himself at length in his own shape and stature.

—THOMAS CARLYLE

Most men lead lives of quiet desperation.

—HENRY DAVID THOREAU

Many people live in only one room of their house, while the house might actually be a palace with towers, banquet halls, sitting rooms, and gardens. They lock themselves in the kitchen or the cellar, believing this room to be the whole house.

—JAMES LYNWOOD WALKER

Every weed is a potential flower.

—LUTHER BURBANK

FUNDAMENTALISM

Believe those who are seeking truth. Doubt those who find it.

—ANDRE GIDE

The future is uncertain ... but this uncertainty is at the very heart of human creativity.

—ILYA PRIGOGINE

We can build a community out of seekers of truth, but not out of possessors of truth.

—WILLIAM SLOAN COFFIN

The greatest haughtiness is that of excessive piety.

—HASIDIC SAYING

Most people prefer the certainty of misery to the misery of uncertainty.

—VIRGINIA SATIR

Whoever undertakes to set himself as judge in the field of Truth and Knowledge is shipwrecked by the laughter of the gods.

—ALBERT EINSTEIN

Be careful to avoid the teacher who says there is only one valid meaning to the text-his or her own! The teacher who gives you the answers rather than the questions, who sees Judaism as an authoritarian system rather than a journey of inquiry and discovery, is not a true Jewish teacher.

—DAVID S. ARIEL

GENERATIVITY

Man is so constituted that he needs to be needed, lest he suffer the mental deformation of self-absorption. Generativity is expressed in parenthood but also in work and creative thought. Man needs to teach.

—ERIK ERIKSON

GENEROSITY

Honor the Lord with your wealth,
With the best of all your income,
And your barns will be filled with grain,
Your vats will burst with new wine.

—BIBLE (PROVERBS 3:9-10)

Liberality consists less in giving much than in giving at the right moment.

—JEAN DE LA BRUYERE

True charity is the desire to be useful to others without thought of recompense.

—EMANUEL SWEDENBORG

GOALS

Hell is to drift; heaven is to steer.

—GEORGE BERNARD SHAW

To be a leader, you have to make people want to follow you, and nobody wants to follow someone who doesn't know where he's going.

—JOE NAMATH

People's feet will lead them to the destination of which they have really decided in the innermost recesses of their heart.

—MIDRASH: MEKHILTA OF RABBI YISHMAEL

I set a goal of becoming a starter on the varsity. That's what I focused on all summer. When I worked on my game, that's what I thought about. When it happened, I set another goal, a reasonable, manageable goal that I could realistically achieve if I worked hard enough.

—MICHAEL JORDAN

The tragedy in life doesn't lie in not reaching your goal. The tragedy lies in having no goal to reach.

—BENJAMIN E. MAYS

People who expect to achieve their goals don't stand around talking about them.

—LES BROWN

GOD

If we wager that God does not exist and He does, then we have everything to lose and nothing to win. If we wager that God does exist and He does, then we have everything to gain and nothing to lose.

—BLAISE PASCAL

When you try to understand the invisible, don't overlook the visible.

—ANONYMOUS

If God is great, he is not good,
If God is good, he is not great.

—ARCHIBALD MACLEISH

I say, not God Himself can make man's best
Without best men to help Him....
'Tis God gives skill,
But not without man's hands.

—GEORGE ELIOT

God is near unto all who call upon God, to all who call upon God in truth.

—BIBLE (PSALMS 145:18)

I've not seen the robin but I know he is there because I heard him singing through my window from the tree-top outside.

I have not seen God. But I have looked at my child's eye, and have been overwhelmed by the miracle of unfolding life.

I have watched the trees bedeck themselves with new garbs of green in the spring, and have been stirred by the miracle of continual rebirth.

I have looked at the stars, and have been overcome by the miracle of the grandeur and majesty of the universe.

I know that God exists, because I have heard the song of His presence from all the tree-tops of creation.

—RABBI BEN ZION BOSKER

Without God, life would be without problems, without anguish, without hope. For God is not only the answer to those who suffer as a result of questions; God is also the question to those who think they have found the answer.

—*ELIE WIESEL*

A person asked God: "Why in ordinary times are there two sets of footprints following me, Yours and mine; but in hard times there is only one, and I feel so alone?" And God responded: "Ah, in the hard times I was carrying you."

—*RICHARD LEVY*

A soul can split the sky in two and let the face of God shine through.

—*EDNA ST. VINCENT MILLAY*

While God's face is above, God's heart is down below.

—*MIDRASH*

The real question is whether we can make a leap of love, not a leap of faith. To make a leap of love means to love God whether or not He (or She, or It) exists. It is in loving God, rather than in only talking God, that we move from metaphor to meaning.

—*LEONARD FEIN*

Unless there is within us that which is above us, we shall soon yield to that which is about us.

—*PETER FORSYTHE*

One must worship something; if one does not worship God, one will worship an idol made of wood, or of gold, or of ideas.

—*FYODOR DOSTOYEVSKY*

God is like a mirror, which stays the same, yet everyone who looks into it sees a different face.

—*TALMUD*

God who gave us life gave us liberty. Can the liberties of a nation be secure when we have removed a conviction that these liberties are the gift of God?

—*THOMAS JEFFERSON*

Religion is not what man does with his solitariness, but rather what man does with God's concern for all men.

—*RABBI ABRAHAM JOSHUA HESCHEL*

Saying you believe in God is about the most gratuitous utterance one can make. Belief in God is an inference from one's actions and life; if we show love and depth we are rooted in the Divine, whatever we say. We can even say we are freethinkers and atheists ... and still be rooted in God. Or we can invoke God until we are blue in the face, but if we go off in our actual life on a totally different basis, what good is the assertion?

—HENRY SLONIMSKY

God can be addressed, not expressed.

—MARTIN BUBER

Heedfulness leads to cleanness; cleanness to purity; purity to holiness; holiness to humility; humility to dread of sin; dread of sin to saintliness; saintliness to the awareness of the Spirit of the Divine.

—RABBI ZEV NELSON

For God, to me, it seems, is a verb, not a noun.

—BUCKMINSTER FULLER

One who does the commandments out of love [of God] is superior to one who does them out of fear.

—TALMUD

At times one must act as though one were an atheist. When poor people ask you for help, don't tell them to have faith in God, who will never let you down. Act as if there is no God, and only you could help them.

—HASIDIC TEACHING

Called or not called, God is present.

—CARL JUNG

Where there is no God, all is permitted.

—FYODOR DOSTOYEVSKY

When you are My witnesses, I am God, and when you are not My witnesses, I am not God.

—TALMUD

The wisdom which a person requires is, first, to know and contemplate the mystery of God and, second, to know yourself.

—ZOHAR HADASH

In the beginning God ... in the end God.

—BISHOP DESMOND TUTU

As a medieval Jewish philosopher, Shem Tov ibn Falquera, said, "If you know yourself, you know God."

—DAVID S. ARIEL

There isn't a certain time we should set aside to talk about God. God is part of our every waking moment.

—MARVA COLLINS

I decided that purpose, meaning, and order in nature emanated from God and that the same must be true for me.

—ANDREW YOUNG

People see God everyday, they just don't recognize Him.

—PEARL BAILEY

What is against life will be destroyed by life, for what is against life is against God.

—HOWARD THURMAN

Make it a habit to begin each day affirming that God is great and that life is a blessing.

—SUSAN L. TAYLOR

One plus God make a majority.

—FREDERICK DOUGLASS

We live inside this unbelievable cosmos, inside our unbelievable bodies- everything so perfect, everything so in tune. I got to think God had a hand in it.

—RAY CHARLES

Atheism is a non-prophet organization.

—GEORGE CARLIN

God gives nothing to those who keep their arms crossed.

—AFRICAN PROVERB

GOSSIP

There is so much good in the worst of us, and so much bad in the best of us, that it hardly behooves any of us to talk about the rest of us.

—ANONYMOUS

Let what you heard die within you; be assured it will not make you burst.

—*TALMUD*

Two things are bad for the heart—running up stairs and running down people.

—*BERNARD BARUCH*

He who throws mud loses ground.

—*MOE UDALL*

> Who steals my purse steals trash;
> 'Tis something, nothing;
> 'Twas mine, 'tis his, and has been slave to thousands;
> But he that filches from me my good name
> Robs me of that which not enriches him,
> And makes me poor indeed.

—*WILLIAM SHAKESPEARE*

GOVERNMENT

That government is best which governs the least, because its people discipline themselves.

—*THOMAS JEFFERSON*

Government is no other than the soul of a city or nation.

—*JAMES HARRINGTON*

Of all the disposition and habits which lead to political prosperity, Religion and Morality are indispensable supports.

—*GEORGE WASHINGTON*

No form of government makes anybody omniscient.

—*THOMAS SOWELL*

The government they devised was defective from the start, requiring several amendments, a civil war, and momentous social transformation to attain the system of constitutional government, and its respect for individual freedoms and human rights that we hold as fundamental today.

—*THURGOOD MARSHALL*

Americans had better watch out, for the political philosophers have warned us that a people will eventually get the kind of government they deserve.

—*PLAYTHELL BENJAMIN*

The problem with depending on a government is that you can't depend on it.

—*TONY BROWN*

GRATITUDE

Mankind will not perish for want of information, but only for want of appreciation.

—*RABBI ABRAHAM JOSHUA HESCHEL*

Things easily granted are taken for granted.

—*ANONYMOUS*

Life is like a mirror. If you frown at it, it frowns back. If you smile, it returns the greeting.

—*WILLIAM THACKERAY*

The man who has forgotten to be thankful has fallen asleep in the midst of life.

—*ROBERT LOUIS STEVENSON*

People would enjoy life more if, once they got what they wanted, they could remember how much they had wanted it.

—*ANONYMOUS*

GREATNESS

No saint, no hero, no discoverer, no prophet, no leader ever did his work cheaply and easily, comfortably and painlessly, and no people was ever great which did not pass through the valley of the shadow of death on its way to greatness.

—*WALTER LIPPMANN*

Lives of great men all remind us
We can make our lives sublime,
And, departing, leave behind us
Footprints on the sands of time.
Footprints, that perhaps another
Sailing o'er life's solemn main,
A forlorn and shipwrecked brother,
Seeing, shall take heart again.

—HENRY WADSWORTH LONGFELLOW

A contemplation of God's works, a generous concern for the good of mankind, and the unfeigned exercise of humility—these only denominate men great and glorious.

—JOSEPH ADDISON

GREED

Greed makes you believe things you would not normally believe.

—IDRIES SHAH

Those who seek more than they need hinder themselves from enjoying what they have.

—SOLOMON IBN-GABIROL

GRIEF

Fill my heart with Love,
that my every teardrop may become a star.

—HAZRAT INAYAT KHAN

GROWTH

I have great faith in a seed. Convince me that you have a seed there and I expect wonders.

—HENRY DAVID THOREAU

Lord, I thank you for the opportunity to grow.

—*LEVI BEN AMITAI*

The great thing in this world is not so much where we stand, as in what direction we are moving.

—*OLIVER WENDELL HOLMES*

A stone is characterized by its finality, whereas man's outstanding quality is in its being a surprise. To claim to be what I am not is a pretension. To insist that I must be only what I am now is a restriction which human nature must abhor. The being of a person is never completed, final.

—*RABBI ABRAHAM JOSHUA HESCHEL*

Friend, don't be a perfectionist. Perfectionism is a curse and a strain. For you tremble lest you miss the bulls-eye. You are perfect if you let be. Friend, don't be afraid of mistakes. Mistakes are no sins. Mistakes are ways of doing something different, perhaps creatively new. Friend, don't be sorry for your mistakes. Be proud of them. You had the courage to give something of yourself.

—*FRITZ PERLS*

This is the journey that men make: To find themselves. If they fail in this, it doesn't matter what else they find. Money, position, fame, many loves, revenge are all of little consequence, and when the tickets are collected at the end of the ride, they are tossed into a bin marked "Failure." But if a man happens to find himself ... then he has found a mansion which he can inhabit with dignity all the days of his life.

—*JAMES MICHENER*

Growth is the only evidence of life.

—*JOHN HENRY NEWMAN*

The mind stretched to a new idea never returns to its original dimension.

—*OLIVER WENDELL HOLMES*

Birth is not one act; it is a process. The aim of life is to be fully born, though its tragedy is that most of us die before we are thus born. To live is to be born every minute. Death occurs when birth stops.

—*ERICH FROMM*

Life has its own urges and only so much patience with the status quo.

—*GEORGE LEONARD*

My pleasure is seeing that I myself grow better day by day.

—EPICTETUS

The true profession of a person is to find the way to oneself.

—HERMAN HESSE

You and I can never be born enough. We are human beings for whom birth is a supremely welcome mystery, the mystery of growing ... which happens only and whenever we are faithful to ourselves.

—e.e. cummings

Our soul ... ferments slowly, quietly, imperceptibly, but is always developing, growing, rising, maturing, and elevating. Almost unnoticed, as we add insight to insight ... good deed to good deed, kindness to kindness, our very interiority begins to expand, our yearning increases, and the curtain between the natural and the supernatural parts ever so slightly, affording us illuminating insights into the realms beyond and within, giving us an awareness of the transcendent, of the Supernatural, and increasing our love for God Himself.

—RABBI NORMANN LAMM

Becoming is superior to being.

—PAUL KLEE

Man never is
But wholly hopes to be.

—ROBERT BROWNING

Our prayers are answered not when we are given what we ask, but when we are challenged to be what we can be.

—MORRIS ADLER

No matter how full the river, it still wants to grow.

—CONGOLESE PROVERB

One might as well try to stop the progress of a mighty railroad train by throwing his body across the tracks; as to try to stop the growth of the world in the direction of giving mankind more intelligence, more culture, and more liberty.

—BOOKER T. WASHINGTON

GUILT

Guilt is ... evidence of moral pain and gives us human stature. To pretend we don't feel guilt is to cheat ourselves of a humanizing emotion.

—RABBI SIDNEY GREENBERG

It is good, even necessary, for a person's development to have intrinsic guilt when he deserves to. It is not just a symptom to be avoided at any cost but is rather an inner guide for growth toward actualization of the real self, and of its potentialities.

—ABRAHAM MASLOW

HABIT

Our virtues are habits as much as our vices. All our life, so far as it has definite form, is but a mass of habits—practical, emotional, and intellectual—systematically organized for our weal or woe. [Such habits] bear us irresistibly toward our destiny.

—WILLIAM JAMES

A habit cannot be tossed out the window. It must be coaxed down the stairs a step at a time.

—MARK TWAIN

In the beginning, sin is like a thread of a spider's web; but in the end, it becomes like the cable of a ship.

—TALMUD

A man should cultivate good deeds in order to improve his character and depart from evil deeds if he wishes his undesirable traits to disappear. Know that good and bad qualities can only be cultivated by repetitive acts. If those actions are good, we acquire a praiseworthy trait, if bad, an undesirable one.

—MOSES MAIMONIDES

A good person is not he who does the right thing, but he who is in the habit of doing the right thing.

—RABBI ABRAHAM JOSHUA HESCHEL

Habit is stronger than reason.

—GEORGE SANTAYANA

HAPPINESS

Stir muddy water,
And it will stay cloudy.
Leave it alone,
And it will become clear.
Let the stream flow,
And it will find its way.
Stop chasing contentment,
And it will come to you.

—TAO TE CHING

Most people are about as happy as they make up their minds to be.

—ABRAHAM LINCOLN

The search for happiness is one of the chief sources of unhappiness.

—ANONYMOUS

While every life has its dark and its cheerful hours, happiness comes from choosing which to remember.

—RABBI SAUL TEPLITZ

O happiness! Our being's end and aim!
Good, pleasure, ease, content; Whate'er thy name:
That something still which prompts the eternal sigh,
For which we bear to live, or dare to die.

—ALEXANDER POPE

True contentment is the power of getting out of any situation all that there is in it.

—G.K. CHESTERTON

Happiness is like a butterfly.
The more you chase it,
The more it will elude you.
But if you turn your attention to other things,
It comes and softly sits on your shoulder.

—L. RICHARD LESSOR

Gratifications lead to only temporary happiness which in turn tends to succeeded by another and (hopefully) higher discontent. It looks as if the human hope for eternal happiness can never be fulfilled. Certainly happiness does come and is obtainable and is real. But it looks as if we must accept its intrinsic transience, especially if we focus on its more intense forms. Peak experiences do not last, and cannot last. Intense happiness is episodic, not continuous.

—ABRAHAM MASLOW

We should try to find happiness as we travel along the road of life. It is foolish to wait until we reach the heights before we view the scenery.

—RABBI SAUL TEPLITZ

Happiness is like those palaces in fairy tales whose gates are guarded by dragons: we must fight in order to conquer it.

—ALEXANDER DUMAS, FILS

Happiness is a perfume, you can't pour on somebody else without getting a few drops on yourself.

—JAMES VAN DER ZEE

My concept of happiness is to be fulfilled in a spiritual sense.

—CORETTA SCOTT KING

HASTE

The slower you drive, the farther you get.

—RUSSIAN PROVERB

What is done in haste is usually regretted in leisure.

—ANONYMOUS

HATE

A man who lives not by what he loves but what he hates is a sick man.

—ARCHIBALD MACLEISH

Those who hate you don't win unless you hate them. And then you destroy yourself.

—RICHARD NIXON

The harboring of hate and resentment against others is ... a biting of oneself. The fruit of hate is always weakness, never strength. We think we are harming others in holding spites, but the deeper harm is to ourselves.

—RABBI SAUL TEPLITZ

Hate wears many masks. It comes disguised as racial or religious superiority, or it can wear the mask of patriotism or revolution. It is the cancer at the root of human relationships—among individuals and entire nations. But strangely, the phenomenon of hate itself and the evil it fosters has rarely been addressed. Although hate has been with humankind since the beginning ... it remains an uncharted sickness in the human soul.

—ELIE WIESEL

Hatred is the coward's revenge for being intimidated.

—ANONYMOUS

Anything, God, but hate;
I have known it in my day,
And the best it does is scar your soul
And eat your heart away.
We must know more than hate,
As the years go rolling on;
For the stars survive and the spring survives,
Only humans deny the dawn.
God, if I have but one prayer
Before the cloud-wrapped end,
I'm sick of hate and the waste it makes.
Let me be another's friend.

—ANONYMOUS

HEALING

People heal with their minds. That's where the power is. Once you tap into it, you have joined up with a universal energy force. And with that power, nothing is impossible.

—GERALD JAMPOLSKY, M.D.

Patients who get well when they're not supposed to are not having accidents or miracles or spontaneous remissions. They're having self-induced healing.... I saw people suddenly having their cancer shrink or disappear. These were things I had never seen before. I was astonished. And, as a physician, I felt uncomfortable with it. They were getting better and I didn't even lift a finger.

—BERNARD SIEGEL, M.D.

The Lord heals broken hearts, and binds up wounds.

—BIBLE (PSALMS 147:2-3)

It is more necessary for the soul to be healed than the body; for it is better to die than to live ill.

—EPICTETUS

The experience of love and peace is the only thing of importance that is communicated. It is this attitude of the heart and not what is said between two people that does healing work in both directions. One party's accumulation of verbal knowledge is of little use to deep inner healing.

—GERALD JAMPOLSKY, M.D.

HEALTH

Daily must a person groom himself, keeping the body always neat and clean, in honor of the Creator.

—TALMUD

A person's spirit can sustain one through illness;
But low spirits—who can bear them?

—BIBLE (PROVERBS 18:14)

There is no wealth like health.

—BEN SIRA

To keep the body in good health is a duty, for otherwise we shall not b able to trim the lamp of wisdom, and keep our mind strong and clear.

—BUDDHA

A joyful heart makes for good health;
Despondency dries up the bones.

—BIBLE (PROVERBS 17:22)

HEART

If the lights go out all over the world
And if even the candles of the churches are dimmed
and eliminated
Blow on the coal of the heart, my dear.
Blow on the coal of the heart,
And we will have a light to see
And we will have a fire that will warm us.

—ARCHIBALD MACLEISH

Of what avail is an open eye, if the heart is blind?

—SOLOMON IBN-GABIROL

When God measures a person, God puts the tape around the heart, instead of the head.

—ANONYMOUS

Walk in the ways of your heart.

—BIBLE (ECCLESIASTES 11:9)

Grant us the knowledge that we need
To solve the problems of the mind,
But, dear God, light Thou our candle
And keep our hearts from going blind.

—RABBI WILLIAM SILVERMAN

The heart is half a prophet.

—YIDDISH SAYING

Enough of science and of art:
Close up those barren leaves:
Come forth, and bring with you a heart
That watches and receives.

—WILLIAM WORDSWORTH

HEAVEN

Earth's crammed with heaven and every common bush afire with God;
But only he who sees takes off his shoes.

—ELIZABETH BARRETT BROWNING

The main object of religion is not to get a man into heaven, but to get heaven into man.

—THOMAS HARDY

Heaven is under our feet as well as over our heads.

—HENRY DAVID THOREAU

Heaven, to those who truly love all, can be heaven only when it has emptied hell.

—NELS FERRE

HELL

The hell to be endured hereafter, of which theology tells, is no worse than the hell we make for ourselves in this world by habitually fashioning our characters in the wrong way. If we realize the extent to which we are mere walking bundles of habits we would give more heed to their formation. We are spinning our own fates, good or evil, and never to be undone. Every smallest stroke of virtue or of vice leaves its ever-so-little scar.

—WILLIAM JAMES

Hell is the suffering of being unable to love.

—FYODOR DOSTOYEVSKY

Hell is paved with good intentions.

—SAMUEL JOHNSON

HEROES

Most of us will never do great things, but we can do small things in a great way.

—ANONYMOUS

It is personalities not principles that move the age.

—OSCAR WILDE

How we treat the weak and needy is the measure of our heroism. For each of us, the question is not what dragons we have slain, but how we tend sheep.

—RABBI DAVID WOLPE

Lives of saints are our source of whatever morality exists in the world.

—HENRI BERGSON

Through such souls alone
God stooping shows sufficient of his light
For us in the dark to rise by. And I rise.

— ROBERT BROWNING

To believe in the heroic makes heroes.

—BENJAMIN DISRAELI

HISTORY

People and governments never have learned anything from history, or acted on principles deduced from it.

—GEORG HEGEL

History is little more than the register of the crimes, follies and misfortunes of mankind.

—EDWARD GIBBON

Life must be lived forward, but can only be understood backward.

—SOREN KIERKEGAARD

A people's memory is history; and as a person without memory, so a people without history cannot grow wiser.

—Y.L. PERETZ

Take from the altars of the past—the fire—not the ashes!

—JEAN JAURES

The interest of the student of history ought to be in the flower which history puts forth, and not the mulch in which it grew.

—LOUIS GINZBERG

The heritage of the past is the seed that brings forth the harvest of the future.

—ANONYMOUS

Remember your roots, your history, and the forebears' shoulders on which you stand. And pass these roots on to your children and to other children. Young people who do not know where they are now will not know where they are going or what to do for anyone besides themselves if and when they finally get somewhere.

—MARIAN WRIGHT EDELMAN

History is the long and tragic story of the fact that privileged groups seldom give up their privileges voluntarily.

—MARTIN LUTHER KING, JR.

Sometimes history takes things into its own hands.

—THURGOOD MARSHALL

History, like beauty, depends largely on the beholder.

—DESMOND TUTU

History has no vacuum. There are transformations, there are lesions, there are metamorphoses, and there are mysteries that cloak the clashing of individual wills and private interests.

—RALPH ELLISON

We need to haunt the halls of history and listen anew to the ancestors' wisdom.

—MAYA ANGELOU

HOLINESS

It takes three things to attain a sense of significant being: God, a soul, and a moment. And the three are always here.

—RABBI ABRAHAM JOSHUA HESCHEL

The great lesson from the true mystics is that the sacred is in the ordinary, that it is found in one's daily life. In one's neighbors, friends, and family and one's backyard.

—ABRAHAM MASLOW

We may say that holy or sacred places have a "spiritual" dimension. But what does that mean? Spiritual ... is that which establishes a connection between the finite and the Infinite ... Spiritual is where "the window of the moment [opens] to the sky of the eternal." Spiritual implies connectedness, a transcendence of the separated self. Spiritual may mean connection not only with the human community but also with the great chain of life.

—WILLIAM HOUFF

Holiness is a greater deal by far than happiness because it embraces struggle and sees all things—achievement, aspiration, even love—as a part of the moral drama of the world and not as life's end or sole reason for being. Holiness is greater than happiness because it is never achieved, it is ever in process, an elusive goal just beyond our reach. The ladder of holiness is built with the rungs of each human life, each worthy accomplishment, each effort at goodness. Sanctity is the only human ladder that reaches, in the biblical metaphor, to the heavens.

—RABBI DAVID WOLPE

The invariable mark of wisdom is to see the miraculous in the common.

—RALPH WALDO EMERSON

Brothers, love a man even in his sin, for that is the semblance of Divine Love and is the highest love on earth. Love all God's creation, the whole and every grain of sand in it. Love every leaf, every ray of God's light. Love the animals, love the plants, love everything. If you love everything, you will perceive it, you will begin to comprehend it better every day. And you will come at last to love the whole world with an all-embracing love.

—FYODOR DOSTOYEVSKY

Let one always consider oneself as if the Holy One dwells within.

— *TALMUD*

There is something in the world that the Bible regards as a symbol of God—not a temple or a tree, not a statue, nor a star. The one symbol of God is man, every man. God Himself created man, in His image. Human life is holy.... Reverence for God is shown in our reverence for man. Treat yourselves as a symbol of God. What is necessary is not to have a symbol, but to be a symbol.

— *RABBI ABRAHAM JOSHUA HESCHEL*

The belief that a human being is a ladder shapes and determines our approach to understanding the nature and purpose of human life-to refine the image of God within us. Anything that strengthens the divine image is called "holy," anything that detracts from it is "unholy." This requires that we look at other people as "holy" and at our own lives as opportunities to strengthen the divine image.

— *DAVID S. ARIEL*

HOLOCAUST

To live through dramatic events is not enough. One has to share them and transform them into acts of conscience.

— *RABBI WAYNE DORSICK*

The things I saw beggar description.... The visual evidence and verbal testimony of starvation, cruelty, and bestiality were so overpowering as to leave me a bit sick.... I made the visit deliberately, in order to be in a position to give first-hand evidence of these things if ever, in the future, there develops a tendency to charge these allegations merely to "propaganda."

— *DWIGHT EISENHOWER*

First the Nazis went after the Jews, but I wasn't a Jew, so I did not react. Then they went after the Catholics, but I wasn't a Catholic, so I didn't object. Then they went after the workers, but I wasn't a worker, so I didn't stand up. Then they went after the Protestant clergy and by then it was too late for anybody to stand up.

— *REVEREND MARTIN NIEMOELLER*

Only those who cried out against the persecution of the innocent have the right to sing religious chants.

—*DIETRICH BONHOEFFER*

For us [the survivors] to speak with the young becomes ever more difficult. We see it as a duty and, at the same time, as a risk of appearing anachronistic, of not being listened to. We must be listened to: above and beyond our personal experiences, we have collectively witnessed a fundamental, unexpected event.... It happened, therefore it can happen again: this is the core of what we have to say.

—*PRIMO LEVI*

A single death is a tragedy. A million deaths is a statistic.

—*JOSEPH STALIN*

> O never say we have come to journey's end,
> When days are dark and clouds upon our world descend.
> Believe the dark will lift, and freedom yet appear
> Our marching feet will tell the world that we are here.
> From sunny lands of palm to lands bedecked with snow,
> We came with all our grief, with all our people's woe.
> Where our martyrs' precious blood the tyrant drew,
> Our hope will yet revive, our life we shall renew.

—*RABBI BEN ZION BOKSER*

How does one commemorate the death of an entire community? What must one say? How many candles should one light, how many prayers should one recite, and how many times? Perhaps someone knows the answer. I don't. I am still searching.

—*ELIE WIESEL*

HOME

Home is measured not in property values but in human values.

—*RABBI JONATHAN SACKS*

Home is like a bed on a cold night. First you warm it, then it warms you.

—*ANONYMOUS*

Home is that place where they have to let you in, not because you deserve it, but because you are you.

—ROBERT FROST

Home is where you can be silent and still be heard,
Where you can ask and find out who you are,
Where people laugh with you about yourself,
Where sorrow is divided and joy multiplied,
Where we share, love, and grow.

—HENRY DAVID THOREAU

We will never have a healthy society with failing homes, or a composed community with failing families.... Yet our family relationships are fractured or, at best, frozen. We don't know each other, and what is worse, many don't care. We go our separate ways.... We have so many beautiful houses, but with an unprecedented number of broken homes.

—RABBI SAUL TEPLITZ

The history of a nation is not a history of its wars but the history of its households.

—JOHN RUSKIN

The ruin of a nation begins in the homes of its people.

—ASHANTI PROVERB

Home is the place you can go when you're whipped.

—MUHAMMAD ALI

HONESTY

The most dangerous of all dilemmas: When we are obliged to conceal truth in order to help the truth to be victorious.

—DAG HAMMARSKJOLD

Honesty in little things is no little thing.

—ANONYMOUS

An honest man's the noblest work of God.

—ALEXANDER POPE

On honesty God's favor is bestowed,
I never saw one lost in a straight road.

—SHAIKH SAADI

HONOR

The people most preoccupied with titles and status are usually the least deserving of them.

—ANONYMOUS

Every noble crown is, and on earth forever will be, a crown of thorns.

—THOMAS CARLYLE

HOPE

Hope is the thing with feathers—
That perches in the soul—
And sings the tune without the words—
And never stops—at all.

—EMILY DICKENSON

By my love and hope I beseech you:
Do not throw away the hero in your soul!
Hold holy your highest hope.

—FRIEDRICH NIETZSCHE

Life is too precious a thing to permit its devaluation by living pointlessly, emptily, without meaning, without love, and finally, without hope.

—VACLAV HAVEL

The day may dawn when fair play, love for one's fellow men, respect for justice and freedom, will enable tormented generations to march forth serene and triumphant from the hideous epoch in which we have to dwell. Meanwhile, never flinch, never weary, never despair.

—WINSTON CHURCHILL

HUMAN POTENTIAL

Compared with what we ought to be, we are only half awake.

—WILLIAM JAMES

First become a blessing to yourself that you may be a blessing to others.

—RABBI SAMSON RAPHAEL HIRSCH

There is a divine light in every soul. It is dormant and eclipsed by the follies of this world. We must first awaken this light, then the upper light will come upon us.

—RABBI AARON OF KARLIN

I am larger, better than I thought.
I did not know I held so much greatness.

—WALT WHITMAN

What we are born is God's gift to us. What we become is our gift to God.

—RALPH WALDO EMERSON

Faith summons us to become a portrait painter of a soul-landscape that shall be worthy to be hung in any art gallery of the spirit.

—RABBI JOSHUA LOTH LEIBMAN

The growth of the human mind is still high adventure, in many ways the highest adventure on earth.

—NORMAN COUSINS

What we do, compared with what we can do, is like comparing the waves on top of the ocean with the ocean's mighty depths.

—WILLIAM JAMES

Every encounter quickens the steps of the Redeemer; let two beings become one and the world is no longer the same; let two human creatures accept one another and creation will have meaning, the meaning they will have imposed upon it.

—ELIE WIESEL

The full development of each individual is not only a right, but a duty to society.

—LOUIS BRANDEIS

Ah for a man to arise in me,
That the man that I am
May cease to be.

—ALFRED LORD TENNYSON

Lord, we know what we are, but know not what we may be.

—WILLIAM SHAKESPEARE

Nature never repeats herself, and the possibilities of one human soul will never be found in another.

—ELIZABETH CADY STANTON

HUMANISM

One cannot approach the divine by reaching beyond the human; one can approach God through becoming human. To become human is what a person, every individual person, has been created for.

—MARTIN BUBER

It is in humans that God must be loved, because the love of God goes through the love of humans.

—RABBI ISRAEL, BAAL SHEM TOV

The main thing in life is not to be afraid to be human.

—ANONYMOUS

HUMILITY

When humility effects depression it is defective; when it is genuine it inspires joy, courage and inner dignity.

—RABBI AVRAHAM YITZHAK KOOK

Humility does not mean meekness.... Humility means to be clear, confident, and accepting without pride, self-interest, or ambition.

—RABBI DAVID COOPER

Whenever you find the greatness of God, you find God's humility.

—TALMUD

The word "humility" is derived from the Latin "humus," meaning "the soil." Perhaps this is not simply because it entails stopping and returning to earthly origins, but also because, as we are rooted in this earth of everyday life, we find in it all the vitality and fertility unnoticed by people who merely tramp on across the surface, drawn by distant landscapes.

—PIERO FERRUCCI

> Those who know they do not know
> Gain wisdom.
> Those who pretend they know
> Remain ignorant.
>
> Those who acknowledge their weakness
> Become strong.
> Those who flaunt their power
> Will lose it.
>
> Wisdom and power
> Follow truth above all.
>
> *—TAO DE CHING*

Before you can find God, you must lose yourself. For there is no room for God in one who is full of oneself.

—RABBI ISRAEL, BAAL SHEM TOV

Excessive humility easily becomes false humility, which is dangerously close to vanity. Excessive humility may numb both mind and soul.

—ELIE WIESEL

The true way to be humble is not to stop until you are smaller than yourself, but to stand at your real height against some higher nature that will show you what the real smallness of your greatness is.

—PHILLIPS BROOKS

Humble people don't think less of themselves-they just think about themselves less.

—ANONYMOUS

A woman once asked Rabbi Yosi ben Halafta: "If the world was created in only six days, what has God been doing since?" He answered: "Spending time building ladders, for some to ascend, and others to descend."

—GENESIS RABBAH

HUMOR

You grow up the day you have your first real laugh at yourself.

—ETHEL BARRYMORE

Humor is in fact, a prelude to faith; and laughter is the beginning of prayer.

—REINHOLD NIEBUHR

A person without a sense of humor is like a wagon without springs: jolted by every pebble in the road.

—HENRY WARD BEECHER

A light heart lives long.

—WILLIAM SHAKESPEARE

There are three things which are real: God, human folly, and laughter. The first two are beyond our comprehension. So we must do what we can with the third.

—JOHN F. KENNEDY

When people have opened their mouths to laugh, they are more ready to open their minds to learn.

—JOEL GOODMAN

He who laughs, lasts!

—ANONYMOUS

Humor is the great thing, the saving thing after all, the minute it crops up, all our hardnesses yield, all our irritations and resentments slip away and a sunny spirit takes their place.

—MARK TWAIN

A merry heart does good like a medicine; but a broken spirit dries up the bones.

—BIBLE (PROVERBS 17:22)

Humor enables us to transcend the immediate incongruities of life, and faith enables us to transcend the ultimate incongruities of life.

—WILLIAM SLOANE COFFIN, JR.

Laughter is the shortest distance between two people.

—VICTOR BORGE

To be grounded is to ... entertain a self-mockery which keeps us humane. The laughless people are the most dangerous.

—ROBERT RAINES

Humor [is one] of the soul's weapons in the fight for self-preservation. It is well known that humor, more than anything else in the human make-up, can afford an aloofness and an ability to rise above any situation, even if only for a few seconds.

— VIKTOR FRANKL

Angels can fly because they take themselves lightly.

—ANONYMOUS

Humor is your unconscious therapy.

—LANGSTON HUGHES

> The mask of comedy grown thin
> Reveals the face of tragedy within,
> And now, my friend we all must weep
> At stale old jokes, sown to reap.

—ANONYMOUS

HYPOCRISY

Hypocrisy is the tribute which vice pays to virtue.

—LA ROCHEFOUCAULD

Softer than butter is his speech, but war is in his heart;
His words are smoother than oil, but they are drawn swords.

—BIBLE (PSALMS 55:22)

IDEALISM

The greatest danger for most of us is not that our aim is too high and we miss it, but that it is too low and we reach it.
— *MICHELANGELO*

All of us are in the gutter, but some of us are looking up at the stars.
— *OSCAR WILDE*

Each time a man stands up for an ideal, or acts to improve the lot of others, or strikes out against injustice, he sends forth a tiny ripple of hope. And crossing each other from a million different centers of energy and daring, those ripples build a current which can sweep down the mightiest walls of oppression.
— *ROBERT KENNEDY*

Ideals are like the stars; we never reach them, but like the mariners of the sea, we chart our course by them.
— *CHARLES SCHULTZ*

If you have built castles in the air, your work need not be lost; that is where they should be. Now put the foundations under them.
— *HENRY DAVID THOREAU*

It's really a wonder that I haven't dropped all my ideals, because they seem so absurd and impossible to carry out. Yet I keep them, because in spite of everything I still believe that people are really good at heart. I simply can't build up my hopes on a foundation consisting of confusion, misery and death. I see the world gradually being turned into a wilderness, I hear the ever approaching thunder, which will destroy us too. I can feel the sufferings of millions ... and yet, if I look up into the heavens, I think that it will all come right, that this cruelty too will end, and that peace and tranquility will return again. In the meantime, I must uphold my ideals.
— *ANNE FRANK*

IDEAS

An idea isn't responsible for the people who believe in it.
— *DON MARQUIS*

Nurture your mind with great thoughts, for you will never go any higher than you think.
                                                                    —BENJAMIN DISRAELI

There is nothing as powerful as an idea whose time has come.

                                                                    —RALPH WALDO EMERSON

In your lifetime if you can come up with one original idea you have accomplished a great deal.
                                                                    — MAX ROACH

Nothing is more unseemly than to give very long legs to very brief ideas.
                                                                    —JOAQUIM MACHADO DE ASSIS

One cannot kill an idea but it may be delayed for a long while.

                                                                    —ALICE CHILDRESS

IMAGINATION

Those who dream by day are cognizant of many things which escape those who dream only by night.
                                                                    —EDGAR ALLEN POE

The world of reality has its limits; the world of imagination is boundless.

                                                                    —JEAN JACQUES ROUSSEAU

Imagination is the highest kite one can fly.

                                                                    —LAUREN BACALL

The essence of faith is in the power of imagination.
                                                                    —RABBI NAHMAN OF BRATSLAV

Everything you can imagine is real.

                                                                    —PABLO PICASSO

Imagination is more important than knowledge.

                                                                    —ALBERT EINSTEIN

Imagination is the beginning of creation. You imagine what you desire; you will what you imagine; and at last you create what you will.

                                                                    —GEORGE BERNARD SHAW

The imagination is the only truth.

—BERTOLT BRECHT

Imagination rules the world.

—NAPOLEON BONAPARTE

Everything that is was once imagined.

—TED JOANS

IMMORTALITY

Brief is the life of man, and of uncertain duration is his handiwork, be it ships, government or laws. But the echoes from soul to soul will go on as long as human life lasts.

—MORRIS RAPHAEL COHEN

Death cannot kill what never dies.

—THOMAS TRAHERNE

INDEPENDENCE

Independence is never given to a people, it has to be earned; and, once earned, must be defended.

—CHAIM WEIZMANN

There is only one success ... to be able to spend your life in your own way.

—CHRISTOPHER MORLEY

INDIVIDUALS

Strength of numbers is the delight of the timid. The valiant in spirit glory in fighting alone.

—MOHATMAS GANDHI

One man may make a difference. Everyone should strive to be that man.

—ROBERT KENNEDY

Never doubt that a small group of thoughtful, committed citizens can change the world. Indeed, it's the only thing that ever has.

—MARGARET MEAD

> I am only one, but I am one.
> I cannot do everything, but I can do something.
> What I can do, I ought to do.
> By the grace of God, I will do.
>
> *—FREDERICK FARRAR*

If the individual is not truly regenerated in spirit, society cannot be either, for society is the sum total of individuals in need of redemption.

—CARL JUNG

Every person born into this world represents something new, something that never existed before, something original and unique.

—MARTIN BUBER

It is a pleasant fact that you will know no man long, however low in the social scale, however poor, miserable, intemperate, and worthless he may appear to be, a mere burden to society, but you will find at last that there is something which he understands and can do better than any other.

—HENRY DAVID THOREAU

> If I can stop one heart from breaking,
> I shall not live in vain;
> If I can ease one life the aching,
> Or cool one pain,
> Or help one fainting robin
> Unto his nest again,
> I shall not live in vain.
>
> *—EMILY DICKINSON*

INTEGRITY

Integrity and firmness is all I can promise; these ... shall never forsake me, although I may be deserted by all men.

—GEORGE WASHINGTON

To be nobody but myself—in a world that is doing its best, night and day, to make you everybody else—means to fight the hardest battle which any human being can fight, and never stop fighting.

— e. e. cummings

As one anonymous leader said (better than I can) "The world needs more men [and women] who do not have a price at which they can be bought; who do not borrow from integrity to pay for expediency; whose handshake is an ironclad contract; who are not afraid of risk; who are honest in small matters as they are in large ones; whose ambitions are big enough to include others; who know how to win with grace and lose with dignity; who do not believe that shrewdness and cunning and ruthlessness are the three keys to success; who still have friends they made twenty years ago; who are not afraid to go against the grain of popular opinion and do not believe in 'consensus'; who are occasionally wrong and always willing to admit it. In short the world needs leaders."

—MARIAN WRIGHT EDELMAN

INTERFAITH RELATIONS

On each race is laid the duty to keep alight its own lamp of mind as its part in the illumination of the world. To break the lamp of any people is to deprive it of its rightful place in the world festival.

—RABINDRANATH TAGORE

The most significant basis for meeting people of different religious traditions is the level of fear and trembling, of humility and contrition, where our individual moments of faith are mere waves in the endless ocean of humanity's reaching out for God, where all formulations and articulations appear as understatements, where our souls are swept away by the awareness of the urgency of answering God's commandment, while stripped of pretension and conceit we sense the tragic insufficiency of human faith.

—RABBI ABRAHAM JOSHUA HESCHEL

INTUITION

I throw a spark into the dark—that is intuition. Then I have to send an expedition into the jungle to find the way of the spark—that is logic.

—INGMAR BERGMAN

We know truth not only through reason but more so through the heart. It is in this latter way that we know first principles, and it is in vain that reason, which plays no part in this, tries to combat them.

—BLAISE PASCAL

JEWS

We owe to the Jews a system of ethics which, even if it were entirely sep-arated from the supernatural, would be the mot precious possession of mankind, worth, in fact, the fruit of all other wisdom and learning together.

—WINSTON CHURCHILL

The mission of the Jewish people has never been to make the world more Jewish, but to make it more human.

—ELIE WEISEL

JOY

If you don't feel happy, pretend to be. If you are downright depressed, put on a smile. Act happy. Genuine joy will follow. Always remember: Joy is not merely incidental to your spiritual quest. It is vital.

—RABBI NAHMAN OF BRATSLAV

You shall rejoice before the Lord your God.

—BIBLE (DEUTERONOMY 12:12)

Joy is not in things, it is in us. True peacefulness comes from abandoning the illusion that satisfying desires brings pleasure. It is called even-minded-ness. In that state, you regard every moment as an opportunity to live fully, to be aware.

—JOAN BORYSENKO

If the day and the night are such that you greet them with joy, and life emits a fragrance like flowers and sweet-scented herbs, it is more elastic, more starry, more immortal—that is your success.

—HENRY DAVID THOREAU

Sadness is not a sin but it can lead to more wrongdoing than any sin. Joy leads to a life of commandments more than any single good deed.

—*RABBI AARON KARLINER*

O Glad, Exulting, Culminating Song!
A vigor more than earth's is in thy notes....
A reborn race appears—a perfect world, all joy!
Women and men in wisdom, innocence and health—all joy!
Riotous laughing bacchanals fill'd with joy!
War, sorrow, suffering gone—the rank earth purged—
 nothing but joy left!
The ocean fill'd with joy—the atmosphere all joy!
Joy! joy in freedom, worship, love! joy in the ecstasy of life!
Enough to merely be! enough to breathe!
Joy! joy! all over joy!

—*WALT WHITMAN*

Joy comes in our lives when we have something to do, something to love, and something to hope for.

—*JOSEPH ADDISON*

God laughs at our dull and drab need to arrange His program or restrict His performance. He is a God of variety, diversity, creativity, innovation, novelty, and adventure. He is a God of fun and games. He journeys with us, battling the forces of complacency, mediocrity, indifference, discouragement, and boredom.

—*JOHN & LELA HENDRIX*

How good is man's life, the mere living!
How fit to employ
All the heart and the soul and the senses
Forever in joy!

—*ROBERT BROWNING*

I will rejoice in the Lord,
Exult in the God who delivers me.

—*BIBLE (HABAKKUK 3:18)*

JUDAISM

The essence of Judaism seems to me to be the affirmation of life for all creatures. For the life of the individual has meaning only in the service of enhancing and ennobling the life of every living thing. Life is holy.... The sanctification of the life which transcends the individual—brings with it reverence, a peculiarly characteristic trait of the Jewish tradition.

—ALBERT EINSTEIN

Life isn't meant to be easy; it is meant to be life. And no religion defended so tenaciously the ordinary dignity of living [as Judaism]. Judaism never stressed an after-life, an after-death punishment, or a heaven; what was worthy and good was here on this earth today. We seek God so earnestly, not to find Him, but to discover ourselves.

—JAMES MICHENER

The world needs Judaism, its compassion instead of the machismo of today's violence, its optimism in the face of despair, its compassion in the face of human callousness, its reverence for the life of the mind in defiance of emotionalism run riot, its love of learning and passion for justice, its hunger for peace as the apex of God's kingdom and its partnership with God in setting the world aright.

—RABBI MAURICE EISENDRATH

JUDGMENT

Forbear to judge, for we are sinners all.

—WILLIAM SHAKESPEARE

Wise people seek solutions;
The ignorant only cast blame.

—TAO DE CHING

All universal judgments are treacherous and dangerous.

—MICHEL MONTAIGNE

JUSTICE

Justice has nothing to do with expediency. It has nothing to do with any temporary standard whatever. It is rooted and grounded in the fundamental instincts of humanity.

—WOODROW WILSON

Earthly power doth then show likest God's
When mercy seasons justice.

—WILLIAM SHAKESPEARE

One who makes himself overly compassionate toward the cruel will end up being cruel to the compassionate.

—MIDRASH

Let our first act every morning be the following resolve: 'I shall not fear anyone on earth. I shall fear only God. I shall bear ill-will towards no one. I shall not submit to injustice from anyone.

—MOHANDAS GANDHI

God writes national judgments upon national sins, and what may be slumbering in the storehouse of divine justice we do not know.

—FRANCES E.W. HARPER

Righteousness means justice practiced between men and nations.

—IROQUOIS

To demand freedom is to demand justice.

—JAMES CONE

Injustice anywhere is a threat to justice everywhere.

—MARTIN LUTHER KING, JR.

KARMA

To him who has the means and refuses the needy, the Holy One says: "Bear in mind, fortune is a wheel."

—TALMUD

KINDNESS

Three things in human life are important: The first is to be kind. The second is to be kind. The third is to be kind.

—*HENRY JAMES*

Practice random kindness and senseless acts of beauty.

—*ANONYMOUS*

You cannot do a kindness too soon, for you never know how soon it will be too late.

—*RALPH WALDO EMERSON*

We cannot make the Kingdom of God happen, but we can put our leaves as it draws near. We can be kind to each other. We can be kind to ourselves. We can drive back the darkness a little. We can make green places within ourselves where God can make his Kingdom happen.

—*FREDERICK BUECHNER*

Be kind and merciful. Let no one ever come to you without leaving better and happier. Be the living expression of God's kindness; kindness in your face, kindness in your eyes, kindness in your smile, kindness in your warm greeting. In the slums we are the light of God's kindness to the poor. To children, to the poor, to all who suffer and are lonely, give always a happy smile. Give them not only your care, but your heart.

—*MOTHER TERESA*

Man's inhumanity to man makes countless thousands mourn.

—*ROBERT BURNS*

KNOWLEDGE

The most violent element in society is ignorance.

—*EMMA GOLDMAN*

He who knows, and knows not that he knows, he is asleep—awaken him. He who knows not, and knows not that he knows not, he is a fool—

shun him. He who knows not, and knows that he knows not, he is a student—teach him. He who knows, and knows that he knows, he is a teacher—study with him.

—ARAB PROVERB

We know too much for any one person to know much.

—ROBERT OPPENHEIMER

LAUGHTER

The only medicine that needs no prescription, has no unpleasant side effects and costs no money, is laughter.

—ANONYMOUS

In laughter the pain of the heart is eased.

—BIBLE (PROVERBS 14:13)

In the catalogue of human assets, few things provide people with greater strength than the love of life, of which the ability to laugh is a prime manifestation.

—NORMAN COUSINS

Hark to the maidens laughing at the wells! There they recount the righteous acts of God.

—BIBLE (JUDGES 5:11)

LAW

It is jealousy and not confidence which prescribes limited constitutions to bind down those whom we are obliged to trust with power. In questions of power, then, let no more be heard of confidence in man, but bind him down from mischief by the chains of the Constitution.

—THOMAS JEFFERSON

We are in bondage to the law in order that we may be free.

—CICERO

The whip of the law cannot change the heart. But thank God it can restrain the heartless until they change their mind and heart.

—*REINHOLD NIEBUHR*

Law is not a noose around our necks, but a rope by which we climb.

—*ANONYMOUS*

One who acts out of love is greater than one who acts out of fear.

—*TALMUD*

[Law] is a way of life, not a standpoint of life. It involves movement, change, progression, not immobility and standing still.

—*ERNST SIMONE*

It may be true that the law cannot make a man love me, but it can keep him from lynching me.

—*MARTIN LUTHER KING, JR.*

In a government of laws, existence of the government will be imperiled if it fails to observe the law scrupulously. Our government is the potent, the omnipresent teacher. For good or for ill, it teaches the whole people by its example. Crime is contagious. If the government becomes a law-breaker, it breeds contempt for law; it invites every man to become a law unto himself; it invites anarchy.

—*LOUIS BRANDEIS*

Fragile as reason is, and limited as law is as the expression of the institutionalized medium of reason, that's all we have standing between us and the tyranny of mere will and the cruelty of unbridled, undisciplined feeling.

—*FELIX FRANKFURTER*

Would that they forsake Me provided that they observed My law.

—*TALMUD*

As there are laws in poetry, so there is poetry in law.

—*RABBI AVRAHAM YITZHAK KOOK*

LEADERSHIP

Great necessities call forth great leaders.

—*ABIGAIL ADAMS*

The public may, after all, be wrong, in the sense that the polls may reflect serious misapprehensions on the public's part which it is the duty of the legislative representative to expose and to set right rather than to accept passively. That is what leadership really ought to mean.

—GEORGE KENNAN

Leadership is the art of letting someone else have your way.

—ANONYMOUS

A person never gets his head above the crowd unless he is willing to stick his neck out.

—BENJAMIN DISRAELI

There go the people; I must hurry and catch up with them, for I am their leader.

—NAPOLEON BONAPARTE

The way of a prophet has always been profitless.

—F. L. WRIGHT

Woe to leadership, for it buries those who possess it.

—TALMUD

Our people are slow to learn the wisdom of sending character instead of talent to Congress.

—RALPH WALDO EMERSON

If I keep from meddling with people, they take of themselves.
If I keep from commanding people, they behave themselves.
If I keep from preaching at people, they improve themselves.
If I keep from imposing on people, they become themselves.

—LAO-TSE

Those in high places ... are the custodians of a nation's ideals, of the beliefs it cherishes, of its permanent hopes, of the faith which makes a nation out of a mere aggregation of individuals.

—WALTER LIPPMANN

The lives of great men all remind us that we can make our life sublime.

—HENRY WADSWORTH LONGFELLOW

Leadership should be born out of the understanding of the needs of those who would be affected by it.

—MARIAN ANDERSON

It may get me crucified, I may even die. But I want it said even if I die in the struggle that "He died to make men free."

—MARTIN LUTHER KING JR.

Women, in general, are not a part of the corruption of the past, so they can give a new kind of leadership, a new image for mankind.

—CORETTA SCOTT KING

LEARNING

A little learning, indeed, may be a dangerous thing, but the want of learning is a calamity to any people.

—FREDERICK DOUGLASS

Few are too young, and none too old, to make the attempt to learn.

—BOOKER T. WASHINGTON

I try to learn as much as I can because I know nothing compared to what I need to know.

—MUHAMMAD ALI

Learn enough about a given phenomenon and the "unexpected" becomes fairly predictable.

—RALPH ELLISON

The act of learning is equal to all the commandments together.

—TALMUD

LETTING GO

You can clutch the past so tightly to your chest that it leaves your arms too full to embrace the present.

—JAN GLIDEWELL

Stir muddy water, and it will stay cloudy.

Leave it alone, and it will become clear.

Let the stream flow, and it will find its way.

Stop chasing contentment, and it will come to you.

—TAO TE CHING

Don't try to force anything.... See God opening millions of flowers every day without forcing the buds.

—BHAGWAN SHREE RAJNEESH

The art of letting things happen, action through non-action, letting go of oneself ... became for me the key opening the door to the way. We must be able to let things happen in the psyche.

—CARL JUNG

Impermanence—look at it right in this moment. A sound comes and then it's gone. A thought arises and so quickly passes away. Sight, taste, smell, touch, feeling—they are all the same—impermanent, fleeting, ephemeral. Where is yesterday, where is last year, where is our childhood? It all vanishes so quickly. If we want to understand death, we have only to look at the present, because in each moment we are being born and dying. The sound we just heard us already gone, it died, and we died with it. To live fully is to let go and die with each passing moment, and to be reborn in each one.

—JOSEPH GOLDSTEIN & JACK KORNFIELD

You put such a stress on passion when you're young. You learn about the value of tenderness when you grow old. You also learn in late life not to hold, to give without hanging on, to love freely, in the sense of wanting nothing in return.

— JOAN ERIKSON

Grab hold lightly

Let go tightly.

—ZEN MAXIM

LIBERALISM

The narrower a man's mind, the broader are his statements.

—ANONYMOUS

I believe that dogma—and that includes liberal and conservative dogma—must not take precedence over reality. A liberal is a person who believes that water can be made to run uphill. A conservative is someone who believes everybody should pay for his water. I'm somewhere in between. I believe water should be free, but that water flows downhill.

—*THEODORE WHITE*

LIBERTY

We can afford no liberties with liberty itself.

—*ROBERT H. JACKSON*

The world has never had a good definition of the word liberty and the American people, just now, are much in need of one. We all declare for liberty; but in using the same word we do not all mean the same thing. With some, the word liberty may mean for each one to do as he pleases with himself, and the products of his labor; while, with others, the same word may mean for some men to do as they please with other men, and the product of other men's labor. Here are two, not only different, but incompatible things called by the same name—liberty. And it follows that each of the things is, by the respective parties, called by two different and incompatible names— liberty and tyranny.

—*ABRAHAM LINCOLN*

Eternal vigilance is the price of liberty.

—*ANONYMOUS*

The cost of liberty is less than the price of repression.

—*W.E.B. Du Bois*

LIFE

Life is crazy and meaningful at once.

—*CARL JUNG*

All the arts we practice are apprenticeship. The big art is our life.

—*M.C. RICHARDS*

Life is not a vale of tears
But a vale of soul-making.

—*JOHN KEATS*

He who has a why to live for can bear with any how.

—*FRIEDRICH NIETZSCHE*

I cannot but have reverence for all that is called life. I cannot avoid compassion for everything that is called life. That is the beginning and foundation of morality.

—*ALBERT SCHWEITZER*

Life is too brief
Between the budding and the falling leaf,
Between the seed time and the golden sheaf,
For hate and spite.
We have no time for malice or for greed;
Therefore, with love make beautiful the deed;
Fast speeds the night.
Life is too swift
Between the blossom and winter's snow's drift.
Between the silence and the lark's uplift,
For bitter words.
In kindness and in gentleness our speech
Must carry messages of hope, and reach
The Sweetest chords.

—*W.M. VORIES*

Anyone who regards his own life and that of his fellow creatures as meaningless ... is not merely unfortunate, he is almost unqualified to live!

—*ALBERT EINSTEIN*

Life will either grind you down or polish you up, and which it does is our choice.

—*ROGER WALSH*

When you were born, you cried and the world rejoiced. When you die, may your life be such that the world cries and you rejoice.

—*NATIVE AMERICAN PROVERB*

Only that day dawns to which we are awake.

—HENRY DAVID THOREAU

Life is either a daring adventure or nothing.

—HELEN KELLER

> Life is not always lost by dying! Life is lost
> Minute by minute, day by dragging day,
> In all the thousand small, undaring ways.
> Always and always, life can be
> Lost without vision but not lost by death.
> Lost by not daring, willing, going on
> Beyond the ragged edge of fortitude
> To something more—something no one has ever seen.
> Life is not always lost by dying.

—ANONYMOUS

Life is what happens while you are busy making plans.

—JOHN LENNON

Although life is all too short, it can be ever so wide.

—SPANISH SAYING

The most important thing about a person is his philosophy of life.

—G.K. CHESTERTON

The purpose of life is to be that self which one truly is.

—SOREN KIERKEGAARD

Just to be is a blessing. Just to live is holy.

—RABBI ABRAHAM JOSHUA HESCHEL

Life is a mystery to be lived, not a problem to be solved.

—ANONYMOUS

Let your life lightly dance on the edges of time.

—RABINDRANATH TAGORE

The pain of life may teach each of us to understand life and in our understanding of life, to love life.

— HOWARD THURMAN

Life is a shadow and a mist; it passes quickly by, and is no more.

— *MADAGASCAN PROVERB*

LISTENING

One voice can enter ten ears, but ten voices cannot enter one ear.

—*MIDRASH*

No one ever listened himself out of a job.

—*CALVIN COOLIDGE*

Is there a God closer than this, that one can enter a synagogue, hide behind a pillar and whisper, and God still hears?

—*TALMUD*

Note the difference between your ears and your mouth. For the Holy One Blessed be He created for you two ears and one mouth so that you might listen twice as much as you speak.

—*RABBI YOSEF BEN YOSEF NAHMIAS*

The first duty of love is to listen.

—*PAUL TILLICH*

The road to the heart is the ear.

—*VOLTAIRE*

Giving instructions, listening to instructions, just listening, sympathizing, understanding—communication between husband and wife, parents and children, is the very life of a family. When it stops, family life has come to an end.

—*RABBI BERNARD MANDELBAUM*

LONELINESS

A man must get away now and then to experience loneliness.
Only those who learn how to live in loneliness
Can come to know themselves and life.

—*CARL SANDBURG*

Whoever does not have an hour a day alone is not a human being.

—*RABBI MOSHE LEIB OF SASSOV*

People are lonely because they build walls instead of bridges.

—*ANONYMOUS*

Love does not dissolve loneliness. It only makes me rich in my solitude. It is tempting to surrender responsibility for the self and merge into life-in-tandem.... I am a single one and merger is for a moment only. If I trade my freedom for succor, we cling together and nourish each other's fears of the wilderness, excitement withers and love grows wrinkled as a limb with severed nerves.

—*SAM KEEN*

Nothing is worse for the victim that solitude. Maybe we cannot help them ... [but] we must let them know that they are not alone.

—*ELIE WIESEL*

LONGEVITY

A life of short duration ... could be so rich in joy and love that it could contain more meaning than a life lasting eighty years.

—*VIKTOR FRANKL*

LOVE

The greatest disease ... is being unwanted, unloved, and uncared for. We can cure physical diseases with medicine, but the only cure for loneliness, despair, and hopelessness is love. There are many in the world who are dying for a piece of bread, but there are many more dying for a little love.

—*MOTHER TERESA*

Faith makes all things possible. Love makes all things easy.

—*RABBI SIDNEY GREENBERG*

Love does not consist in gazing at each other but in looking together in the same direction.

—*ANTOINE DE SAINT-EXUPERY*

True love is that which not only affirms in subjective feeling the absolute significance of human individuality in another and in oneself, but also justifies this absolute significance in reality, really rescues us from the inevitability of death and fills out our life with an absolute content.

—*VLADIMIR SOLOVYOV*

To love at all is to be vulnerable. Love anything and your heart will be wrung and possibly broken. If you want to make sure of keeping it intact, you must give your heart to no one.... Wrap it carefully round with hobbies and little luxuries; avoid all entanglements; lock it up safe in the casket of your selfishness. But in that casket, safe, dark, motionless, it will change. It will not be broken; it will become unbreakable, impenetrable, irredeemable.

—*C. S. LEWIS*

There's a land of the living and a land of the dead, and the bridge is love. If we love one another, we will be eternal.

—*THORNTON WILDER*

While one is consciously afraid of not being loved, the real though usually unconscious fear is that of loving. To love means to commit one's self— without guarantee, to give one's self completely—in the hope that our love will produce love in the other person. Love is an act of faith ... and whosoever is of little faith is also of little love.

—*ERICH FROMM*

We can do no great things; only small things with great love.

—*MOTHER TERESA*

Love is the wind, the tide, the waves, the sunshine. Its power is incalculable; it is many horse-power. It never ceases, it never slacks; it can move the globe without a resting-place; it can warm without fire; it can feed without meat; it can clothe without garments; it can shelter without roof; it can make a paradise within which will dispense with a paradise without.

—*HENRY DAVID THOREAU*

Life is short and we have not too much time for gladdening the hearts of those who are swift traveling the dark way with us. O be swift to love! Make haste to be kind.

—*HENRI-FREDERIC AMIEL*

To cheat oneself out of love is the most terrible deception; it is an eternal loss for which there is no reparation, either in time or in eternity.

—*SOREN KIERKEGAARD*

Love is what we live by. And yet it is also what we blind ourselves by, what we suffer by, and what we torture each other by.... Love—its presence, its lack, its distortions—is the single cause explaining all the joys and sorrows of humanity.

—*PIERO FERRUCCI*

Love consists in this, that two solitudes protect and touch and greet each other.

—*RAINER MARIA RILKE*

Love is ... a power which breaks through the walls which separate man from his fellow man, which unites him with others; love makes him overcome the sense of isolation and separateness, yet it permits him to be himself, to retain his integrity.

—*ERICH FROMM*

Unless you love someone nothing else makes any sense.

— *e. e. cummings*

Gravity is love. It is gravity that brings things together.... Gravity is thus very much like love ... unexplainable, undetectable by objective technologies, but so dominant everywhere.

—*BOB SAMPLES*

As long as one can admire and love, then one is young forever.

—*PABLO CASSALS*

There is a comfort in the strength of love; T'will make a thing endurable, which else would overset the brain, or break the heart.

—*WILLIAM WORDSWORTH*

Love isn't like a reservoir. You'll never drain it dry. It's much more like a natural spring. The longer and the farther that it flows, the stronger and the deeper and the clearer it becomes.

—*EDDIE CANTOR*

Hell is the suffering of being unable to love.

—*FYODOR DOSTOYEVSKY*

Where there is great love there are always miracles.

—*WILLA CATHER*

It is in us that God must be loved, because the love of God goes through the love of humans.

—RABBI ISRAEL, BAAL SHEM TOV

When the power of love overcomes the love of power, the world will know peace.

—ANONYMOUS

> True love's the gift which God has given
> To man alone beneath the heaven....
> It is the secret sympathy,
> The silver link, the silken tie,
> Which heart to heart and mind to mind
> In body and in soul can bind.

—SIR WALTER SCOTT

MAN

You must not lose faith in humanity. Humanity is an ocean; if a few drops of the ocean are dirty, the ocean does not become dirty.

—GANDHI

One of the most revolutionary concepts to grow out of our clinical experience is the growing recognition that the innermost core of man's nature, the deepest layers of his personality, the base of his 'animal nature', is positive in nature—is basically socialized, forward-moving, rational and realistic.

—CARL R. ROGERS

> Born on this Isthmus of a middle state
> A being darkly wise and widely great
> He hangs between; in doubt to act or rest
> In doubt to deem himself a God or beast
> In doubt his mind or body to prefer,
> Born but to die and reasoning but to err,
> Sole judge of truth in endless error hurled
> The glory, jest and riddle of the world.

—ALEXANDER POPE

Everyone must have two pockets, so that he can reach into one or the other as the need might arise. In one right pocket are the words: "For my sake was the world created,"; and in the other pocket, the words, "I am earth and ashes."

—RABBI SIMHAH BUNAM OF PSHIS'HA

What a piece of work is a man! How noble
In reason! How infinite in faculty!

—SHAKESPEARE

Man is that being who has invented the gas chambers of Auschwitz; however, he is also that being who has entered those gas chambers upright, with the Lord's Prayer, or the Shema Yisrael on his lips.

—VIKTOR E. FRANKL

After Adam and Eve were expelled from the Garden of Eden, God caused a deep sleep to come over them. God then called a council of angels and said to the heavenly hosts: "When Adam and Eve awake, they will know that they are no longer divine and they will go in search of their divinity. Tell me, angels, where shall I hide this divinity?"—First of the angels spoke and said: "Lord of the Universe, let us conceal their divinity within themselves for that is the last place they will go in search of it."

—MIDRASH

Man is not yet human. He is only a candidate for humanity.

—RABBI MORDECAI M. KAPLAN

Why was man created on the sixth day, after the creation of all the other creatures? So that, should he become overbearing, he can be told "The gnat was created before you were."

—MISHNAH

Dressed in a little brief authority,
Most ignorant of what he's most assured,
His glassy essence,
Like an angry ape,
Plays such fantastic tricks before high heaven
As make the angels weep.

—SHAKESPEARE

It is easier to know mankind than any man.

—LA ROCHEFOUCAULD

The greatest lie on earth is the human face.

—PAUL SIMON

I am fearfully and wonderfully made.

—BIBLE (PSALMS 139:14)

It is certain that God attaches more importance to a human than to a lion, but I do not know that we can be sure that he prefers one person to the entire species of lions.

—LEIBNIZ

To feed people and not to love them is to treat them as if they were barnyard cattle. To love them and not to respect them is to treat them as if they were household pets.

—MENCIUS

Of all created creatures man is the most detestable. Of the entire brood he is the only one ... that possesses malice.... Also ... he is the only creature that has a nasty mind.

—MARK TWAIN

Whenever two people meet there are really six people present. There is each man as he sees himself, each man as the other person sees him, and each man as he really is.

—WILLIAM JAMES

Man's inhumanity to man
Makes countless thousands mourn.

—BURNS

Man passes away; his name perishes from record and recollection; his history is as a tale that is told, and his very monument becomes a ruin.

—WASHINGTON IRVING

If man lives in slime-and there is slime always at the core of the soul—it is nevertheless this briefly animated dust that beholds stars, writes symphonies, and imagines God.

—IRWIN EDMAN

Know then thyself, presume not God to scan;
The proper study of mankind is Man.

—ALEXANDER POPE

If man is not rising upwards to be an angel, depend upon it, he is sinking downwards to be a devil. He cannot stop at the beast.

—SAMUEL TAYLOR COLERIDGE

Man is the only creature in the animal kingdom that sits in judgment on the work of the Creator and finds it bad—including himself and Nature.

—ELBERT HUBBARD

I decline to accept the end of man. It is easy enough to say that man is immortal simply because he will endure; that when the last ding-dong of doom has clanged and faded from the last worthless rock hanging tideless in the last red and dying evening, that even then there will be one more sound: that of his puny inexhaustible voice, still talking.

I refuse to accept this. I believe that man will not merely endure: he will prevail. He is immortal, not because he alone among creatures has an inexhaustible voice, but because he has a soul, a spirit capable of compassion and sacrifice and endurance.

—WILLIAM FAULKNER

The measure of a man is in the lives he's touched.

—FRED HAMPTON

MARRIAGE

Marriage bonds are like financial bonds. They aren't worth much unless the interest is kept up.

—ANONYMOUS

Marriage is the high sea for which no compass has yet been invented.

—HEINRICH HEINE

A man in love is incomplete until he is married. Then he is finished.

—ZSA ZSA GABOR

A fight a day keeps the divorce court away.

—*ANONYMOUS*

Marriage is that relation between man and woman in which the independence is equal, the dependence mutual and the obligation reciprocal.

—*LOUIS KAUFMAN ANSPACHER*

It is a strange thing that two people can live together for half a lifetime and only understand one another at the very end.

—*DUKE OF WELLINGTON*

Marriage must incessantly contend with a monster which devours everything, that is, familiarity.

—*HONORE DE BALZAC*

Marriage is an edifice that must be rebuilt every day.

—*ANDRE MAUROIS*

People marry for many reasons, and few people marry for love, because few people are able to love the person they love at the time that they marry them. In our society, people commonly marry in a romantic haste, usually ignorant of the traits, needs, and aims of their spouses. They marry an image, not a person.... Following the ceremony, reality often sets in with an unpleasant shock.... Shortly after the people are married, trouble begins, and it should, if the couple are growing people. Trouble is normal, to be expected, even desirable.

—*SIDNEY JOURARD*

If any persons have been hindered by the marriage state, let them know that marriage is not the hindrance but their purpose which made an ill use of marriage.... It is not wine which makes drunkenness, but the evil purpose, and the using it beyond measure.

—*ST. JOHN CHRYSOSTOM*

God help the man who won't marry until he finds the perfect woman, and God help him still more if he finds her.

—*BENJAMIN TILLET*

MATERIALISM

If you want your children to turn out well, spend twice as much time with them, and half as much money on them.

—ABIGAIL VANBUREN

I'd rather have roses on my table than diamonds on my neck.

—EMMA GOLDMAN

I want you to know that possessions have made more people unhappy than happy, because they define the limits of your life and keep you from the freedom of choice that comes with traveling light upon the earth.

I want you to know that possessions are chameleons that change from fantasies into responsibilities once you hold them in your hands and that they take your eye from the heavens and rivet it squarely on the earth.

And I want you to know that possessions that increase your own value are empty in comparison to those that increase the value of the lives around you.

But most of all I want you to know that possessions become what you make them. If they increase your capacity to give, they become something good. If they increase your focus on yourself and become standards by which you measure other people, they become something bad. It is in your hands to give them meaning.

Periodically purge yourself. Give away what you don't use. Go on a long trip and take only a single pack. Do something to remind yourself that most of the possessions you thought were important are nothing more than unimportant decorations on who you really are.

—KENT NERBURN

Man has had to pay dearly for his material achievements. His life has become richer, broader, and more stimulating, but at the same time more complicated and exhausting. Its rapidly increasing tempo, the opportunities it offers for gratifying his desires, and the intricate economic and social machinery in which it has enmeshed him make ever more insistent demands on his energy, his mental functions, his emotions, and his will.

—ROLLO MAY

Money buys everything except love, personality, freedom, immortality, silence, peace.

—CARL SANDBURG

I got plenty o' nuttin, and nuttin's plenty fo' me.

—PORGY, IN GERSHWIN'S "PORGY AND BESS"

A blackbird found a large piece of food in the village and lit out into the sky with the food in its beak. A flock of his brothers chased after him and raucously attacked the food, pulling it from his beak. The blackbird finally let go of the last piece of bread and the frenzied flock left him alone. The bird swooped and dived and thought, "I have lost the food but I have regained the peaceful sky."

—SUFI

Why it's so
I really don't know—
The more I make,
The more I owe.

— W.E. MORGAN

What you feel about physical things is true—there is a consciousness in them, a life which is not the life and consciousness of man and animal which we know, but still secret and real. That is why we must have respect for physical things and use them rightly, not misuse and waste, ill-treat or handle them with a careless roughness. The feeling of all being consciousness or alive comes when our own physical consciousness—and not the mind only—awakes out of its obscurity and becomes aware of the One in all things, the Divine everywhere.

—PIERO FERRUCCI

To be upset over what you don't have ...
Is to waste what you do have.

—KEN KEYES, JR.

A man is rich in proportion to the number of things he can do without.

—HENRY DAVID THOREAU

Civilization is a process by which yesterday's luxuries become today's necessities.

—ANONYMOUS

Money can buy the husk of things, but not the kernel. It brings you food but not appetite, medicine but not health, acquaintances, but not friends, servants but not faithfulness, days of joy but not peace or happiness.

—HENRIK IBSEN

[Advertising] has made a fine art of taking advantage of human silliness. It rams unwanted material goods down surfeited throats when two-thirds of all human beings now alive are in desperate need of the bare necessities of life. This is an ugly aspect of the affluent society; and, if I am told that advertising is the price of affluence, I reply without hesitation, that affluence has been bought too dear.

—*ARNOLD J. TOYNBEE*

In this world there are only two tragedies. One is not getting what one wants, and the other is getting it. The last is the real tragedy.

—*OSCAR WILDE*

Two things I ask of you, O Lord: keep me from poverty, keep me from too much wealth.

—*BIBLE (PROVERBS 30:7-8)*

I find that the Americans have no passions, they have appetites.

—*RALPH WALDO EMERSON*

Adversity makes the man,
Prosperity makes the monster.

—*VICTOR HUGO*

Fame is a vapor, popularity an accident, riches take wings. Only one thing endures and that is character.

—*ABRAHAM LINCOLN*

MATURITY

I believe I've found the missing link between animal and civilized man. It is us.

—*KONRAD LORENZ*

For the healthy student reaching such a state is not synonymous with completion, but rather a state of heightened readiness for continued growth and for the regularized broadening of competencies, skills, and interests. Adaptive maturity involves confronting the options in one's life, the ability to respond with choices, and the courage to accept the consequences of one's decisions.

—*RICHARD A. & PATRICIA A. SCHMUCK*

Maturity is coming to terms with yourself somewhere between your ambitions and your limitations.

—LEE SAUL DUSHOFF

I have removed one source of confusion by confining the concept very definitely to older people. By the criteria I used, self-actualization does not occur in young people. In our culture at least, youngsters have not yet achieved identity, or autonomy, nor have they had time enough to experience and enduring, loyal, post-romantic love relationship, nor have they generally found their calling, the altar upon which to offer themselves. Nor have they worked out their own system of values; nor have they had experience enough (responsibility for others, tragedy, failure, achievement, success) to shed perfectionistic illusions and become realistic; nor have they generally made their peace with death; nor have they learned how to be patient; nor have they learned enough about evil in themselves and others to be compassionate; nor have they had time to become post-ambivalent about parents and elders, power and authority; nor have they generally become knowledgeable and educated enough to open the possibility of becoming wise; nor have they generally acquired enough courage to be unpopular, to be unashamed about being openly virtuous, etc.

—ABRAHAM H. MASLOW

Maturation is the transcendence from environmental support to self-support.

—FRITZ PERLS

Knowledge and timber shouldn't be much used till they are seasoned.

—OLIVER WENDELL HOLMES, JR.

The young man who has not wept is a savage, and the old man who will not laugh is a fool.

—GEORGE SANTAYANA

MEANING

If I thought at the end of the year that all I did was make a living, I'd regard it as a pretty incomplete year.

—PAUL O'DWYER

We have had the experience but missed the meaning.

—T. S. ELIOT

When the purpose of living fails, the will to live dies. Old people deprived of responsibility for tasks to be performed, suddenly disintegrate and hardly survive their retirement.

—*RABBI THEODORE FRIEDMAN*

I do not beg you to reveal to me the secret of your ways. I could not bear it! But show me one thing; show it to me more clearly and more deeply: show me what this, which is happening at this very moment, means to me, what it demands of me, what you, Lord of the world, are telling me by way of it. Ah, it is not why I suffer that I wish to know, but only whether I suffer for your sake.

—*HASIDIC*

In the Nazi concentration camps, one could have witnessed that those who knew that there was a task waiting for them to fulfill were most apt to survive.

—*VIKTOR E. FRANKL*

I have told the story of a life that cannot be said to have bubbled over with sweetness and joy. But it is a life that has had worthy moments, because actuated by efforts after things that are of perennial value, efforts which have proved sustaining in dark hours and which I think will strengthen human hearts in the future, as they have in the past.

Brief is the life of man, and of uncertain duration is his handiwork, be it ships, houses, government or laws. But the echoes from soul to soul will go on as long as human life lasts.

—*MORRIS RAPHAEL COHEN*

We are the hollow men,
We are the empty men.

—*T. S. ELIOT*

It is clear to me that in therapy ... commitment to purpose and to meaning in life is one of the significant elements of change. It is only when the person decides, "I am someone; I am someone worth being; I am committed to being myself," that change becomes possible.

—*CARL R. ROGERS*

What most people want—young or old—is not merely security, or comfort, or luxury, although they are glad enough to have these. Most of all, they want meaning in their lives.

—*ROCKEFELLER FOUNDATION, 1958*

There is no beginning, no movement, no peace and no end
But noise without speech, food without taste....
And the wind shall say: 'Here were decent godless people:
Their only monument the asphalt road
And a thousand lost golf balls.'

—T. S. ELIOT

MEDITATION

For one who enters the woods noisily, the woods are silent. For one who enters the woods silently, the woods are filled with sound.

—OLD PROVERB

First, you quit trying.
Second, you quit trying to quit.
Third, you quit quitting.

—EDWARD THORNTON

It is possible to cut through the noise and reach the quiet zone.

—SAUL BELLOW

And Isaac went out to meditate in the field at eventide.

—BIBLE (GENESIS 25:63)

Without knowledge there is no meditation, without meditation there is no knowledge. He who has knowledge and meditation is near to Nirvana.

—DHAMMAPADA

A free person thinks of death least of all things; and his wisdom is a meditation not of death but of life.

—BARUCH SPINOZA

It is meditation that leads us in spirit into the hallowed solitudes wherein we find God alone-in peace, in calm, in silence, in recollection.

—J. CRASSET

It is of primary importance that a certain space of time be allotted daily to meditation on eternal things. No priest can omit this without a serious manifestation of negligence and without a grave loss to his soul.

—POPE PIUS X

That happiness which belongs to a mind which by meditation has been washed clear of all impurity and has entered with the Self, cannot be described by words; it can be felt by the inward power only.

—MAITRANYANA BRAHMANA UPANISHAD

Meditation, because it is free of dogma, of historical commitments and narrow prejudices, because it is practiced for the most part silently and therefore secretly, and because it is practiced by some members of all religions-meditation is a channel for seekers of all faiths or no faith, a river into which many streams can freely flow.

—BRADFORD SMITH

MEMORY

Redemption lies in remembering.

—RABBI ISRAEL, BAAL SHEM TOV

The threat of oblivion is the heaviest stone that melancholy can throw at a man.

—THOMAS BROWNE

And when I am old, and my body has begun to fail me, my memories will be waiting for me. They will lift me and carry me over mountains and oceans. I will hold them and turn them and watch them catch the sunlight as they come alive once more in my imagination. I will be rich and I will be at peace.

—KENT NERBURN

Memory is the receptacle and the sheath of all knowledge.

—CICERO

Forgetfulness is to obliterate the past and lose all the possible joy and growth in what has been: memory is to take those same experiences and illuminate the future. To remember is what marks us as human beings—may we use that power well.

—RABBI BARRY DOV SCHWARTZ

The word "lethal," meaning deadly, comes from the word "Lethe," the legendary name of a river in Hades, the water of which, when drunk, produced forgetfulness of the past.

—ANONYMOUS

There exists no greater sorrow than, in our misery, to recall happy times.

—DANTE

It's a pleasure to share one's memories. Everything remembered is dear, endearing, touching, precious.

—SUSAN SONTAG

My memories are of moving, constantly moving.

—ALVIN AILEY

An individual who loses his or her memory is disabled. So it is with a people.

—ASA HILLIARD

MESSIAH

The Baal Shem Tov asked the Messiah:

"When will you come, Sir?"

The Messiah responded:

"When the wellsprings of your teachings spread to the outermost limits."

—HASIDIC

Many people await the coming of the Messiah and the "better days" it will bring. In truth, however, these are the best days there are. What the Messiah will do is reveal the hidden goodness of our present-day existence.

—RABBI SHOLOM DOV BER OF LUBAVITCH

> For the vision is yet for the appointed time,
> And it declares of the end, and does not lie;
> Though it tarry, wait for it;
> Because it will surely come, it will not delay.

—BIBLE (HABAKKUK 2:3)

If there be a plant in your hand when they say to you, behold the Messiah, go and plant the plant and afterward go out and greet him.

—RABBAN YOHANAN BEN ZAKKAI

Seek Allah, but tether your camel first.

— KORAN

A Hasidic sage was once asked by his disciples when he thought the Messiah would arrive. To their total surprise he indicated that he did not expect the Messiah at all. He went on to say, however, that in each person there resides a spark of the Messiah. If we could combine all these little sparks it would make for a resplendent flame which would light up the universe with Messianic peace and harmony for all people everywhere.

—RABBI JOSHUA L. GOLDBERG

Today we do not believe in a personal Messiah, or a Messiah people, but in humankind, acting as its own Messiah.

—RABBI LOUIS I. NEWMAN

MIDDLE AGE

Middle Age is when it takes longer to rest than get tired.

—JOEY ADAMS

It's a feeling you get reading a report that tells of crumbling road, bridges and sewers and reveals most of them to be younger than you.

— BILL TAMMEUS

Middle Age is when you're sitting at home on Saturday night and the telephone rings and you hope it isn't for you.

—OGDEN NASH

Middle Age is when the broad mind and narrow waist change places!

—ANONYMOUS

MIRACLES

A miracle, my friends, is an event which creates faith. That is the purpose and nature of miracles. They may seem very wonderful to the people who witness them, and very simple to those who perform them. That does not matter: if they confirm or create faith they are true miracles.

—GEORGE BERNARD SHAW

Transformation is one of the most common events of nature. The seed becomes the flower. The cocoon becomes the butterfly. Winter becomes spring and love becomes a child.

We never question these, because we see them around us every day. To us they are not miracles, though if we did not know them they would be impossible to believe.

—KENT NERBURN

Invite the Sacred to participate in your joy in little things, as well as in your agony over the great ones. There are as many miracles to be seen through a microscope as through a telescope. Start with little things seen through the magnifying glass of wonder, and just as a magnifying glass can focus the sunlight into a burning beam that can set a leaf aflame, so can your focused wonder set you ablaze with insight. Find the light in each other and just fan it.

—ALICE O. HOWELL

A hundred million miracles
Are happening every day.
And those who do not agree
Are those who do not hear or see.

—RODGERS AND HAMMERSTEIN

The world will not starve for want of wonders, but only for want of wonder.

—G.K. CHESTERTON

Referring not to miracles or startling phenomena, but to the natural order of things, they insist that the world of the known is a world unknown; hiddenness, mystery. What stirred their souls was neither the hidden nor the apparent, but the hidden in the apparent; not the order but the mystery of the order that prevails in the universe.

—RABBI ABRAHAM JOSHUA HESCHEL

The achievement by spirit of what by every law of logic and common sense seems impossible.... When the immovable is moved, when the insuperable is conquered, when the impossible is achieved, what else is that but a miracle?

—RABBI MILTON STEINBERG

God acts against the wonted course of nature, but by no means does God act against the supreme law; because Divinity does not act against Itself.

—ST. AUGUSTINE

That miracles have been, I do believe; that they may yet be wrought by the living, I do not deny; but I have no confidence on those which are fathered on the dead.

—*THOMAS BROWNE*

All is miracle. The stupendous order of nature, the revolution of a hundred millions of worlds around a million of suns, the activity of light, the life of animals, all are grand and perpetual miracles.

—*VOLTAIRE*

Depend upon it, it is not the want of greater miracles but of the soul to perceive such as are allowed us still, that makes us push all the sanctities into the far spaces we cannot reach. The devout feel that wherever God's hand is, there is miracle.

—*JAMES MARTINEAU*

There are only two ways to live your life. One is as though nothing is a miracle. The other is as though everything is a miracle.

—*ALBERT EINSTEIN*

MISSION

It is not that men strive, but that they
Strive so dreamlessly,
Not that they sow, but that they seldom reap,
Not that they serve, but have not gods to serve,
Not that they die, but that they die like sheep.

—*T. S. ELIOT*

In order to promote life it is necessary to value something more than mere life. Life devoted to life is without real human value, incapable of preserving men permanently from weariness and the feeling that all is vanity. Those who best promote life do not have life for their purpose.

—*BERTRAND RUSSELL*

Each child carries his or her own unique blessing into the world.

—*RABBI WAYNE DOSICK*

Up and down, to and fro, round and round: this is the monotonous and meaningless rhythm of the universe.

—MARCUS AURELIUS

Each man is a soldier in a cosmic campaign, the plan of which he does not know.

—OLIVER WENDELL HOLMES

Life means to have something definite to do-a mission to fulfill-and in the measure in which we avoid setting our life to something, we make it empty. Human life, by its very nature, has to be dedicated to something.

— JOSE ORTEGA Y GASSET

In working with people who are dying and in reading a lot about near-death experiences, people seem to arrive at a sense of what life's purpose is—and it is not to be a doctor or to be well-known or even to make a social contribution. The purpose of life, as these people tell it, is simpler than this. The purpose of life is to grow in wisdom and to learn to love better. If life serves these purposes, then health serves them as well, because illness is part of life.

—RACHEL NAOMI REMEN

In each person there is a priceless treasure that is in no other. Therefore, one shall honor each person for the hidden value that only that person and none of the person's comrades has.

—MARTIN BUBER

Spiritual practice always involves going beyond simply finding out who one is to a level of finding out also what one needs to do in the world.

—GERALD MAY

MISTAKES

An Expert is a guy who has made all his mistakes in one field.

—ANONYMOUS

To err is human; to blame it on someone else is even more human.

—ANONYMOUS

We learn wisdom from failure more than from success; we often discover what will do by finding out what will not do; and probably he who never made a mistake never made a discovery.

— *SAMUEL SMILES*

Lucy: Another ballgame lost!!! Good Grief.

Charlie Brown: I get tired of losing.... Everything I do, I lose!

Lucy: Look at it this way, Charlie Brown. We learn more from losing than we do from winning.

Charlie Brown: THAT MAKES ME THE SMARTEST PERSON IN THE WORLD!!!

— *CHARLES SCHULZ*

Experience is the name everyone gives his mistakes.

— *OSCAR WILDE*

Friend, don't be a perfectionist. Perfectionism is a curse, and a strain. For you tremble lest you miss the bulls-eye. You are perfect if you let be.

Friend, don't be afraid of mistakes. Mistakes are not sins. Mistakes are ways of doing something different, perhaps creatively new.

Friend, don't be sorry for your mistakes. Be proud of them. You had the courage to give something of yourself.

— *FRITZ PERLS*

There is nothing final about a mistake, except its being taken as final.

— *PHYLLIS BOTTOME*

To gild refined gold, to paint the lily,
To throw a perfume on the violet,
To smooth the ice, or add another hue
Unto the rainbow, or with taper light
To seek the beauteous eye of heaven to garnish,
Is wasteful and ridiculous excess.

— *SHAKESPEARE*

MORALITY

There comes a time in every man's life when he has to abandon his principles and do the right thing.

—*HARRY S. TRUMAN*

A people is judged not by its standard of living, but by its standard of life.

—*HONORE DE BALZAC*

> If all the good people were clever,
> And all clever people were good,
> The world would be nicer than ever
> We thought that it possibly could.
> But somehow, 'tis seldom or never
> The two hit it off as they should;
> The good are so harsh to the clever,
> The clever so rude to the good!

—*ELIZABETH WORDSWORTH*

There is but one morality, as there is but one geometry.

—*ELTON TRUEBLOOD*

The greater part of morality is of a fixed eternal nature, and will endure when faith shall fail.

—*JOSEPH ADDISON*

The fundamental principle of all morality is that the human is a being naturally good, loving justice and order; that there is not any original perversity in the human heart, and that the first movements of nature are always right.

—*JEAN JACQUES ROUSSEAU*

There are moral laws of the universe just as abiding as the physical laws, and when we disobey these moral laws we suffer tragic consequences.

—*MARTIN LUTHER KING, JR.*

MOTHERS

An ounce of mothers is worth a pound of clergy.

—*SPANISH PROVERB*

Mother is the name of God in the lips and hearts of little children.

—*WILLIAM MAKEPEACE THACKERAY*

Men are what their mothers made of them.

— *RALPH WALDO EMERSON*

The mother's heart is the child's schoolroom.

— *HENRY WARD BEECHER*

MOURNING

Our tears can drive us to discover the deeper sources of comfort available to every human being. The word comfort, from the Latin "cum forte," literally means "with strength." And there is, deep inside every one of us, a strength greater than we ever dreamed, a strength which is only discovered when we are driven to the extremities of feeling.

—*ANTHONY FRIES PERRINO*

After the storm the birds sing, so why shouldn't we?

—*ROSE KENNEDY*

These things are beautiful beyond belief
The pleasant weakness that comes after pain
The radiant greenness that comes after rain
The deepened faith that follows after grief
And the awakening to love again.

—*ANONYMOUS*

So they sat down with him upon the ground seven days and seven nights, and none spoke a word unto him; for they saw that his grief was very great.

—*BIBLE (JOB 2:13)*

The wise in heart mourn not for those who live, nor for those who die.

—*BHAGAVAD-GITA*

The house of mourning teaches charity and wisdom.

—*ST. JOHN CHRYSOSTOM*

MUSIC

Without music, life would be a mistake.

—*FRIEDRICH NIETZSCHE*

To stop the flow of music would be like the stopping of time itself, incredible and inconceivable.

—*AARON COPLAND*

God respects me when I work
But He loves me when I sing.

—*RABINDRANATH TAGORE*

All of God's wisdom is encased in a garment: it is in the music. When we speak, you may say 'yes' and I say 'no' and we are already opposed to each other. In music, what is absolutely unbelievable, is that I can sing a melody, you can sing different notes, and it's the deepest harmony. The greatest revelation of God's oneness in the world is music.

—*RABBI SHLOMO CARLEBACH*

The most direct means for attaching ourselves to God from this material world is through music and song, so even if you can't sing well, sing. Sing to yourself. Sing in the privacy of your own home.

—*RABBI NAHMAN OF BRATSLAV*

Music puts our being as men and women in touch with that which transcends the sayable, which outstrips the analyzable.... It continues to be the unwritten theology of those who lack or reject any formal creed.... For many human beings, religion has been the music which they believe in.

—*GEORGE STEINER*

Music can name the unnamable and communicate the unknowable.

—*LEONARD BERNSTEIN*

There is a special Temple in Heaven, whose gates can be opened only through music.

—*ZOHAR*

I will sing unto the Lord as long as I live,
I will sing praise to my God while I have any being.

—*BIBLE (PSALM 104:3)*

The man that hath no music in himself,
Nor is not mov'd with concord of sweet sounds,
Is fit for treason, stratagems, and spoils;
The motions of his spirit are dull as night,
And his affections dark as Erebus:
Let no such man be trusted.

—*SHAKESPEARE*

Music is a universal language and need not be translated. With it, soul speaks to soul.

—*B. AUERBACH*

Music is what is awakened in us when we are reminded by the instruments.

—*WALT WHITMAN*

Nature is saturated with melody;
Heaven and earth are full of song.

—*RABBI NAHMAN OF BRATZLAV*

Music is the way that our memories sing to us across time. The loveliest quality of music involves its modulation upon the theme of time. Songs, playing in the mind, become the subtlest shuttles across years.

—*LANCE MORROW*

There are three ways in which man expresses his deep sorrow; the man on the lowest level cries; the man on the second level is silent; the man on the highest level knows how to turn his sorrow into song.

—*RABBI ABRAHAM JOSHUA HESCHEL*

What passion cannot Music raise and quell!

—*JOHN DRYDEN*

Listening to great music is a shattering experience, throwing the soul into an encounter with an aspect of reality to which the mind can never relate itself adequately.... The shattering experience of music has been a challenge to my thinking on ultimate issues. I spend my life working with thoughts. And one problem that gives me no rest is: do these thoughts ever rise to the heights rendered by authentic music? Music leads to the threshold of repentance, of unbearable realization of our own vanity and frailty and of the terrible relevance of God. I would define myself as a person who has been smitten by music, as a person who has never recovered from the blows of music.

—RABBI ABRAHAM JOSHUA HESCHEL

Let my song go forth like the path of the sun!
May all sons of the Immortal listen —
They who have reached their heavenly homes!

—SVETESVARA UPANISHAD

Heard melodies are sweet, but those unheard
Are sweeter.

—JOHN KEATS

Our fathers have broken even the strong fortresses by their hymns, the rock by their shouting. They have opened to us the path of the great heaven.

—RIG-VEDA

There is sweet music here that softer falls
Than petals from blown roses on the grass....
Music that gentler on the spirit lies,
Than tired eyelids upon tired eyes.

—ALRED LORD TENNYSON

MYSTICISM

To see a world in a grain of sand
And a Heaven in a wild flower,
Hold Infinity in the palm of your hand
And Eternity in an hour.

—WILLIAM BLAKE

Faith is an oasis in the heart which will never be reached by the caravan of thinking.
—KAHLIL GIBRAN

If everything on earth were rational, nothing would happen.
—DOSTOYEVSKY

In all your ways acknowledge God,
And God will direct your paths.
—BIBLE (PROVERBS 3:6)

Mysticism asserts that there is a level of reality beyond the phenomenal world; and this reality, hidden to the naked eye and undisclosed to those who exist on the surface of life, embodies the true meaning of existence. As we rise out of the surface of life we transcend the ugliness and pain of mundane existence, and find the true beatitude which the heart seeks.

The goal of the mystic is not to gain conceptual knowledge, to discover confirmation that a higher reality exists; it is rather to establish an emotional bond with it. It is to embrace the vibrations of the higher reality which pulsate throughout existence. It is to establish union with, or ... a cleaving to God. The fruits of this experience are a reconciliation to life as something noble and exalted, a surge of creative energy that enables a person to pursue tasks hitherto deemed too arduous, and an inner illumination which reveals a wisdom beyond the reach of dialectical reason.
—RABBI BEN ZION BOKSER

But as for me, the nearness of God is my good;
I have made the Lord God my refuge,
That I may tell of all Your works.
—BIBLE (PSALMS 73:28)

The seers, the mystics, the visionaries smash the mirror again and again. They restore man to the primordial flux, they put him back in the stream like a fisherman emptying his net.
—HENRY MILLER

They desire to know, only that they may love; and their desire for union with the principle of things in God, who is the sum of them all, is founded on a feeling which is neither curiosity nor self-interest.
—E. RECÉJAC

To be a mystic is simply to participate here and now in that real and eternal life.

—EVELYN UNDERHILL

A mystic is not one who sees God in nature, but one for whom God and nature fit into one plane.

—BEDE JARRETT

True mystics simply open their souls to the oncoming wave.... That which they have allowed to flow into them is a stream flowing down and seeking through them to reach their fellow humans; the necessity to spread around them what they have received affects them like an onslaught of love.

—HENRI BERGSON

Broadly speaking, I understand it to be the expression of the innate tendency of the human spirit towards complete harmony with the transcendental order.

—EVELYN UNDERHILL

Mysticism is essentially ... leading to immediate contact with God.

—THOMAS HUGHES

What is the world? The world is God, wrapped in robes of God, so as to appear to be material. And who are we? We are God, wrapped in robes of God, and our task is to unwrap the robes and to discover, uncover, that we are God.

—RABBI MENAHEM NAHUM OF CHERNOBYL

MYTH

Myths are public dreams. Dreams are private myths....

Myths are the sign language the unconscious uses to communicate with the conscious mind.

—JOSEPH CAMPBELL

It would not be too much to say that myth is the secret opening through which the inexhaustible energies of the cosmos pour into human cultural manifestations. Religions, philosophies, arts, the social forms of primitive and historic man, prime discoveries in science and technology, the very dreams that blister sleep boil up from the black magic ring of myth.

—JOSEPH CAMPBELL

Storyteller's Creed:

I believe that imagination is stronger than knowledge.

That myth is more potent than history.

That dreams are more powerful than facts.

That hope always triumphs over experience.

That laughter is the only cure for grief.

And I believe that love is stronger than death.

—ROBERT FULGHUM

The myth is mostly invented, but the faith at the back of it has at least a good deal of probability about it.

—GILBERT MURRAY

Fiction was invented to discover the truth.

—MILAN KUNDERA

NATIONALISM

Our true nationality is mankind.

—H.G. WELLS

We should behave toward our country as women behave toward the men they love. A loving wife will do anything for her husband except to stop criticizing and trying to improve him. That is the right attitude for a citizen. We should cast the same affectionate but sharp glance at our country. We should love it, but also insist on telling it all its faults.

—J. B. PRIESTLEY

Had I but served my God with half the zeal I served the king, he would not in mine age have left me naked to mine enemies.

—SHAKESPEARE

The Lord is high above all nations,
God's glory is above the heavens.

—BIBLE (PSALM 113:4)

In the world as it is constituted today, a man may be a citizen of one land only, and his country is an extremely jealous shrew. Our conception of patriotism—"my county right or wrong"—is one of the nastiest sins of mankind. Jealous, vindictive, suspicious, it possesses the bodies, minds, and souls of men; countless millions of lives have been sacrificed to the obscene goddess of blind patriotism, untold millions of fortune. What men built over generations—schools, hospitals, shrines, sanctuaries—were demolished in an hour and less. Our earth has been raked over and over because of lawless patriotism. We shall know no redemption until a nobler conception of patriotism is achieved, a broader base of citizenship. Before a man is a national of any one country he is a human being, a child of God.

—RABBI BERYL D. COHON

Nationalism is simply one of the effective ways in which the modern man escapes life's ethical problems. Delegating his vices to larger and larger groups, he imagines himself virtuous.

—REINHOLD NIEBUHR

Nationalism is a heretical religion based on the erroneous doctrine that nations have a soul and that this soul is more permanent, more "eternal," so to speak, than the soul of an individual.

—FRANZ WERFEL

NATURE

Hills are always more beautiful than stone buildings, you know. Living in a city is an artificial existence. Lots of people hardly ever feel real soil under their feet, see plants grow except in flower pots, or get far enough beyond the street light to catch the enchantment of a night sky studded with stars. When people live far from scenes of the Great Spirit's making, it's easy for them to forget his laws.

—WALKING BUFFALO

Nature abhors a vacuum.

—FRANCOIS RABELAIS

The best remedy for those who are afraid, lonely or unhappy is to go outside, somewhere where they can be quite alone with the heavens, nature and God. Because only then does one feel that all is as it should be and that God wishes to see people happy, amidst the simple beauty of nature. As long as this exists, and it certainly always will, I know that then there will always be comfort for every sorrow, whatever the circumstances may be.

—ANNE FRANK

All things in nature work silently. They come into being and possess nothing. They fulfill their function and make no claim. All things alike do their work, and then we see them subside. When they have reached their bloom, each returns to its origin.... This reversion is an eternal law. To know that law is wisdom.

—LAO-TZE

Let children walk with Nature, let them see the beautiful blendings and communions of death and life, their joyous inseparable unity, as taught in woods and meadows, ... and they will learn that death is stingless indeed, and as beautiful as life.

—JOHN MUIR

Whatever befalls in the course of nature should be considered good.

—CICERO

> Oh, when I am safe in my sylvan home,
>   I tread on the pride of Greece and Rome;
> And when I am stretched beneath the pines
>   Where the evening star so holy shines,
> I laugh at the lore and the pride of man,
>   At the sophist schools and the learned clan;
> For what are they all in their conceit,
>   When man in the bush with God may meet?

—RALPH WALDO EMERSON

> And this our life, exempt from public haunt,
> Finds tongues in trees, books in the running brooks,
> Sermons in stones and good in everything.

—SHAKESPEARE

Material nature is the principle of becoming and is so evil that it fills with evil any being which is not yet in it and which does no more than look at it.

—PLOTINUS

There is a pleasure in the pathless woods,
There is a rapture on the lonely shore,
There is society where none intrudes
By the deep sea, and music in its roar:
I love not man the less but nature more
From these our interviews, in which I steal
From all I may be or have been before
To mingle with the universe and feel
What I can ne'er express, yet cannot all conceal.

—GEORGE LORD BYRON

Follow the order of nature, for God's sake! Follow it! It will lead who follows; and those who will not, it will drag along anyway.

—MICHEL DE MONTAIGNE

Nature is not governed except by obeying her.

—FRANCIS BACON

Be open-eyed to the great wonders of nature, familiar though they may be or people are more likely to be astonished at the sun's eclipse than at its unfailing rise.

—ORHOT TZADIKIM 15C

NOSTALGIA

Nostalgia is when we find the present tense and the past perfect.

—ANONYMOUS

We should be certain we do not fall into the trap of yearning for 'the good old days.' Nostalgia is marvelous for the fashion and record industry. But, it should not blind us to what we have really left behind. The '30s with their depression, Nazis, American fascists; the '40s with World War II, Dachau, Buchenwald; the '50s with McCarthy and Korea; the '60s with student riots, etc., etc., etc., are as much a part of the past for which some of us crave. Of course, we have our own concerns and our own challenges. These problems are enormous and frightening. Yes, challenges require suitable responses.

—RABBI GERALD I. WOLPE

OLD AGE

Forty is the old age of youth; fifty is the youth of old age.

—*VICTOR HUGO*

Let us take care of the children, for they have a long way to go. Let us take care of the elders, for they have come a long way. Let us take care of those in between, for they are doing the work.

—*ANONYMOUS*

People don't grow old merely by living a certain number of years. Aging is an activity of the mind, an attitude. We grow old when we give up our sense of fun. We age when we relinquish our ideals, our dignity, our hope, our belief in miracles. Age comes when we cease reveling in the game of life, when we are no longer excited by the new and challenged by the dream. As long as we celebrate the richness of the world, hear the laughter in the voice of love and continue to believe in ourselves, age is incidental.

—*LEO BUSCAGLIA*

My wife is going blind; and on the whole she is glad of it; there is nothing worth seeing. She says she hopes she will also become deaf; for there is nothing worth hearing. The best thing about being old is that you are near the goal.

—*JOHANN AUGUST STRINDBERG*

I have gotten used to my arthritis ... to my dentures I'm resigned ...
I can cope with my trifocals ... but oh, my, how I miss my mind.

—*ANONYMOUS*

So feeble are many old people that they cannot execute any task or duty or any function of life whatever, but that in truth is not the peculiar fault of old age, but belongs to bad health.

—*CICERO*

Aging is a matter of the mind; if you don't mind, it doesn't matter.

—*JACK BENNY*

You know you're old when the candles cost more than the cake.

—*BOB HOPE*

I'm going to die young ... as late in life as possible.

—*ASHLEY MONTAGUE*

Never have I enjoyed youth so thoroughly as I have in my old age.

—*GEORGE SANTAYANA*

Old age is like everything else. To make a success of it, you've got to start young.

—*FRED ASTAIRE*

Age cannot wither her,
Nor custom stale her infinite variety.

—*SHAKESPEARE*

You can't help getting older, but you don't have to get old.

—*GEORGE BURNS*

Age is opportunity no less
Than youth itself, though in another dress,
And as the evening twilight fades away
The sky is filled with stars invisible by day.

—*HENRY WADSWORTH LONGFELLOW*

You are as young as your faith, as old as your doubt; as young as your confidence, as old as your fear; as young as your hope, as old as your despair.

In the central place of every heart there is a recording chamber; so long as it receives messages of beauty, hope, cheer and courage, so long are we young. When the wires are all down and your heart is covered with snows of pessimism and the ice of cynicism, then and then only are you grown old.

—*DOUGLAS MacARTHUR*

They shall still bring forth fruit in old age;
They shall be full of sap and richness;
To declare that the Lord is upright,
My Rock, in whom there is no unrighteousness.

—*BIBLE (PSALM 92:15-16)*

Don't regret growing old. It's a privilege denied to many.

—*POSTER*

You shall rise up before the hoary head, and honor the face of the old, and you shall fear your God: I am the Lord.

—*BIBLE (LEVITICUS 19:32)*

Abraham took along to the Akedah "two of his servants." The Hebrew words ... a Hasidic interpretation points out, can also be translated, "the years of his youth." It is worth noting in this regard that according to tradition, Abraham was 137 years old at this time. He could have pleaded infirmity and the disabilities of age as an excuse for not fulfilling the onerous Divine command. But the Bible makes a point of letting us know that despite the anguish and the indescribable heartbreak involved in fulfilling the Divine command, Abraham gathered up his youthful energy and determination in order to fulfill God's word. His zeal not only commands our admiration but also calls for emulation.

—RABBI SIDNEY GREENBERG

It's not how old you are, but it's how you are old.

—MARIE DRESSLER

The test of a people is how it behaves toward the old. It is easy to love children. Even tyrants and dictators make a point of being fond of children, but the affection and care for the old, the incurable, the helpless are the true gold mines of a culture.

—RABBI ABRAHAM JOSHUA HESCHEL

Grow old along with me,
The best is yet to be;
The last of life
For which the first was made.

—ROBERT BROWNING

One ought not be alarmed when one's hair turns gray. Yes, if it turned green or blue, then one ought to see a doctor. But if it turns gray, it simply means that there is so much gray matter in the skull that there is no longer room for it and it comes out and discolors the hair.... Hence there is no reason to be ashamed of one's gray hair.

—WILLIAM LYONS PHELPS

Do not go gentle into that good night,
Old age should burn and rave at close of day;
Rage, rage, against the dying of the light.

—DYLAN THOMAS

As long as one can admire and love, then one is young forever.

—PABLO CASSALS

Most people say that as you get old, you have to give up things. I think you get old because you give up things.
—SENATOR THEODORE GREEN

The true prosperity of a country is measured by its treatment of the elderly.
—RABBI NAHMAN OF BRATSLAV

A busy, highly involved person somewhat advanced in years once complained to his physician, whose prescription for his severe cold had not improved his condition. He was slated to take a long overseas trip in a few days and his frustration, upset, and even anger at the doctor, was beginning to show. The doctor angrily reacted by saying that he was not a magician, he could not turn the clock back and make him young again. To which the patient responded-that is not what I want, to become young again. What I do want is to go on getting older.
—ANONYMOUS

OPENMINDEDNESS

Just as important as having ideas is getting rid of them.
—FRANCIS CRICK

I have steadily endeavored to keep my mind free so as to give up any hypothesis, however much beloved (and I cannot resist forming one on every subject), as soon as facts are shown to be opposed to it.
—CHARLES DARWIN

O Lord, help me not to despise or oppose what I do not understand.
—WILLIAM PENN

There is a tide in the affairs of men,
Which, taken at the flood, leads on to fortune;
Omitted, all the voyage of their life
Is bound in shallows and in miseries.
On such a full sea are we now afloat;
And we must take the current when it serves,
Or lose our ventures.
—SHAKESPEARE

OPPORTUNITY

It is one of life's laws that as soon as one door closes, another opens. But the tragedy is that we look at the closed door and disregard the open one.

—*ANDRE GIDE* .

A wise man will make more opportunities than he finds.

—*FRANCIS BACON*

OPPRESSION

It is not power that corrupts, but fear. Fear of losing power corrupts those who wield it, and fear of the courage of power corrupts those who are subject to it.

—*AUNG SAN SUU KYI*

There comes a time when people get tired of being trampled over by the iron feet of oppression!

—*MARTIN LUTHER KING, JR.*

OPTIMISM

Pessimism is a waste of time.

—*NORMAN COUSINS*

Over-optimism is waiting for your ship to come in when you haven't sent one out.

—*ANONYMOUS*

I live as an optimist because I find I cannot live at all as a pessimist.

—*BERNARD MALAMUD*

All human wisdom is summed up in two words—wait and hope.

—*ALEXANDER DUMAS, ELDER*

A pessimist is one who, given two bad choices, takes them both.

—*ANONYMOUS*

The optimist thinks this is the best of all possible worlds, and the pessimist knows it.

—*J. ROBERT OPPENHEIMER*

One summer night two frogs fell into a bucket of milk. The first frog, realizing the hopelessness of his situation, promptly gave up and drowned. The second frog began thrashing about furiously with all his might. The following morning the farmer was surprised to find his bucket of milk turned to butter and there was a frog sitting on the top of it.

—*ANONYMOUS*

Hell is the place where one has ceased to hope.

—*A.J. CRONIN*

The pessimist may be proven right at the end of the trip, but the optimist enjoys the ride more.

—*ANONYMOUS*

The commander who took counsel only of all the gloomy intelligence estimates would never win a battle; he would be forever sitting, waiting for the predicted catastrophes.

—*DWIGHT D. EISENHOWER*

We are moving through a period of extreme danger and splendid hope.

—*WINSTON CHURCHILL*

Man is born with rainbows in his heart. And you'll never read him unless you consider the rainbows.

—*CARL SANDBURG*

Do not despair—there is no such thing as despair.

—*RABBI NAHMAN OF BRATZLAV*

There is no tonic so powerful as expectation of a better tomorrow; there is no medicine like hope. It is the adrenaline of the soul.

—*RABBI SAUL TEPLITZ*

An optimist is a person who falls from the Empire State Building and upon seeing horrified workers rush to the window of the 47th floors, gaily waves and says: "So far so good! Don't worry about me."

—*ANONYMOUS*

If you wish to find the fire, look for it in the ashes.

—*REB MOSHE-LEIB OF SASSOV*

In the face of uncertainty, there is always hope.

—*WILLIAM SAROYAN*

An optimist is an inverse paranoid: he thinks the world is out to do him good.

—*ANONYMOUS*

Tough times never last, but tough people do.

—*ANONYMOUS*

It is a peculiarity of man that he can only live by looking to the future.

—*VIKTOR E. FRANKL*

A man was shipwrecked on a desert island. He built a crude hut, in which he placed the few belongings he had accumulated and saved. Every day he prayed for deliverance and regularly scanned the horizon to look for ships.

One day, returning from a hunt for food, he was horrified to find his hut in flames. All he owned was gone. The worst thing that could happen to him had just happened. He cursed one and all. The next day a ship arrived, and the captain said: "We saw your smoke signal."

—*ANONYMOUS*

Let us admit half of the terrible picture that Jonathan Swift drew of humanity; let us agree that in every generation of man's history, and almost everywhere, we find superstition, hypocrisy, corruption, cruelty, crime, and war; in the balance against them we place the long roster of poets, composers, artists, scientists, philosophers, and saints. That same species upon which poor Swift revenged the frustration of his flesh wrote the plays of Shakespeare, the music of Bach and Handel, the odes of Keats, the Republic of Plato, the Principia of Newton, and the Ethics of Spinoza; it built the Parthenon and painted the ceiling of the Sistine Chapel; it conceived and cherished, even if it crucified, Christ. Man did all this: let him never despair.

—*WILL DURANT*

In Paris there is a painting in the Louvre showing Faust and the Devil sitting on opposite sides of a chessboard. The Devil wears a smile of triumph, while Faust sits dejected. The caption beneath the painting consists of one word: "Checkmate!"

People viewing the painting usually marvel at its beauty and power, but soon are overwhelmed by its message of hopelessness and despair. One man, however, who studied the chessboard made a discovery:

"There is one more move possible," he shouted, "Faust can still win!"

—*RABBI C. J. TEICHMAN*

With some qualifications I suggest that nothing is more characteristic of mental well-being than a healthy self-respect, a regard for one's body and its functions, and a reasonably optimistic outlook on life.

—BRUCE BETTELHEIM

Optimism is the madness of maintaining that everything is right when it is wrong.

—VOLTAIRE

God's in his Heaven—
All's right with the world!

—ROBERT BROWNING

Nothing is too great or too good to be true. Do not believe that we can imagine things better than they are. In the long run, in the ultimate outlook, in the eye of the Creator, the possibilities open to us, are beyond our imagination.

—OLIVER LODGE

A pessimist is one who has been intimately acquainted with an optimist.

—ELBERT HUBBARD

Do you know what a pessimist is? A man who thinks everybody as nasty as himself, and hates them for it.

—GEORGE BERNARD SHAW

All sunshine makes a desert.

—ARAB PROVERB

An optimist is a believer in the best, and any man who believes that anything less than the best is the ultimate purpose of God, and so the ultimate possibility of God's children, has no business to live upon the earth.

—PHILLIPS BROOKS

PAIN

Without your wounds where would your power be? The very angels themselves cannot persuade the wretched and blundering children on earth as can one human being broken in the wheels of living. In love's service, only the wounded soldiers can serve.

—THORTON WILDER

There was a faith healer from Deal
Who said, "Although pain is not real,
When I sit—on a pin
And it punctures my skin,
I dislike—what I fancy—I feel.

—ANTHONY FRIES PERRINO

From youth until old age Rabbi Yitzchak Eisik suffered from an ailment which was known to involve very great pain. His physician once asked him how he managed to endure such pain without complaining or groaning. He replied: "You would understand that readily enough if you thought of the pain as scrubbing and soaking the soul in a strong solution. Since this is so, one cannot do otherwise than accept such pain with love and not grumble. After a time, one gains the strength to endure the present pain. It is always the question of a moment, for the pain which has passed is no longer, and who would be so foolish as to concern himself with future pain!

—MARTIN BUBER

Your pain is the breaking of the shell that encloses your understanding.

—KAHLIL GIBRAN

You know quite well,
Deep within you,
That there is only
A single magic,
A single power,
A single salvation ...
And that is called loving.
Well then, love your suffering.
Do not resist it, do not flee from it
It is only your aversion that hurts, nothing else.

—HERMAN HESSE

We, by our suff'rings, learn to prize our bliss.

—JOHN DRYDEN

If we could read the secret history of our enemies, we should find in each man's life sorrow and suffering enough to disarm all hostility.

—HENRY WADSWORTH LONGFELLOW

It's wonderful to be alive; but why does it always hurt?

—BORIS PASTERNAK

If a nasty jagged stone
Gets into your shoe,
Thank the Lord it came alone,
What if it were two?

—ANONYMOUS

There was never yet a philosopher who could bear the toothache patiently.

—SHAKESPEARE

I walked a mile with pleasure.
She chatted all the way;
But left me none the wiser
For all she had to say.
I walked a mile with sorrow,
And ne'er a word said she;
But, oh, the things I learned from her
When sorrow walked with me!

—ROBERT BROWNING

If I accept the sunshine and warmth then I must also accept the thunder and lightning.

—KAHLIL GIBRAN

The enemy of development is the pain phobia—the unwillingness to do a tiny bit of suffering. You see, pain is a signal of nature. The painful leg, the painful feeling, cries out, "Pay attention to me—if you don't pay attention things will get worse."

—FRITZ PERLS

The pearl of great price always begins as a pain in the oyster's stomach!

—JOHN E. LARGE

PARENTING

Don't worry that children never listen to you; worry that they are always watching you.

—ROBERT FULGHUM

Nothing must separate parents from their duty to their children.

—MARIAN WRIGHT EDELMAN

Advise and counsel them; if they do not listen, let adversity teach them.

—ETHIOPIAN PROVERB

If your son laughs when you scold him, you ought to cry, for you have lost him; if he cries, you may laugh, for you have a worthy heir.

—SENEGALESE PROVERB

My mother would always go into the bathroom to pray. One day, when I was about ten years old, while she was in the bathroom praying, I walked in just as she was calling my name in prayer. That experience had such a tremendous impact on my life because from that moment on, I know that no matter where I went in the world, or whatever circumstances I found myself in, my mother was praying for me!

—REV. RODNEY T. FRANCIS

A school system without parents at its foundation is just like a bucket with a hole in it.

—REVEREND JESSE JACKSON

You didn't have a choice about the parents you inherited, but you do have a choice about the kind of parent you will be.

—MARIAN WRIGHT EDELMAN

PATH

Truth is a pathless land.

—JIDDU KRISHNAMURTI

Where is the way to the dwelling of light,
And as for darkness, where is its place;
That you should take it to its boundary,
And that you should know the paths to its house?
You know it, for you were then born,
And the number of your days is great!

—BIBLE (JOB 38:19-21)

Each person's life represents a road toward oneself, an attempt at such a road, the intimation of such a path.

—*HERMAN HESSE*

Happy is the one who finds wisdom,
And the one who obtains understanding....
Her ways are ways of pleasantness,
And all her paths are peace.

—*BIBLE (PROVERBS 3:13-17)*

The individual is the path. The only one who matters is the one who takes the path.

—*ANTOINE DE SAINT-EXUPERY*

Let us not be uneasy that the different roads we may pursue, as believing them the shortest, to that of our last abode; but, following the guidance of a good conscience, let us be happy in the hope that by these different paths we shall all meet in the end.

—*THOMAS JEFFERSON*

As one can ascend to the top of a house by means of a ladder or a bamboo or a staircase or a rope, so diverse are the ways and means to approach God, and every religion in the world shows one of these ways.

—*SRI RAMAKRISHNA*

Go Godward: thou wilt find a road.

—*RUSSIAN PROVERB*

PATIENCE

Do not be desirous of having things done quickly. Do not look at small advantages. Desire to have things done quickly prevents their being done thoroughly. Looking at small advantages prevents great affairs from being accomplished.

—*CONFUCIUS*

Justice is not to be taken by storm. She is to be wooed by slow advances.

—*JUSTICE BENJAMIN CARDOZO*

There are two cardinal sins from which all the others spring: impatience and laziness.

—FRANZ KAFKA

No! Tell a man whose house is on fire to give a moderate alarm; tell him moderately to rescue his wife from the hands of a ravisher; tell the mother to extricate her babe gradually from the fire into which he has fallen-but urge me not to rise moderately in a cause like the present.

—WILLIAM LLOYD GARRISON

Patience is the companion of wisdom.

—ST. AUGUSTINE

The two powers which in my opinion constitute a wise person are those of bearing and forbearing.

—EPICTETUS

Be patient, and endure.

—OVID

Study to be patient in hearing the defects of others and their infirmities be they what they may: for you have many things which another must bear as well.

—THOMAS Á KEMPIS

PATRIOTISM

The real patriots are those who love America as she is, but who want the beloved to be more loveable. This is not treachery. This, as every parent, every teacher, every friend must know, is the truest and noblest affection.

—ADLAI STEVENSON

Patriotism is the egg from which wars are hatched.

—GUY DE MAUPASSANT

I wish I could love my country as much as I love justice.

—ANONYMOUS

Patriotism is the last refuge of a scoundrel.

—SAMUEL JOHNSON

Our country, right or wrong.
When right—to be kept right.
When wrong—to be put right.

—CARL SCHURZ

Patriotism is entering into praiseworthy competition with one's forebears.

—TACITUS

Next to love of God, the love of country is the best preventive of crime. He who is proud of his country will be particularly cautious not to do anything which is calculated to disgrace it.

—GEORGE BARROW

Standing as I do, in view of God and Eternity, I realize that patriotism is not enough. I must have no hatred or bitterness for anyone.

—EDITH CAVELL

PEACE

Our security is the total product of our economic, intellectual, moral and military strengths.... There is no way in which a country can satisfy the cravings for absolute security—but it can easily bankrupt itself, morally and economically, in attempting to reach that illusory goal through arms alone.

— DWIGHT D. EISENHOWER

One day we must come to see that peace is not merely a distant goal that we must seek but a means by which we arrive at that goal.

—MARTIN LUTHER KING, JR.

What a waste it would be, after four billion tortuous years of evolution, if the dominant organism on earth contrived its own self-destruction. We are the first species to have devised the means. There is no issue more important than the avoidance of nuclear war. It is incredible for any thinking person not to be concerned with this issue!

—CARL SAGAN

Ultimately the only way to prevent more and more nations from developing nuclear arms is for those who have them to begin to disarm.

—*BENJAMIN SPOCK*

Friendships have defended more borders than arms and cannon ever have.

—*DWIGHT D. EISENHOWER*

Since wars are born in the minds of men, it is in the minds of men that we must erect ramparts of peace.

—*UNESCO CHARTER*

You can't hug kids with nuclear arms.

—*BUMPER STICKER*

Every gun that is made, every warship launched, every rocket fired, signifies, in the final sense, a theft from those who hunger and are not fed, those who are cold and are not clothed. This world in arms is not spending money alone. It is spending the sweat of its laborers, the genius of its scientists, the hope of its children....

This is not a way of life at all, in any true sense. Under the cloud of threatening war, it is humanity hanging from a cross of iron.

—*DWIGHT D. EISENHOWER*

A time to love, and a time to hate;
A time for war, and a time for peace.

—*BIBLE (ECCLESIASTES 3:8)*

Indeed, it is part of the general pattern of misguided policy that our country is now geared to an arms economy which has bred in an artificially induced psychosis of war hysteria and nurtured upon an incessant propaganda of fear. While such an economy may produce a sense of soaring prosperity for the moment, it rests on an illusionary foundation of complete unreliability and renders among our political leaders almost a greater fear of peace than is their fear of war.

—*DOUGLAS MACARTHUR*

Mankind must put an end to war or war will put an end to mankind.

—*JOHN F. KENNEDY*

The world's a puzzle from which a 'peace' is missing.

—*ANONYMOUS*

People want peace so much that one of these days governments had better get out of their way and let them have it.

—*DWIGHT D. EISENHOWER*

Mercy and truth are met together;
Righteousness and peace have kissed each other.

—*BIBLE (PSALMS 85:11)*

There is a story told about a Chinese sage who was once asked by a farmer, "When will the world truly know peace?"

The sage replied, "Follow me," and he took the farmer to a brook, put his hand on the farmer's head, and pressed it into the water until the farmer came up gasping for breath. The sage then said to the farmer, "This is your answer. When people want peace as much as you wanted air, when one comes up gasping for peace, when we are ready to give everything in ourselves to have peace, as you have given to air, then, and only then, will we have peace.

—*ANONYMOUS*

One nuclear bomb could ruin your whole day.

—*BUMPER STICKER*

The work of righteousness shall be peace;
And the effect of righteousness quietness and confidence for ever.

—*BIBLE (ISAIAH 32:17)*

Smile, God loves your enemies.

—*BUMPER STICKER*

Ask not that events should happen as you will, but let your will be that events happen as they do, and you shall have peace.

—*EPICTETUS*

No peace can last, or ought to last, which does not recognize and accept the principle that governments derive all their just powers from the consent of the governed; and that no right anywhere exists to hand people about from sovereignty to sovereignty, as if they were property. The world can be at peace only if its life is stable; and there can be no stability where there is not tranquility of spirit and a sense of justice, of freedom and right.

—*WOODROW WILSON*

The first and fundamental law of Nature ... to seek peace and follow it.

—*THOMAS HOBBES*

It is one thing to see the land of peace from a wooded ridge ... and another to tread the road that leads to it.

—ST. AUGUSTINE

The grim fact is that we prepare for war like precocious giants and for peace like retarded pygmies.

—LESTER B. PEARSON

The only excuse for war is that it be undertaken to ensure a peace injurious to none.

—CICERO

PEAK EXPERIENCE

In Karlin the Hasid was constantly singed by sacred fire; and as he burned he shouted for more—such was his yearning to become flame and thus reach the divine source. And to forget who he was on this earth, to forget everything on this earth; to become an offering.

—ELIE WIESEL

If a man could pass through paradise in a dream, and have a flower presented to him as a pledge that his soul had really been there, and if he found that flower in his hand when he awoke, ay, what then!

—SAMUEL TAYLOR COLERIDGE

Apparently most people, or almost all people, have peak experiences, or ecstasies. The question might be asked in terms of the single most joyous, happiest, most blissful moment of your life.... How did you feel different about yourself at that time? How did the world look different? What did you feel like? What were your impulses? How did you change if you did?

—ABRAHAM MASLOW

PERFECTIONISM

Nature does not require that we be perfect. It only requires that we grow.

—ANONYMOUS

Total freedom from error is what none of us will allow to our neighbors; however we may be inclined to flirt a little with such spotless perfection ourselves.

—CHARLES CALEB COLTON

The creature, by the very fact of its creation, can only be imperfect. God will bring it gradually to perfection.

—ST. IRENAEUS

It is not enough to serve God in the hope of future reward; one must do right and avoid wrong because one is a human, and owes it to his humanity to seek perfection.

—MAIMONIDES

Perfection and imperfection are really only modes of thought; that is to say, notions which we are in the habit of forming from the comparison with one another of individuals of the same species or genus.

—BARUCH SPINOZA

The love of God never looks for perfection in created beings. It knows that it dwells with God alone. As it never expects perfection, it is never disappointed.

—FRANÇOIS FÉNELON

PERSEVERANCE

If a man has any greatness in him, it comes to light, not in one flamboyant hour, but in the ledger of his daily work.

—BERYL MARKHAM

Success is just getting up just one more time than you fall down.

—ANONYMOUS

Poetry, like all birth and creativity, is accompanied by pain and sacrifice.

—ROBERT FROST

The saints are the sinners who keep on going.

—ROBERT LOUIS STEVENSON

Nothing in the world can take the place of persistence. Talent will not; nothing is more common than unsuccessful men with talent. Genius will not; unrewarded genius is almost a proverb. Education will not; the world is full of educated derelicts. Persistence and determination alone are omnipotent. The slogan 'Press on' has solved and always will solve the problems of the human race.

—*CALVIN COOLIDGE*

I never have frustrations
The reason is to wit—
If at first I don't succeed
I quit!

—*ANONYMOUS*

A hero is the same as anyone else except that he has courage five minutes longer.

—*ANONYMOUS*

A diamond is just a piece of coal that stayed on the job.

—*ANONYMOUS*

Never let your head hang down. Never give up and sit and grieve. Find another way. And don't pray when it rains if you don't pray when the sun shines.

—*SATCHEL PAIGE*

Never give in, never never-in nothing great or small, large or petty-never give in-except in conviction of honor and good sense.

—*TOM BRADLEY*

It's not that I'm so smart, it's just that I stay with problems.

—*ALBERT EINSTEIN*

PERSONAL GROWTH

The aim of our worship is the purification, enlightenment, and uplifting of our inner selves.

—*RABBI SAMSON RAPHAEL HIRSCH*

One who covers transgressions shall not prosper;
But whoso confesses and forsakes them shall obtain mercy.
Happy is the one who fears always;
But one who hardens the heart shall fall into evil.

—*BIBLE (PROVERBS 28:13-14)*

PERSPECTIVE

Miracles result from our recognition that even the worst news is only a short story: the whole plot is an unfolding mystery. Be humble in your perpetual uncertainty.

—*PAUL PEARSALL*

A man whose axe was missing suspected his neighbor's son. The boy walked like a thief, looked like a thief, and spoke like a thief. But the man found his axe while he was digging in the valley, and the next time he saw his neighbor's son, the boy walked, looked, and spoke like any other child.

—*TRADITIONAL GERMAN TALE*

When you think that there are at least four billion suns in the Milky Way, which is just one of billions of galaxies spaced about one million light years apart; and that the further you go into space, the thicker the galaxies become. When you think of all of this, isn't it kind of silly to worry whether the waitress brought you string beans instead of limas?

—*HARRY GOLDEN*

Both read the Bible day and night,
But thou reads't black where I read white.

—*WILLIAM BLAKE*

We have our nose to the ground to ferret out the scent of the adversary; we have our ears to the ground to hear the distant rumbling; before we know it, something decisive has happened to us. We are no longer upright. Our gaze is no longer fixed on God and man in charity.

—*KARL STERN*

The illusion that times that were are better than those that are, has probably pervaded all ages.

—*HORACE GREELEY*

Two men look out through the same bars;
One sees mud, and one the stars.

—FREDERICK LANGBRIDGE

PERSUASION

If you can't convince them, confuse them.

—HARRY S. TRUMAN

We are more easily persuaded, in general, by the reasons we ourselves discover than by those which are given to us by others.

—BLAISE PASCAL

Let any man speak long enough, he will get believers.

—ROBERT LOUIS STEVENSON

PHILOSOPHY

A little philosophy inclineth men to atheism, but depth in philosophy bringeth man's mind about to religion.

—BACON

In earnestly investigating and attempting to discover the reason of all things, every means of attaining to a pious and perfect doctrine lies in that science and discipline which the Greeks call philosophy.

—JOHANNES SCOTUS ERIGENA

Metaphysics is the finding of bad reasons for what we believe on instinct.

—F. H. BRADLEY

In theology the weight of Authority, but in philosophy the weight of Reason is valid.

—JOHANNES KEPLER

Be a philosopher; but, amidst all your philosophy, be still a man.

—DAVID HUME

Philosophy is written in that vast book which stands forever open before our eyes. I mean the universe.

—GALILEO

There are more things in heaven and earth, Horatio,
Than are dreamt of in your philosophy.

—SHAKESPEARE

Philosophy ... is not a presumptuous effort to explain the mysteries of the world by means of any superhuman insight or extraordinary cunning, but has its origin and value in an attempt to give a reasonable account of our personal attitude toward the more serious business of life.

—JOSIAH ROYCE

PLEASURE

Life is a gift to be used every day,
Not to be smothered and hidden away...
Get out and live it each hour of the day,
Wear it and use it as much as you may.

—EDGAR GUEST

Pleasure is, and must remain, a side-effect,... by-product, and is destroyed and spoiled to the degree to which it is made a goal in itself.

—VIKTOR E. FRANKL

From pleasure comes grief, from pleasure comes fear; he who is free from pleasure knows neither grief nor fear.

—DHAMMAPADA

Pleasure is very seldom found where it is sought.

—SAMUEL JOHNSON

Love of pleasure is the disease which makes humans most despicable.

—LONGINUS

Pleasure and action make the hours seem short.

—*SHAKESPEARE*

POLARITY

Only liars never contradict themselves. People who tell the truth are full of contradictions.

—*RABBI SHLOMO CARLEBACH*

At the still point of the turning world, neither flesh, nor fleshless;
Neither from nor towards; at the still point, there the dance is,
But neither arrest nor movement. And do not call it fixity,
Where past and future are gathered. Neither movement from nor
    towards,
Neither ascent nor decline. Except for the point, the still point,
There would be no dance, and there is only the dance.

—*WILLIAM H. HOUFF*

That great principle of Undulation in nature that shows itself in the inspiring and expiring of the breath; in desire and satiety; in the ebb and flow of the sea; in day and night; in heat and cold; and, as yet more deeply ingrained in every atom and every fluid, is known to us under the name of Polarity, —these "fits of easy transmission and reflection," as Newton called them, are the law of nature because they are the law of spirit.

—*RALPH WALDO EMERSON*

Teach us to care and not to care.
Teach us to sit still.

—*T. S. ELIOT*

The opposite of a trivial truth is plainly false. The opposite of a great truth is also true.

—*NIELS BOHR*

Do I contradict myself? Very well then I contradict myself, (I am large, I contain multitudes).

—*WALT WHITMAN*

Self-expression, paradoxically enough, requires the capacity to lose oneself in the pursuit of objectives not primarily related to the self.

—GORDON ALLPORT

This discovery of the complexity of human nature was accompanied by another—the discovery of the complexity and irrationality of human motive, the discovery that one could love and hate simultaneously, be honest and cheap, be arrogant and humble, be any pair of opposites that one had supposed to be mutually exclusive. This, I believe, is not common knowledge and would be incomprehensible to many. It has always been known, of course, by the dramatists and novelists. It is, in fact, a knowledge far more disturbing to other people than writers, for to writers it is the grist of their mills.

—ALAN PATON

I have always felt sorry for people afraid of feeling, of sentimentality, who are unable to weep with their whole heart. Because those who do not know how to weep do not know to laugh either.

—GOLDA MEIR

Primitive people do not differentiate their world of experience into two realms that oppose or compliment each other. They seem to maintain a consistent understanding of the unity of all experience.

—VINCE DELORIA

Paradoxically, the only way to stop experiencing something is to be totally willing to experience it.

—GAY HENDRICKS

It's a beautiful paradox: the more you open your consciousness, the fewer unpleasant events intrude themselves into your awareness.

—THADDEUS GOLAS

We have to befriend paradox: that love can complete us only if we grow whole; that union makes us feel our separateness all more acutely; that in love we have everything only if we possess nothing. If we are steadfast in our loving, relationships can be like the repetitive experiments that lead scientists to discoveries they had never anticipated, or the Zen practice that creates the "empty sky" for enlightenment's thunderbolts.

—MARK BARASCH

At the very roots of Chinese thinking and feeling there lies the principle of polarity, which is not to be confused with the ideas of opposition or conflict. In the metaphors of other cultures, light is at war with darkness, life with death, good with evil, and the positive with the negative, and thus and idealism to cultivate the former and be rid of the latter flourishes throughout much of the world. To the traditional way of Chinese thinking, this is as incomprehensible as an electric current without both positive and negative poles, for polarity is the principle that + and - , north and south, are different aspects of one and the same system, and that the disappearance of either one of them would be the disappearance of the system.

—*ALAN WATTS*

Dichotomizing pathologizes (and pathology dichotomizes). Isolating two interrelated parts of a whole from each other, parts that need each other, parts that are truly "parts" and not wholes, distorts them both, sickens and contaminates them.

—*ABRAHAM H. MASLOW*

A paradox is a contradiction in which you take sides—both sides.

—*GREGORY BATESON*

Defects of character, like physical ailments, may at times require drastic methods of treatment. Although extremes are normally to be rejected, the only way a man with a normal tendency towards one extreme can heal himself is to go for a time to the opposite extreme until the balance is achieved. Maimonides' commentators give the illustration of a bamboo cane that is bent. The only way to make it straight is to bend it in the opposite direction.

—*LOUIS JACOBS*

If enough individuals learn to integrate the polarities of existence—such as love and hate; caution and risk; certainty and ambiguity; separateness and relatedness; agency and communion—they will be able to utilize energy, hitherto applied to the mainstreams of a good, fixed character, in the development of a society which will support, rather than destroy, uniqueness and individuality.

—*JAMES LYNWOOD WALKER*

'Tis well to learn that sunny hours
May quickly change to mournful shade;
'Tis well to prize life's scattered flowers
Yet be prepared to see them fade.

—*ELIZA COOK*

Gradually I am beginning to accept my polarities as a person. I have pride; I am humble. I am selfish; I am unselfish. I am assertive, yet dependent. I love; I hate. I admire; yet am overly competitive. How much guilt have I known because of some unaware source of condemnation for the ambition which I possessed! How much joy in achievement have I missed because the achievement was all mixed up in my overall program of professional success.

—EVERETT L. SHOSTROM

At the end of the first creation story stand a double blessing—of the first man and the first Shabbat; at end of the second creation story stands a double curse—on the first man and the earth. Between both stand Sin. Natural man is established by a blessing; historical man by a curse. Both together form the dual nature and the dual fate of man.

—MARTIN BUBER

"Self-pity doesn't jibe with power," he said. "The mood of a warrior calls for control over himself and at the same time it calls for abandoning himself."

"How can that be?" I asked. "How can he control and abandon himself at the same time?"

"It is a difficult technique," he said.

—CARLOS CASTANEDA

These are the three principles I want you to follow:

Learn how to kneel and stand erect; to dance and remain motionless; to shout and be silent—all at the same time.

—RABBI MENDEL OF VORKE

The test of a first-rate intelligence is the ability to hold two opposed ideas in mind at the same time and still retain the ability to function.

—F. SCOTT FITZGERALD

In peak-experiences, the dichotomies, polarities, and conflicts of life tend to be transcended or resolved. That is to say, there tends to be a moving toward the perception of unity and integration in the world. The person himself tends to move toward fusion, integration, and unity and away from splitting, conflicts, and oppositions.

—ABRAHAM MASLOW

To be a hero, he must think of himself as anything but a hero.

—ELIE WIESEL

How significant it is that in the Indo-European languages, as Darmsteter has pointed out, the root meaning 'two' should connote badness. The Greek prefix dys- (as dyspepsia) and the Latin dis- (as in dishonorable) are both derived from 'duo.' The cognate bis- gives a pejorative sense to such modern French words as bevue ('blunder,' literally 'two-sight'). Traces of that "second which leads you astray" can be found in 'dubious,' 'doubt' and Zweifel—for to doubt is to be double-minded. Bunyan has his Mr. Facing-both-ways, and modern American slang its 'two-timers.' Obscurely and unconsciously wise, our language confirms the findings of the mystics and proclaims the essential badness of division—a word, incidentally, in which our old enemy 'two' makes another decisive appearance.

—ALDOUS HUXLEY

The Amish love the sunshine and shadow quilt pattern. It shows two sides-the dark and light, spirit and form-and the challenge of bringing the two into a larger unity. It's not a choice between extremes: conformity or freedom, discipline or imagination, acceptance or doubt, humility or raging ego. It's a balancing act that includes opposites.

—SUE BENDER

Psychic life is governed by a necessary opposition.

—C.G. JUNG

We might find this division into positive and negative poles childishly simple except for one difficulty: which one is positive, weight or lightness?

Parmenides responded: lightness is positive, weight negative.

Was he correct or not? That is the question. The only certainty is: the lightness/weight opposition is the most mysterious, most ambiguous of all.

—MILAN KUNDERA

When you learn to love hell, you will be in heaven.

—THADDEUS GOLAS

The Ancient Greeks believed that the gateway to the Aegean Sea was guarded by a rock and a whirlpool, called respectively, Scylla and Charybdis. If you became obsessed with the danger of the whirlpool you ran smack into the rock and wrecked your ship and your fortunes. If you railed against the rock, vowing to skirt it by the widest margin, the whirlpool would catch you and you'd soon be spiraling giddily and gurgling downwards....

—CHARLES HAMPDEN-TURNER

POPULATION

In 1830 the planet first reached the point of a population of a billion people. In July 1986 we reached the 5 billion point. The latest billion took just 11 years. By 2021 we will have increased our numbers by 3 billion more.

—UN STATISTICS

The recent explosive growth of the world's population could be a greater threat to world peace and prosperity than the atomic bomb.

—KARL SAX

The world population problem forms the first world problem in history ... the implications of which are of direct importance to the welfare of universal humanity.

—GEORGE H.L. ZEEGERS

POTENTIAL

Capacities clamor to be used, and cease their clamor only when they are well used. Not only is it fun to use our capacities, but it is also necessary. The unused capacity or organ can become a disease center or else atrophy, thus diminishing the person.

—ABRAHAM H. MASLOW

For the potential of the oak lies vibrating within the atomic structure of the acorn, as does the flower live within the bud and the Self within a human.

—MASTER SUBRAMUNIYA

To be what we are and to become what we are capable of becoming, is the only end of life.

—ROBERT LOUIS STEVENSON

The ultimate creative capacity of the brain may be, for all practical purposes, infinite.

—DR. W. ROSS ADEY, BRAIN RESEARCH INSTITUTE, UCLA

God created the world "in the beginning"—in the beginning stages. It is the human's task to finish it.

—MIDRASH

I have no doubt whatever, that most people live whether physically, intellectually, or morally, in a very restricted circle of their potential being .... The so-called 'normal man' of commerce, so to speak ... is a mere extract from the potentially realizable individual he represents, and we all have reservoirs of life to draw upon of which we do not dream.

—WILLIAM JAMES

Compared with what we ought to be, we are only half awake. Our fires are damped, our drafts are checked. We are making use of only a small part of our possible mental and physical resources.

—WILLIAM JAMES

POVERTY

Wars of nations are fought to change maps. But wars of poverty are fought to map changes.

—MUHAMMAD ALI

When you're poor, you grow up fast.

—BILLIE HOLIDAY

There is something about poverty that smells like death.

—ZORA NEALE HURSTON

POWER

Remember, strength is not force. It is an attribute of the heart. Its opposite is not weakness and fear, but confusion, lack of clarity, and lack of sound intention. If you are able to discern the path with heart and follow it even when at the moment it seems wrong, then and only then are you strong.

Remember the words of the Tao te Ching:

"The only true strength is that people do not fear."

Strength based in force is a strength people fear.

Strength based in love is a strength people crave.

—KENT NERBURN

Ignorance with weakness does little harm.
Ignorance with power is cause for alarm.
Wisdom with weakness does little good.
Only wisdom and power combine as they should.

—SANDY KERR

Let us have faith that Right makes Right, and in that faith, let us to the end dare to do our duty as we understand it.

—ABRAHAM LINCOLN

When power leads man toward arrogance, poetry reminds him of his limitations. When power narrows the area of man's concern, poetry reminds him of the richness and diversity of existence. When power corrupts, poetry cleanses.... The men who create power make an indispensable contribution to the nation's greatness. But the men who question power make a contribution just as indispensable ... for they determine whether we use power or power uses us.

—JOHN F. KENNEDY

For all power is from the Lord God, and has been with Him always, and is from everlasting. The power which the prince has is therefore from God, for the power of God is never lost, nor severed from Him.

—JOHN OF SALISBURY

Give me somewhere to stand, and I shall move the earth.

—ARCHIMEDES

The highest proof of virtue is to possess boundless power without abusing it.

—T. B. MACAULAY

Power tends to corrupt, and absolute power corrupts absolutely.

—LORD ACTON

PRAYER

Prayer is the means through which we sacrifice our selfishness and greed and get in touch with our powers for truth, mercy, and love.

—RABBI ABRAHAM JOSHUA HESCHEL

In nature, one never really sees a thing for the first time until one has seen it for the fiftieth.

—*JOSEPH WOOD KRUTCH*

Repetition is reality, and it is the seriousness of life ... repetition is the daily bread which satisfies with benediction.

—*SÖREN KIERKEGAARD*

Prayer is like a bed on a cold winter night. One must warm it up before it provides warmth.

—*ANONYMOUS*

When God has put a dream in your heart, He means to help you fulfill it. To gain His help you must ask for it ... and this asking is prayer.

—*WILLIAM TUBMAN*

Prayer cannot mend a broken bridge, rebuild a ruined city, or bring water to parched fields. Prayer can mend a broken heart, lift up a discouraged soul, and strengthen a weakened will. Moreover, prayer can help lighten the burdens we bear in the knowledge that there's a listening ear, and an eternal source of courage, strength and hope to draw upon, when we have used up all of our own.

—*FERDINAND M. ISSERMAN*

Humor is the prelude to faith and laughter is the beginning of prayer.

—*REINHOLD NIEBUHR*

I pray to the birds because I believe they will carry the messages of my heart upward. I pray to them because I believe in their existence, the way their songs begin and end each day-the invocations and benedictions of Earth. I pray to the birds because they remind me of what I love rather than what I fear. And at the end of my prayers, they teach me how to listen.

—*TERRY TEMPEST WILLIAMS*

Most middle-class Americans tend to worship their work, to work at their play, and to play at their worship.

—*GORDON DAHL*

The time of business does not differ with me from the time of prayer; and in the voice and clatter of my kitchen, while several persons are at the same time calling for different things, I possess God in as great tranquility as if were on my knees at the Blessed Sacrament.

—*BROTHER LAWRENCE*

Prayer, in short, though it accomplishes nothing material constitutes something material. In rational prayer the soul may be said to accomplish new things important to its welfare. It withdraws within itself and loses for a moment its self pre-occupations. It accommodates itself to destiny and it grows toward the ideal which it utters.

—GEORGE SANTAYANA

More things are wrought by prayer
Than this world dreams of. Wherefore, let thy
Voice rise like a fountain for me night and day.
For what are men better than sheep or goats
That nourish a blind life within the brain,
If, knowing God, they lift not hands of prayer
Both for themselves and those who call them friend?
For so the whole round earth is every way
Bound by gold chains about the feet of God.

—ALFRED LORD TENNYSON

Prayer is the food of the soul.

—GERALD JAMPOLSKY, M.D.

Prayer may not save the world, but it might make the world worth saving.

—RABBI ABRAHAM JOSHUA HESCHEL

What people usually ask for when they pray is that two and two may not make four.

—RUSSIAN PROVERB

Prayer is not the endeavor to get God to do what we want. Rather, it is the attempt to put ourselves into such a relationship with God that God can do in, for, and through us what God wants. It is not so much begging from God, as cooperation with God. To pray is, therefore, not a way changing God to get what we want, but rather a way of changing ourselves to become what God wants us to be. The experience of prayer has been likened to the long rope which is cast out from a ship as it approaches land. The purpose of the rope is not to draw the land to the ship, but to bring the ship close to the land.

—RABBI SAUL I. TEPLITZ

Do not pray for easy lives. Pray to be stronger men. Do not pray for tasks equal to your powers. Pray for powers equal to your tasks.

—PHILLIPS BROOKS

Some keep the Sabbath going to church;
I keep it staying at home,
With a bobolink for a chorister,
And an orchard for a dome....
God preaches,—a noted clergyman,—
And the sermon is never long;
So instead of getting to heaven at last,
I'm going all along!

—*EMILY DICKINSON*

Man in prayer does not seek to impose his will upon God; he seeks to impose God's will and mercy upon himself.

—*RABBI ABRAHAM JOSHUA HESCHEL*

All is lost, all is lost!
To prayer, to prayer.

—*SHAKESPEARE*

When I recite words I do not believe, it is not out of humility, a sense that perhaps I may be wrong in my rejection of their meaning. It is out of deference. The principle of community means more to me than the principle of consistency.

—*LEONARD FEIN*

If I were to pray today the same way I prayed yesterday, I had better not pray at all.

—*HASIDIC*

Prayer is meaningless unless it is subversive, unless it seeks to overthrow and to ruin the pyramids of callousness, hatred and opportunism and falsehood. The liturgical movement must become a revolutionary movement, seeking to overthrow the forces that continue to destroy the promise, the hope and the vision.

—*RABBI ABRAHAM JOSHUA HESCHEL*

To do righteousness and justice
Is more acceptable to the Lord than sacrifice.

—*BIBLE (PROVERBS 21:3)*

Pray as if everything depended on God,
Act as if everything depended on you.

—*ANONYMOUS*

If you have questions, prayer leads to answers. If you have answers, prayer brings questions.
—ELIE WIESEL

The archimedian point outside the world is the little chamber where the true supplicant prays in all sincerity—where one lifts the world off its hinges.
—SÖREN KIERKEGAARD

Lord, I do not ask for the faith to move mountains.
I pray only for the energy to move me.
—ANONYMOUS

If Psalms could cure, you could buy them in a drug store.
—YIDDISH EXPRESSION

Prayer must come not from the top of the head but from the bottom of the heart.
—ANONYMOUS

The right relationship between prayer and conduct is not that conduct is supremely important and prayer may help it, but that prayer is supremely important and conduct tests it.
—ARCHBISHOP WILLIAM TEMPLE

One's prayer is not heeded unless God is approached with one's heart in one's hands.
—TALMUD

Pray, for all men need the aid of the gods.
—HOMER

Pray not for lighter burdens but for stronger backs.
—THEODORE ROOSEVELT

O God, from whom to be turned is to fall,
To whom to be turned is to rise,
And with whom to stand is to abide forever;
Grant us in all our duties
Your help,
In all our perplexities your guidance
In all our dangers Your protection,
And in all our sorrows Your peace.
—ST. AUGUSTINE

Between the humble and the contrite heart and the majesty of heaven there are no barriers; the only password is prayer.

—*HOSEA BALLOU*

And why pierceth it heaven, this little short prayer of one syllable [God]? For it is prayed with a full spirit, in the height and in the depth, in the length and in the breadth of the spirit that prayed it.

—*THE CLOUD OF UNKNOWING*

A musician must practice by pre-arranged schedule, regardless of his inclination at the moment. So with the devout soul.... It must work. The person who folds his hands, waiting for the spirit to move him to think of God—who postpones worship for the right mood and the perfect setting, a forest or mountain peak—will do little of meditating or praying.

—*RABBI MILTON STEINBERG*

PREJUDICE

Once you label me, you negate me.

—*SÖREN KIERKEGAARD*

Prejudice is a labor saving device. It enables one to form opinions without bothering to dig up the facts.

—*ANONYMOUS*

A woodsman came into a forest and asked the trees to give him a handle for his axe. It seemed so modest a request that the principal trees at once agreed on it. They decided that a plain, homely ash, the least important among them, should be sacrificed. No sooner had the woodsman fitted the staff into his axe than he began chopping down the noblest trees in the woods. The oak, now understanding the whole matter, whispered to the cedar, "The first concession lost everything for us. If we had not sacrificed our humblest neighbor, we might have stood for ages ourselves."

—*AESOP*

A prejudiced person has a mind like concrete-all mixed up and permanently set.

—*ANONYMOUS*

Our method of transferring our own sickness to others. It is our ruse for disliking others rather than ourselves.

—BEN HECHT

Every one is forward to complain of the prejudices that mislead other men and parties, as if he were free, and had none of his own. What now is the cure? No other but this, that every man should let alone others' prejudices and examine his own.

—JOHN LOCKE

Prejudice, put theologically, is one of man's several neurotic and perverted expressions of his will to be God.

—KYLE HASELDEN

The man who never alters his opinion is like standing water, and breeds reptiles of the mind.

—WILLIAM BLAKE

PRIDE

Some have status. Others bring stature.

—ANONYMOUS

Far better a sinner who knows he is a sinner than a saint who knows he is a saint.

—HASIDIC TEACHING

Holding himself good, one loses his goodness.

—SHU CHING

I have been more and more convinced, the more I think of it, that, in general, pride is at the bottom of all great mistakes. All the other passions do occasional good; but whenever pride puts in a word, everything goes wrong; and what might really be desirable to do, quietly and innocently, it is mortally dangerous to do proudly.

—JOHN RUSKIN

Some glory in their birth, some in their skill,
Some in their wealth, some in their bodies' force,
Some in their garments, though new-fangled ill;
Some in their hawks and hounds, some in their horse;
And every humour hath his adjunct pleasure,
Wherein it finds a joy above the rest.

—SHAKESPEARE

If ever humans become proud, let them remember that a mosquito preceded them in the divine order of creation!

—SANHEDRIN

Haughtiness toward others is rebellion to God.

—MOSES NAHMANIDES

Pride may be allowed to this or that degree, else a man cannot keep up his dignity.

—JOHN SELDEN

PRIVACY

The right to be let alone is the most comprehensive of rights and the right most valued by civilized man.

—JUSTICE LOUIS D. BRANDEIS

There are societies that have no word for privacy, and when the idea is explained to them they think it is horrible. In one society in which I worked—Samoa—a curtain hung between me and the other members of the household gave me a certain privacy; but in a house without walls nothing separated me from the rest of the village, from whose eyes, obviously, I did not need the protection of privacy. Nevertheless, some sort of privacy, some small, identifiable spatial territory of one's own—even if it is only a hook on which to hang one's own hat—seems to be a basic need.

—MARGARET MEAD

PROCESS

Flowing water does not decay.

—CHINESE ADAGE

Life, at its best, is a flowing, changing process in which nothing is fixed.... It is always in process of becoming.

—CARL ROGERS

PROGRESS

What can you learn from parking meters? That we lose money standing still.

—ANONYMOUS

Progress requires that the subject be enlarged in itself, alteration, that it be transformed into something else.

—ST. VINCENT OF LÉRINS

To wish to progress is the larger part of progress.

—SENECA

The vice of the modern notion of mental progress is that it is always something concerned with the breaking of bonds, the effacing of boundaries, the casting away of dogmas.

—G. K. CHESTERTON

Real human progress depends upon a good conscience.

—ALBERT EINSTEIN

Life must progress in part by the imprudence of those who undertake the impossible, not knowing what they do.

—WILLIAM E. HOCKING

PROJECTION

Everything that irritates us about others can lead us to an understanding of ourselves.

—CARL JUNG

People seem not to see that their opinion of the world is also a confession of character. We can only see what we are, and, if we misbehave, we suspect others.

—RALPH WALDO EMERSON

My wife was very immature. Whenever I was in the bathtub she came and sank my little ships.

—WOODY ALLEN

Sinners are mirrors. When we see faults in them we should realize that they only reflect the evil in ourselves.

—RABBI ISRAEL, BAAL SHEM TOV

We hate the criminal and deal severely with him because we view, in his deed, as in a distorting mirror, our own instincts.

—SIGMUND FREUD

What we see depends mainly on what we look for.

—ANONYMOUS

Human nature is something that makes you swear at a pedestrian when you are driving and at the driver when you are a pedestrian.

—OREN ARNOLD

We do not see things as they are but as we are.

—ANONYMOUS

PSYCHIATRY

The heart is deceitful above all, and desperately sick, who can know it?

—BIBLE (JEREMIAH 17:9)

Psychiatry is the only business in which the customer is always wrong.

—ANONYMOUS

Don't pull yourself up by the roots to see how you are growing.

—ANONYMOUS

Only a priestly man can be a complete psychiatrist. For with him the relation to the patient and the inner activities of the patient have been lifted out of the realm of the subjectivity of the finite into the inclusive life of the eternal.

—PAUL TILLICH

It is doubtless true that religion has been the world's psychiatrist throughout the centuries.

—KARL M. MENNINGER

Love—incomparably the greatest psychotherapeutic agent—is something that professional psychiatry cannot of itself create, focus, nor release.

—GORDON W. ALLPORT

It always fascinates me to realize—despite the jargon of even pagan psychiatrists-that the terminology of psychiatry is simply a roundabout and veiled corroboration of Christian doctrine.

—JOHN E. LARGE

Any system of psychiatry which totally ignores man's obligations and aspirations in the spiritual order cannot but diminish his stature and be incomplete.

—J. DOMINIAN

PURITY

Heedfulness leads to cleanness; cleanness to purity; purity to holiness; holiness to humility; humility to dread of sin; dread of sin to saintliness; saintliness to the awareness of the Spirit of the Divine.

—RABBI PINHAS BEN YAIR

Purity and stillness are the correct principles for humankind.

—LAO-TZU

All created things perish, he who knows and sees this becomes passive in pain; this is the way to purity.

—*DHAMMAPADA*

To the virtuous all is pure.

—*TRIPITAKA*

Purity of soul cannot be lost without consent.

—*ST. AUGUSTINE*

By purity God is made captive in me, purity makes me God-conscious and conscious of naught beside God, purity begets detachment. The pure soul has a light—birth as it were, purity is satisfied with God alone.

—*MEISTER ECKHART*

The Sun is never worse for shining on a Dunghill.

—*THOMAS FULLER*

Man flows at once to God when the channel of purity is opened.

—*HENRY DAVID THOREAU*

[Purity] is not an inactive virtue; it does not merely consist in not committing certain sins. It means using your life in the way God wants, exercising constant restraint.

—*FRANCIS DEVAS*

QUESTIONS

Computers are useless. They only give you answers.

—*PABLO PICASSO*

There is always an easy solution to every problem—neat, plausible and wrong.

—*H. L. MENCKEN*

Children enter school as question marks and leave as periods.

—*NEIL PORTMAN*

An algorithm for solving problems:

    1. Write down the problem

    2. Think real hard

    3. Write down the answer

—RICHARD FEYNMAN

The only stupid question is the one that is not asked.

—ANONYMOUS

You are so young, so before all beginning, and I want to beg you, as much as I can, dear sir, to be patient toward all that is unsolved in your heart and to try to love the questions themselves like locked rooms and like books that are written in a very foreign tongue. Do not now seek the answers, which cannot be given to you because you would not be able to live them. And the point is, to live everything. Live the questions now. Perhaps you will then gradually, without noticing it, live along some distant day into the answer.

—RAINER MARIA RILKE

Without God, life would be without problems, without anguish, without hope. For God is not only the answer the to those who suffer as a result of questions; God is also the question to those who think they have found the answer.

—ELIE WIESEL

An intelligent person's question is half the answer.

—SOLOMON IBN GABIROL

REASON

If a person spurns reason, his faith will be full of distortion and falsehood.

—RABBI AVRAHAM YITZHAK KOOK

What the good person ought to do he does; for reason in each of its possessors chooses what is best for itself, and the good person obeys his reason.

—ARISTOTLE

My reason is not framed to bend or stoop; my knees are.

—*MICHEL DE MONTAIGNE*

Passion and prejudice govern the world; only under the name of reason.

—*JOHN WESLEY*

I am immortal, imperishable, eternal, as soon as I form the resolution to obey the laws of reason.

—*J. G. FICHTE*

Reason is Thought conditioning itself with perfect freedom.

—*G. W. F. HEGEL*

If there is no higher reason—and there is not—then my own reason must be the supreme judge of my life.

—*LEO TOLSTOY*

Reason inspired by love of truth is the only eye with which man can see the spiritual heavens above us.

—*CHARLES E. GARMAN*

Reason is man's imitation of divinity.

—*GEORGE SANTAYANA*

Reason in my philosophy is only a harmony among irrational impulses.

—*GEORGE SANTAYANA*

It is doubtful if a truly good world, a better and fuller life for man, can ever be established through reason alone.

—*EDMUND W. SINNOT*

I do not believe man possesses an avenue to truth which is superior to his reason.

—*RABBI ROLAND B. GITTELSOHN*

Those whom God wishes to destroy, God first deprives of their senses.

—*EURIPIDES*

The Almighty does nothing without reason, though the frail mind of humans cannot explain the reason.

—*ST. AUGUSTINE*

I do not feel obliged to believe that the same God who has endowed us with sense, reason, and intellect has intended us to forgo their use.

—GALILEO

No man serves God with a good conscience, who serves him against his reason.

—SAMUEL TAYLOR COLERIDGE

Reason will find God, but reason will find, too, the need to transcend reason, the promise of more than reason can offer.

—GEORGE BRANTLE

If we submit everything to reason, our religion will have nothing in it mysterious or supernatural. If we violate the principles of reason, our religion will be absurd and ridiculous.

—BLAISE PASCAL

Is it really too much to ask and hope for a religion whose content is perennial but not archaic, which provides ethical guidance, teaches the lost art of contemplation, and restores contact with the supernatural without requiring reason to abdicate?

—ARTHUR KOESTLER

For till it be resolved how far we are to be guided by reason, and how far by faith, we shall in vain dispute, and endeavor to convince one another in matters of religion.

—JOHN LOCKE

Faith ... can be nothing but the annihilation of reason, a silence of adoration at the contemplation of things absolutely incomprehensible.... Faith, therefore, is nothing but submissive or deferential incredulity.

—VOLTAIRE

Faith ... is not a lord that tyrannizes over reason, nor does it contradict it: the seal of truth is impressed by God no differently upon faith than upon reason.

—POPE PIUS XII

If faith cannot be reconciled with rational thinking, it has to be eliminated as an anachronistic remnant of earlier stages of culture and replaced by science dealing with facts and theories which are intelligible and can be validated.

—ERICH FROMM

RELIGION

It is about time that we stopped talking of the failure of religion, education and civilization to improve man, and began to talk of the failure of man to improve religion, education and civilization.

—RABBI MORDECAI M. KAPLAN

A soap-maker approached a rabbi and asked, "What good is religion?" He continued, "Religion teaches honesty. Look at all the dishonest people in the world. Religion teaches peace. Look how many wars there are. What good is religion?"

The rabbi shook his head, "My dear soap-maker, there are so many wonderful soaps in the world, but look how many dirty people there are. Religion is like soap—it works when you use it."

—ANONYMOUS

And let us with caution indulge the supposition that morality can be maintained without religion. Whatever may be conceded to the influence of refined education on minds of peculiar structure, reason and experience both forbid us to expect that national morality can prevail in exclusion of religious principle.

—GEORGE WASHINGTON

Religion must be some intuition of the infinite in the finite.

—FRIEDRICH SCHLEIERMACHER

Religion is not primarily a set of beliefs, a collection of prayers, or a series of rituals. Religion is first and foremost a way of seeing. It can't change the facts about the world we live in, but it can change the way we see those facts, and that in itself can often make a real difference.

—HAROLD KUSHNER

If Jesus were here today the last thing he'd be is a Christian.

—MARK TWAIN

Puritanism is the terrible fear that someone might be happy.

—G. K. CHESTERTON

Religion is least compelling when it offers us answers about the past; it is most compelling when it offers us questions about the future.

—LEONARD FEIN

The code of conduct is like the score to a musician. Rules, principles, forms may be taught; insight, feeling, the sense of rhythm must come from within. Ultimately, then, the goal of religious life is quality rather than quantity, not only what is done, but how it is done.

—RABBI ABRAHAM JOSHUA HESCHEL

The men in the Bible are sinners like ourselves, but there is one sin they do not commit, our arch-sin: they do not dare confine God to a circumscribed space or division of life, to "religion,"... they do not presume to draw boundaries around God's commandments and say to Him: "Up to this point, You are sovereign, but beyond these bounds begins the sovereignty of science or society or the state."

—MARTIN BUBER

We have enough religion to make us hate, but not enough to make us love one another.

—JONATHAN SWIFT

Theology is talking about God.
Religion is experiencing God.

—MARTIN BUBER

The Church is like Noah's Ark; it would be impossible to stand the stench from within, were it not for the flood-waters from without.

—REINHOLD NIEBUHR

The error of the psychoanalytic theory of religion—to state the error in its own terminology—lies in locating religious beliefs exclusively in the defensive functions of the ego rather than in the core and center and substance of the developing ego itself. While religion certainly fortifies the individual against the inroads of anxiety, doubt, and despair, it also provides the forward intention that enables him at each stage of his becoming to relate himself meaningfully to the totality of Being.

—GORDON W. ALLPORT

The test of one's religion is in the quality of existence that it evokes, in the meaning it gives to life, and in the life-enhancing effect it has in the midst of life itself. Religion, in its truest sense, is a relentless search for life. Organized religion—the churches—frequently provide answers, and interfere with, even prevent, the search.

—SIDNEY M. JOURARD

Religion is the way we share our predicament.

—*RICHARD RUBENSTEIN*

I say the whole earth and all the stars in the sky are for
    religion's sake.
I say no man has ever yet been half devout enough,
None has ever yet adored or worshipped half enough,
None has begun to think how divine he himself is, and how
    certain the future is.
I say that the real and permanent grandeur of these States
    must be their religion,
Otherwise there is no real and permanent grandeur;
Nor character nor life worthy the name without religion,
Nor land nor man or woman without religion.

—*WALT WHITMAN*

Among my patients in the second half of life, that is to say, over thirty-
five, there has not been one whose problem in the last resort was not that
of finding a religious outlook on life.

—*C.G. JUNG*

Religion should be the rule of life, not a casual incident in it.

—*BENJAMIN DISRAELI*

Religion is not beliefs. Beliefs are intellectual constructs; they are the
subject matter of theology. They are important, but they are not the substance of religion itself. Religion has to do primarily with values.

—*REV. RICHARD GILBERT*

Anything that makes religion a second object makes religion no object.
God will put up with many things in the heart, but this is one thing he will
not put up with—second place. He who offers God second place offers no
place.

—*JOHN RUSKIN*

Religion errs when it becomes primarily a source of controls, rules, and
duties, and loses its ability to lift, inspire, and energize the totality of one's
life.... There is more than enough drabness in life without making religion
into a force that further squeezes the enjoyment out of living!

—*HOWARD J. CLINEBELL*

The fairest thing we can experience is the mysterious. It is the fundamental emotion which stands at the cradle of true art and true science. He who knows it not, and can no longer wonder, no longer feel amazement, is as good as dead, a snuffed-out candle. It was the experience of mystery ... that engendered religion. A knowledge of the existence of something we cannot penetrate, our perceptions of the profoundest reason and the most radiant beauty, which our minds seem to reach only in their most elementary forms; it is this knowledge and this emotion that constitute the truly religious attitude.

—ALBERT EINSTEIN

Religion is not what man does with his solitariness, but rather what man does with God's concern for all men.

—RABBI ABRAHAM JOSHUA HESCHEL

The foundation of all religion is one, and God's is the East and the West; and wherever ye turn, there is God's face.

—KORAN

In the long run, morals without religion will wither and die like seed sown upon stony ground, or among thorns.

—SAMUEL I. PRIME

Every religion is four elements fused into an organic unity: It is an interpretation of reality as a whole, the ethical implications which flow from it, a system of ritual acts, and a complex of emotional drives and associations.

—RABBI MILTON STEINBERG

If man is wicked with religion, what would he be without it?

—BENJAMIN FRANKLIN

The dogmas of the quiet past are inadequate to the stormy present.... We must think anew and act anew. Let us disenthrall ourselves.

—ABRAHAM LINCOLN

Religion is a disease, but it is a noble disease.

—HERACLITUS

Man is by his constitution a religious animal.

—EDMUND BURKE

There is only one religion, though there are a hundred versions of it.

—GEORGE BERNARD SHAW

Every religion is good that teaches man to be good.

— *THOMAS PAINE*

Men hate and despise religion, and fear it may be true.

— *BLAISE PASCAL*

Be still, and know that I am God.

— *BIBLE (PSALMS 46:11)*

A good life is the only religion.

— *THOMAS FULLER*

Compulsion in religion is distinguished peculiarly from compulsion in every other thing. I may grow rich by an art I am compelled to follow; I may recover health from medicines I am compelled to take against my own judgment; but I cannot be saved by a worship I disbelieve and abhor.

— *THOMAS JEFFERSON*

RELIGIOUS LEADERSHIP

I probably would have entered the ministry except so many clergymen look like undertakers.

— *OLIVER WENDELL HOLMES*

And I will raise up a faithful priest, that shall do according to that which is in My heart and in My mind; and I will build him a sure house; and he shall walk before Mine anointed forever.

— *BIBLE (I SAMUEL 2:35)*

Probably the most effective minister is one who knows sin, who knows the short-run pleasures and longer-run hell of sneaking and who has learned how to find satisfaction and meaning in a more righteous life. Because he knows sin, he can address the sinner with empathy. But he won't get many to accept his invitation unless his very being as a man is living proof that one can be righteous without being joyless, priggish, or bored.

— *SIDNEY M. JOURARD*

The three qualifications for the Ministry are the grace of God, knowledge of the sacred Scriptures, and gumption.

—SAMUEL JOHNSON

God said to Moses:

"You doubted me, but I forgive you that doubt. You doubted your own self, and failed to believe in your own powers as a leader; and I forgave that also. But you lost faith in this people and doubted the divine possibilities of human nature. That I cannot forgive. The loss of faith makes it impossible for you to enter the Promised Land."

—MIDRASII

The whole of the relation, then, between the (religious leader) and the congregation is plain. They belong together. But neither can absorb or override the other. They must be filled with mutual respect. He is their leader, but his leadership is not one constant strain and never is forgetful of the higher guidance upon which they both rely. It is like the rope by which one ship draws another out into the sea. The rope is not always tight between them, and all the while the tide on which they float is carrying them both. So it is not mere leading and following. It is one of the very highest pictures of human companionship that be seen on earth.... It has much of the intimacy of the family with something of the breadth and dignity that belongs to the state. It is too sacred to be thought of as a contract. It is a union which God joins together for purposes worthy of His care.

—PHILLIPS BROOKS

The message of a rabbi is not the preaching, but the man himself.

—RABBI LEO BAECK

I don't know the key to success, but the key to failure is trying to please everybody.

—BILL COSBY

You should know, my child, that peace in a community is a sign that the community is without a man of great intellect, for if there were such a man then some would agree with him and some would fight against him. But when the man of great intellect is missing, there is peace but no intellect.

—RABBI NAHMAN OF BRATZLAV

The true art of pleasing lies not in giving people what they want (for they quickly tire of that), but in making them learn to want what you are giving them.

—SYDNEY J. HARRIS

You drop a stone in a pool, and the circles spread. Who knows on what far shore of the pool the last circle breaks?

—*ANDRÉ MALRAUX*

A minister ought to be dominant, but not domineering; he ought to exercise leadership, but not lordship.

—*REV. MILTON R. SCHEMM*

I'm the spirit's janitor. All I do is wipe the windows a little bit so you can see out for yourself.

—*GODFREY CHIPS, LAKOTA MEDICINE MAN*

The purpose of a rabbi is to establish trust.

—*MARTIN BUBER*

I live in fear of not being misunderstood.

—*OSCAR WILDE*

> The Lord God hath given me
> The tongue of them that taught,
> That I should know how to sustain with words him that is
>   weary;
> He wakeneth morning by morning,
> He wakeneth mine ear
> To hear as they that are taught.
> The Lord God hath opened mine ear,
> And I was not rebellious,
> Neither turned away backward.

—*BIBLE (ISAIAH 50:4-5)*

I have always considered a clergyman as a father of a larger family than he is able to maintain.

—*SAMUEL JOHNSON*

The pastors are to be fervidly zealous about the inner wants of their subjects, without neglecting the care of their outer wants.

—*POPE ST. GREGORY THE GREAT*

Pastor: One employed by the wicked to prove to them by his example that virtue doesn't pay.

—*H. L. MENCKEN*

The clergy are in a special way tempted to take to themselves the sacredness that belongs to the things that they represent.

—*JOHN C. BENNETT*

The minister's task is to lead men from what they want to what they need.

—*RALPH W. SOCKMAN*

Vainly does the preacher utter the Word of God exteriorly unless he listens to in interiorly.

—*ST. AUGUSTINE*

The test of a preacher is that his congregation goes away saying, not "What a lovely sermon," but "I will do something!"

—*ST. FRANCIS OF SALES*

The preacher of the Gospel must be ready to afflict the comfortable as well as comfort the afflicted.

—*AELRED GRAHAM*

The paradox of the pulpit is that its occupant is a sinner whose chief right to be there is his perpetual sense that he has no right to be there, and is there only by grace and always under a spotlight of divine judgment.

—*A.C. CRAIG*

Preacher's silent prayer:
Lord, fill my mouth with worthwhile stuff,
And nudge me when I've said enough.

—*ANONYMOUS*

The preaching of divines helps to preserve well-inclined men in the course of virtue, but seldom or never reclaims the vicious.

—*JONATHAN SWIFT*

Preach faith till you have it; and then, because you have it, you will preach faith.

—*JOHN WESLEY*

A congregation except in the rarest instances, does not dismiss its minister because of what he preaches, but because of what he does not preach.

—*RAYMOND CALKINS*

Preaching is an art, and in this, as in all other arts, the bad performers far outnumber the good.

—*ALDOUS HUXLEY*

Priests are no more necessary to religion that politicians to patriotism.

—*JOHN HAYNES HOLMES*

RENEWAL

The myth of perfection is one in which we constantly are dissatisfied with what is currently happening. We are never "here" because we are always trying to be "there," wherever that is. But understand this important teaching: When we accept each moment as a new opportunity for fulfilling our purpose, we are always present, always succeeding, always changing the world for the better. And we are always "here."

—*DAVID A. COOPER*

Man's mind stretched to a new idea never goes back to its original dimension.

—*OLIVER WENDELL HOLMES*

When you feel that you have reached the end
And that you cannot go one step further,
When life seems drained of all purpose,
What a wonderful opportunity to start all over again.

—*EILEEN CADDY*

We must be willing to get rid of the life we've planned, so as to have the life that is waiting for us. The old skin has to be shed before the new one can come.

—*JOSEPH CAMPBELL*

Most of us grow stale while we are still young. We look upon the days to come as repetitive of days gone by. We are afraid of the unprecedented. We see what we know; we do not know what we see.

—*RABBI ABRAHAM JOSHUA HESCHEL*

We shall not cease from exploration
And the end of all our exploring
Will be to arrive where we started
And know the place for the first time.

—T.S. ELIOT

He alone is worthy of life and freedom
Who each day does battle for them anew.

—GOETHE

Age cannot wither her,
Nor custom stale her infinite variety.

—SHAKESPEARE

The Life span of man running toward death would inevitably carry every-thing human to ruin and destruction if it were not for the faculty of inter-rupting and beginning something new, a faculty which is inherent in action like an ever-present reminder that men, though they must die, are not born in order to die, but in order to begin again.

—HANNAH ARENDT

Here is Eternal Spring; for You
The very Stars of Heaven are New.

—ROBERT BRIDGES

The light did not come to me just by chance,
And from my father I did not inherit it:
I scratched it out of my rock and my stone,
And hewed it out of my heart.

—CHAIM NACHMAN BIALIK

If your everyday life seems poor to you, do not accuse it; accuse your-self, tell yourself you are not poet enough to summon up its riches, since for the creator there is no poverty and no poor or unimportant place.

—RAINER MARIA RILKE

A new heart also will I give you, and a new spirit will I put within you; and I will take away the stony heart out of your flesh, and I will give you a heart of flesh.

—BIBLE (EZEKIEL 36:26)

God says to Moses: "Put off thy shoes from thy feet."

Put off the habitual which encloses your foot, and you will know that the place on which you are now standing is holy ground. For there is no rung of human life on which we cannot find the holiness of God everywhere and at all times.

—THE RABBI OF KOBRYN

Surely the Lord's mercies are not consumed,
Surely His compassions fail not.
They are new every morning;
Ample is Thy grace!

—BIBLE (LAMENTATIONS 3:23)

REPENTANCE

No man is rich enough to buy back his past.

—OSCAR WILDE

The sins we commit, these are not the worst thing. After all, temptation is powerful and man is weak. The great human crime is that we could turn at any time and we don't.

—RABBI SIMCHA BUNAM OF PSHIS'CHA

One who covers up faults will not succeed;
One who confesses and gives them up will find mercy.
Happy is the one who is anxious always,
But one who hardens the heart falls into misfortune.

—BIBLE (PROVERBS 28:13-14)

If you're heading in the wrong direction, God allows U-turns.

—BUMPER STICKER

The Rebbe asks:
How far do you have to travel to be on the other side of the world?
Answer: Just one step.
Turn around—and you'll face the opposite direction.

—HASIDIC

And like bright metal on a sullen ground,
My reformation, glittering o'er my fault,
Shall show more goodly and attract more eyes
Than that which hath no foil to set it off.

—SHAKESPEARE

Repent means now, this minute and forever.... I'm not religious or anything like that, but I know I don't have to be next year what I was last year.
I've been at one end and I can get to the other.

—SAUL BELLOW

He who approaches near to Me one span, I will approach to him one
cubit; and he who approaches near to Me one cubit, I will approach to him
one fathom, and whoever approaches Me walking, I will come to him running, and he who meets Me with sins equivalent to the whole world, I will
greet him with forgiveness equal to it.

—MISHKAT AL-MASABIH

Every weed is a potential flower.

—LUTHER BURBANK

Caterpillar: "... and who are you?"
Alice: "I hardly know Sir, just at present—at least I know who I was when
I got up this morning, but I think I must have changed several times since
then."

—LEWIS CARROLL

Experience is the name we give to our mistakes.

—MARK TWAIN

Going on means going far;
Going far means return.

—TAO TE CHING

The mark of a civilized man is his willingness to re-examine his most
cherished beliefs.

—OLIVER WENDELL HOLMES

Every human being is endowed by the Maker with two eyes. With one he
is expected to look at his neighbor, fastening his gaze on his virtues, his
excellences, his desirable qualities. With the other eye, he is to turn inward
to see his own weaknesses, his imperfections, and his shortcomings, in
order to correct them.

—RABBI ISRAEL SALANTER

Finish every day and be done with it. You have done what you could. Some blunders and absurdities no doubt crept in; forget them as soon as you can. Tomorrow is a new day; begin it well and serenely and with too high a spirit to be cumbered with your old nonsense. This day is all that is good and fair. It is too dear, with its hopes and invitations, to waste a moment on the yesterdays.

—*RALPH WALDO EMERSON*

As long as you live, keep learning how to live.

—*SENECA*

Don't ever be afraid to admit you were wrong. It's like saying you're wiser today than you were yesterday.

—*ANONYMOUS*

A stone is characterized by its finality, whereas man's outstanding quality is in its being a surprise. To claim to be what I am not is a pretension. To insist that I must be only what I am now is a restriction which human nature must abhor. The being of a person is never completed, final.

—*RABBI ABRAHAM JOSHUA HESCHEL*

The conscience is a little three-cornered thing in the heart that stands still when we're good, but when we're bad, it turns around a lot. If we keep on going wrong, soon the corners wear off and it does not hurt any more.

—*NATIVE AMERICAN TEACHING*

It has been said that blaming your faults on your nature does not change the nature of your faults. Thus, "I am like that" does not help anything. "I can be different" does.

—*THOMAS A. HARRIS*

The highest moment in a man's career is the hour when he beats upon his breast and tells all the sins of his life.

—*OSCAR WILDE*

Let every dawn of morning be to you as the beginning of life, and every setting sun be to you as its close. Then let every one of these short lives leave its sure record of some kindly thing done for others, some goodly strength or knowledge gained for yourself.

—*JOHN RUSKIN*

The unexamined life is not worth living.

—*SOCRATES*

Write injuries in dust, kindness in marble.

—*ANONYMOUS*

Lord, make all our words gracious and tender today for tomorrow we may have to eat them.
— *DIANA McCARTHY*

One person finds pleasure in improving land, another horses. My pleasure is seeing that I myself grow better day by day.
— *EPICTETUS*

And as for the wickedness of the wicked, it shall not be a source of stumbling to one on the day of turning from wickedness.
— *BIBLE (EZEKIEL 33:12)*

If you feel far from God, who moved?
— *BUMPER STICKER*

Every human being has the freedom to change at any instant... A human being is a self-transcending being.
— *VIKTOR E. FRANKL*

A disciple once said to his Hasidic master, "You continually reiterate the need for forgiveness. Teach me the true meaning of repentance, as you understand it to apply to me." The Rebbe said, "Go my son, to the creek at the outskirts of the town. Watch what transpires, and then report to me." After he carried out the instructions, he returned even more baffled than before. "All I saw was women doing their laundry by the creek. They come with dirty garments, scrub them clean, and at the end of the week return with more dirty garments to scrub them all over again." "This is the wisdom you need to learn," said the Rebbe. "Our souls are like those garments. Repentance is a kind scrubbing, to remove the soil and filth which accumulates in our souls as we live in the world. No one can live in the world without being stained by it. The person who seeks spiritual cleanliness is the person who practices the art of forgiveness."

Let us forgive each other, before we ask the Almighty to be forgiving of us.
— *RABBI SAUL I. TEPLITZ*

RESENTMENT

Resentment is like taking poison and waiting for the other person to die.
— *ANONYMOUS*

RESPONSIBILITY

No snowflake will take the blame for an avalanche.

—ANONYMOUS

The ten most powerful two-letter words:
If it is to be, it is up to me.

—ANONYMOUS

I am only one, but I am one.
I cannot do everything, but I can do something.
What I can do, I ought to do.
By the grace of God, I will do.

—FREDERICK FARRAR

We are all manufacturers—some make good, others make trouble, and still others make excuses.

—ANONYMOUS

Each player must accept the cards life deals him/her.
But once they are in hand, s/he alone must decide how to play the cards in order to win the game.

—VOLTAIRE

People are always blaming their circumstances for what they are. I don't believe in circumstances. The people who get on in this world are the people who get up and look for the circumstances they want, and, if they can't find them, make them.

—GEORGE BERNARD SHAW

When we are sick in fortune, often the surfeit of our own behavior, we make guilty of our disasters the sun, the moon and the stars; as if we were villains on necessity; fools by heavenly compulsion; knaves, thieves and teachers by spherical predomination; drunkards, liars and adulterers by an enforced obedience of planetary influence.

—SHAKESPEARE

Most of the evil that befalls individuals comes from the imperfections within themselves. Out of these imperfections of ours we cry out demands. The evil we inflict upon ourselves, of our own volition, and which pains us— this evil we ascribe to God.

—MAIMONIDES

If people see that sufferings come upon them, let them scrutinize their own deeds.

—TALMUD

If you want to praise, praise God. If you want to blame, blame yourself.

—RABBI ISRAEL, BAAL SHEM TOV

The fault, dear Brutus, lies not in our stars but in ourselves.

—SHAKESPEARE

I am the master of my fate:
I am the captain of my soul.

—WILLIAM HENLEY

We will live together as brothers or die together as fools.

—MARTIN LUTHER KING, JR.

Life will either grind you down or polish you up, and which it does is our choice.

—ROGER WALSH

You have to take life as it happens, but you should try to make it happen the way you want to take it.

—GERMAN SAYING

I have put before you life and death, blessing and curse. Choose Life!

—BIBLE (DEUTERONOMY 30:19)

A youth once inquired of an older person:
What is life's heaviest burden?
The older person answered:
To have nothing to carry.

—ANONYMOUS

One is always responsible, whether the act is intentional or inadvertent, whether one is awake or asleep.

—TALMUD

A hundred times every day I remind myself that my inner and outer life depend on the labors of other men, living and dead, and that I must exert myself in order to give in the measure as I have received and am still receiving.

—ALBERT EINSTEIN

A scientist once proudly proclaimed, "I invented a computer that's almost human."

When a friend asked, "Does it think?" the scientist replied, "No, but when it makes a mistake it blames another computer."

—ANONYMOUS

When I was a child I read an old legend which at the time I did not understand. The legend said, before the gates of Rome there sits a leprous beggar and he waits. This is the Messiah, the redeemer of the world. At that time I came to an old man and I asked him, "For whom does he wait?" And the old man answered me then and it was only much much later that I really understood his reply. He said, "He waits for you."

—MARTIN BUBER

Our grand business in life is not to see what lies dimly at a distance, but to do what clearly lies at hand.

—THOMAS CARLYLE

Let everyone sweep in front of his or her own door, and the whole world will be clean.

—GOETHE

You have brains in your head.
You have feet in your shoes.
You can steer yourself
any direction you choose.

—DR. SEUSS

REVELATION

The surest way of misunderstanding revelation is to take it literally, to imagine that God spoke to the prophet on a long-distance telephone. Yet most of us succumb to such a fancy, forgetting that the cardinal sin in thinking about ultimate issues is literal mindedness. The error of literal mindedness is in assuming that things and words have only one meaning.

—RABBI ABRAHAM JOSHUA HESCHEL

Those who deny Revelation shall not enter Paradise until the camel goes through the eye of needle.

—KORAN

Moses may have gotten his ideas about morality from the same place that Shakespeare got his poetry and Mozart his music, but the process surpasses my understanding. I describe them as "God-given" to convey the idea that they are a permanent part of life, not subject to human approval or disapproval.

—RABBI HAROLD KUSHNER

If you say you have a revelation from God, I must have a revelation from God too before I can believe you.

—BENJAMIN WHICHCOTE

What education is to the individual, revelation is to the whole human race.

—G. E. LESSING

I gradually came to disbelieve in Christianity as a divine revelation ... and have never since doubted even for a single second that my conclusion was correct.

—CHARLES DARWIN

He who does not believe that revelation is continuous does not believe in revelation at all.

—GEORGE BERNARD SHAW

We Jews do not believe in such a thing as continual revelation. God spoke once, at Sinai, and never before or since has there been a moment like that one. But we do believe in continual interpretation! We do believe that the gates of interpretation are never locked and that each generation has the right and the duty to read the Torah afresh, from where it is, and to see what it says to them at this moment, in this place.

—RABBI ABRAHAM JOSHUA HESCHEL

Revelation when genuine is simply the record of the immediate experience of those who are pure enough in heart and poor enough in spirit to be able to see God.

—ALDOUS HUXLEY

When one has sought long for the clue to a secret of nature, and is rewarded by grasping some part of the answer, it comes as a blinding flash or revelation.... This conviction is of something revealed, and not something imagined.

—LAWRENCE BRAGG

Revealed truths are above our intelligence, and I would not dare submit them to the feebleness of my reason.

—RENÉ DESCARTES

252 MOMENTS OF THE SPIRIT

It is universally acknowledged that revelation itself is to stand or fall by the test of reason.

—EDMUND GIBSON

The transition to a new order of things ought rather to be effected by the principle of a pure religion according to reason, considered as a Divine revelation constantly being made to all people through their reason only.

—IMMANUEL KANT

RISK

Avoidance of risk creates risk.

—ANONYMOUS

If you have tried to do something and failed, you are vastly better off than if you had tried to do nothing and succeeded.

—ANONYMOUS

Most people prefer the certainty of misery to the misery of uncertainty.

—VIRGINIA SATIR

It is common sense to take a method and try it: If it fails, admit it frankly and try another. But above all, try something.

—FRANKLIN DELANO ROOSEVELT

Take a chance! All life is a chance. The man who goes farthest is generally the one who is willing to do and dare. The sure-thing boat never gets far from shore.

—DALE CARNEGIE

Don't be afraid to go out on a limb.
That's where the fruit is.

—ANONYMOUS

Do not be too timid and squeamish about actions. All life is an experiment. The more experiments you make the better. What if they are a little coarse, and you get your coat soiled or torn? What if you do fail, and get fairly rolled in the dirt once or twice? Up again, you shall never be so afraid of a tumble.

—RALPH WALDO EMERSON

A ship in port is safe, but that is not what ships are for.

—ANONYMOUS

It is the business of the future to be dangerous.

—ALFRED NORTH WHITEHEAD

One cannot discover new oceans unless one has the courage to lose sight of the shore.

—ANDRE GIDE

The important thing is this: to be able at any moment to sacrifice what we are for what we could become.

—CHARLES DeBOIS

Trust is the result of a risk successfully survived.

—JACK R. GIBB

So far as man stands for anything and is productive or originative at all, his entire vital function may be said to deal with maybes. Not a victory is gained, not a deed of faithfulness or courage is done, except upon a maybe; not a service, not a sally of generosity, not a scientific exploration or experiment or textbook, that may not be a mistake. It is only by risking our persons from one hour to another that we live at all.

—WILLIAM JAMES

For without risk there is no faith, and the greater the risk, the greater the faith.

—SÖREN KIERKEGAARD

RITUAL

A religion without ritual is like a suit of clothes without buttons.

—RABBI MORDECAI M. KAPLAN

Anything that can be done at any time and any place will likely be done at no time and no place.

—RABBI SOLOMON GOLDMAN

Rituals never change—they are independent of life's circumstances and can be repeated in times of war or in times of peace, in poverty or in wealth, in youth or in old age, in happiness or in despair. They represent a timeless dimension, untouched by chance, doubt, or decay—a true stronghold. Furthermore, the deliberate attention with which they are carried out, their solemnity, the concentrated attention of the participants, and the movements of the body suggest a suprasensible reality. All these factors generate a situation in which consciousness is naturally led to transpersonal levels.

—PIERO FERRUCI

Rituals are forms in which people can experience and express deep feelings. A ritual is a focusing lens for emotions. Weddings and funerals allow strong feelings, arising from marriage or death, to be shared and channeled. The ritual intensifies the feelings and gives them a beginning, a middle and an end.

—HOWARD R. LEWIS & HAROLD S. STREIFELD

A ritual is a socially programmed use of time where everybody agrees to do the same thing. It is safe, there is no commitment to or involvement with another person, the outcome is predictable, and it can be a pleasant insofar as you are "in step" or doing the right thing. There are worship rituals, greeting rituals, cocktail party rituals, bedroom rituals. The ritual is designed to get a group of people through the hour without having to get close to anyone. They may, but they don't have to.... Rituals, like withdrawal, can keep us apart.

—THOMAS A. HARRIS

The meticulous observance of ritual is always a temptation to self-righteousness.

—RABBI MORDECAI M. KAPLAN

Ritual is a kind of shorthand by which we say things that we do not take time to put into words or could not if we would. Religious symbols body forth unutterable aspirations, gratitudes, devotions. We have ritual in courtesy when the hand is extended or the hat lifted—in love when the endearing name is used or the kiss bestowed—in law, without which the procedure of the courts would be impossible—in business as anyone will soon discover who tries to display conspicuous originality in making out a check. God cares not anything about our meticulous performance of a ceremony, if it does not issue in private and public righteousness.

—REV. HARRY EMERSON FOSDICK

Rituals can be fun ... in that they repeat again and again joyous moments which can be anticipated, counted on, and remembered.

— THOMAS A. HARRIS

The Church has succumbed to the temptation to believe in the goodness and power of her own tradition, morality and religious activity. So the Church has come to believe in images of man, of the world, and of God which she has fabricated of her own means.

— KARL BARTH

To do righteousness and justice
Is more acceptable to the Lord than sacrifice.

— BIBLE (PROVERBS 21:3)

Spiritual narcissism is the unconscious use of spiritual practice, experience, and insight to increase rather than decrease self-importance.

— GERALD MAY

A fanatic is a person who does one commandment more than you, and a heretic is someone who does one commandment less than you.

— ANONYMOUS

Excess in the ritual realm can often lead to zealotry and hypocrisy. It is enough to do what God commands. We can then be fairly certain that we are serving God and not our own egos, that we are acting in pursuit of divine service and not excessive passion.

— RABBI SHLOMO RISKIN

I hate, I despise your feasts,
And I will take no delight in your solemn assemblies.
Yea, though ye offer me burnt-offerings and your meal offerings,
I will not accept them;
Neither will I regard the peace-offerings of your fat beasts.
Take thou away from Me the noise of thy songs;
And let Me not hear the melody of thy psalteries.
But let justice well up as waters,
And righteousness as a mighty stream.

— BIBLE (AMOS 5:21-24)

SACRIFICE

No religion is worth its salt which does not make great demands upon its adherents....Too many of our people want an easy-going religion, one which does not interfere with their leisure, their sleep, or their television, which calls for no study no observance, which does not challenge or disturb them, a religion without any spiritual travail, without any stab of thought or conscience, without any sacrifices, the religion of a self-pampering people. No religion has ever survived in that kind of an emotional and intellectual vacuum.

—RABBI ABBA HILLEL SILVER

The sacrifice most acceptable to God is complete renunciation of the body and its passions. This is the only real piety.

—ST. CLEMENT OF ALEXANDRIA

Sacrifice signifies neither amputation nor repentance. It is, in essence, an act. It is the gift of oneself to the being of which one forms a part.

—ANTOINE DE SAINT-EXUPÉRY

Nothing that we consider evil can be offered to God in sacrifice. Therefore, to renounce life in disgust is no sacrifice.

—THOMAS MERTON

Self-sacrifice is the real miracle out of which all the reported miracles grew.

—RALPH WALDO EMERSON

It is only through the mystery of self-sacrifice that one may find oneself anew.

—CARL G. JUNG

SCIENCE

Science is built up with facts as a house is with stones. But a collection of facts is no more a science than a heap of stones is a house.

—HENRI POINCARÉ

Science can only be created by those who are thoroughly imbued with the aspirations toward truth and understanding. This source of feeling, however, springs from the sphere of religion. To this there also belongs the faith in the possibility that the regulations valid for the world of existence are rational; that is, comprehensive to reason. I cannot conceive of a genuine scientist without that profound faith. The situation may be expressed by an image: Science without religion is lame, religion without science is blind.

—*ALBERT EINSTEIN*

If we define science as a search for truth, insight, and understanding, and as a concern with important questions, we must be hard put to differentiate between the scientists on the one hand, and the poets, artists, and philosophers on the other hand.

—*ABRAHAM H. MASLOW*

The possible destructive uses of scientific products do not make me fear new knowledge, for my faith is firm in the scientist as humanist.

—*MICHAEL E. DEBAKEY*

I submit that the tension between science and faith should be resolved not in terms either of elimination or duality, but in terms of a synthesis.

—*TEILHARD DE CHARDIN*

In the days when an idea could be silenced by showing that it was contrary to religion, theology was the greatest single source of fallacies. Today, when any human thought can be discredited by branding it as unscientific, the power previously exercised by theology has passed over to science; hence science has become in its turn the greatest single source of error.

—*JOHN CHARLES POLANYI*

A little science estranges people from God, but much science leads them back to God.

—*LOUIS PASTEUR*

Science is infallible but scientists err all the time.

—*ANATOLE FRANCE*

We may well go to the moon, but that is not very far. The greatest distance we have to cover still lies within us!

—*CHARLES DE GAULLE*

Anyone who has seriously studied science is filled with a conviction that a spirit tremendously superior to the human spirit manifests itself in the law-abidingness of the world, before whom we, with our simple powers, must humbly stand back. So, the study of science leads to religious feeling which is certainly to be distinguished from the religiousness of less informed people.

—*ALBERT EINSTEIN*

Science without conscience is but the ruin of the soul.

—*FRANÇOIS RABELAIS*

We are not born to solve the problems of the universe, but to find out where the problem begins, and then to restrain ourselves within the limits of the comprehensible.

—*GOETHE*

True science teaches, above all, to doubt and to be ignorant.

—*MIGUEL UNAMUNO*

With all your science, can you tell me how and whence it is that light comes into the soul?

—*HENRY DAVID THOREAU*

Science may prove the insignificance of this globe in the scale of creation, but it cannot prove the insignificance of man.

—*BENJAMIN DISRAELI*

Science must constantly be reminded that her purposes are not the only purposes and that the order of uniform causation which she has such use for, and is therefore right in postulating, may be enveloped in a wider order, on which she has no claim at all.

—*WILLIAM JAMES*

Science knows nothing about the first cause of things.

—*SIR OLIVER LODGE*

SEARCH

Show me a thoroughly satisfied man and I will show you a failure.

—*THOMAS EDISON*

A man was lost in the forest. He had been wandering for many days, but he could not find his way. Finally he met another man in the forest, and he said to him: "My friend, I am lost. I have been trying to find my way for many days, but I cannot. Can you show me the way?" The other man answered: "I am lost too. But I can tell you this. Do not go the way I have come, because that way does not lead anywhere. And now let us search for the way together."

—RABBI HAYYIM OF ZANZ

And never to be hungry at all is also a curse. Said Rebbe Pinhas of Koretz: Rather than possess what I desire, I prefer to desire what I possess. And Reb Mendel of Kotzk, echoing Reb Moshe-Leib's words, said: For having seduced Eve, the serpent was sentenced to forever crawl in, and eat, dust. What kind of punishment is that? asked the Master of Kotzk. Condemned to eat dust, the serpent would never be hungry—is that a punishment? Yes, answered the Kotzker. That is the worst punishment of all: never to be hungry, never to seek, never to desire anything.

—ELIE WIESEL

There is no solution.
Seek it lovingly.

—POGO

We have not succeeded in answering all your problems. The answers we have found only serve to raise a whole set of new questions. In some ways we feel we are as confused as ever, but we believe we are confused on a higher level and about more important things.

—ANONYMOUS

I want the hunger for love and beauty to be in the depths of my spirit, for I have seen those who are satisfied are the most wretched of people. I have heard the sigh of those in yearning and longing, and it is sweeter than the sweetest melody.

—KAHLIL GIBRAN

I thought I had all the answers until I discovered that the questions to which I had the answers were not the important questions.

—REINHOLD NIEBUHR

The journey is more important than the inn.

—SPANISH PROVERB

Instead of giving young people the impression that their task is to stand a dreary watch over the ancient values, we should be telling them the grim but bracing truth that it is their task to recreate those values continuously in their own time.

—JOHN GARDNER

The important thing is not to win, but to take part. The important thing in life is not the triumph but the struggle; the essential thing is not having conquered but to have fought well.

—PIERRE DE COUBERTIN

When one wants to go from one mountain top to the next mountain top, one cannot step lightly from one to the other as the legendary Siegfried did. It is necessary rather to go down into the valley before a new ascent can begin.

—IRA PROGROFF

To have succeeded is to have finished one's business on earth, like the male spider, who is killed by the female the moment he has succeeded in his courtship. I like a state of continual becoming, with a goal in front and not behind.

—GEORGE BERNARD SHAW

SELF-ACCEPTANCE

The woods would be very silent if no birds sang except the best.

—YIDDISH PROVERB

None of us, no not one, is perfect; and were we to love none who had imperfections, this world would be a desert for our love.

—THOMAS JEFFERSON

To the ego, life is a game of hide-and-seek. We hide the love that is within us from ourselves and then we seek it outside ourselves, where it can never be found.

—GERALD JAMPOLSKY, M.D.

So you think you are a failure? Well, you probably are. What's wrong with that? In the first place, if you have any sense at all you must have learned by now that we pay just as dearly for our triumphs as we do for our defeats. Go ahead and fail. Embrace failure! Seek it out! Learn to love it. That may be the only way any of us will ever be free.

—*TOM ROBBINS*

Spirituality means the ability to find peace and happiness in an imperfect world, and to feel that one's own personality is imperfect but acceptable. From this peaceful state of mind come both creativity and the ability to love unselfishly, which go hand and hand. Acceptance, faith, forgiveness, peace and love are the traits that define spirituality for me.

—*BERNARD SIEGEL*

When one makes peace with oneself, one will able to make peace with the whole world.

—*RABBI SIMHAH BUNAM*

Once you begin to behave in the knowledge that no being is greater or lesser than you, then you are free to change, because you will feel stable no matter what level you are on. You will feel calm and sure of yourself with or without a body, with or without a job, a brain, a book to read, or a book to write.

—*THADDEUS GOLAS*

This advice—more than any saying uttered by any Master—summarizes the attitude of the Hasidic movement: Ask the utmost of man, but accept him as he is.

—*ELIE WIESEL*

Self-acceptance means self-discovery.

—*RICHARD PERRY*

SELF-ACTUALIZATION

Every human's foremost task is the actualization of his unique, unprecedented and never-recurring potentialities, and not the repetition of something that another, and be it even the greatest, has already achieved.

—*MARTIN BUBER*

All shall know and consider that in their qualities they are unique in the world and that none like them ever lived, for had there ever before been someone like them, then they would not have needed to exist. But each is in truth a new thing in the world, and they shall make perfect their special characteristics, for it is because they are not perfect that the coming of the Messiah tarries.

—RABBI NAHMAN OF BRATZLAV

> May you find the path
> Which will lead you
> To the Highest and
> Truest of Yourself!
> Keep the right path
> Upwards—and hope
> For Perpetual Discovery—
> And Trust Life.
> That's All.

—TEILHARD DE CHARDIN

First become a blessing to yourself that you may be a blessing to others.

—RABBI SAMSON RAPHAEL HIRSCH

To be what we are, and to become what we are capable of becoming is the only end of life.

—SPINOZA

There is never a finished man.

—RALPH WALDO EMERSON

The truth is that there is nothing noble in being superior to somebody else. The only real nobility is in being superior to your former self.

—WHITNEY YOUNG

Trust yourself. Think for yourself. Act for yourself. Speak for yourself. Be yourself. Imitation is suicide.

—MARVA COLLINS

SELF-DISCLOSURE

Where two stand side by side on an equal footing and are open to each other without reservation, there God is.

—*MARTIN BUBER*

Whatever the meaning of the word 'truth' may be in other realms, in the interhuman realm it means that people communicate themselves to one another as what they are. It does not depend on one saying to the other everything that occurs to him, but only on his letting no seeming creep in between himself and the other. It does not depend on one letting himself go before another, but on granting to the man to whom he communicates himself a share in his being.

—*MARTIN BUBER*

SELF-ESTEEM

To be a person of truth, be swayed neither by approval nor disapproval. Work at not needing approval from anyone and you will be free to be who you really are.

—*RABBI NAHMAN OF BRATZLAV*

Our crown has been bought and paid for. All we must do is put it on our heads.

—*JAMES BALDWIN*

Looking down on others is the lazy person's path to self-esteem.

—*GEORGE F. WILL*

Self-esteem isn't everything; it's just that there's nothing without it.

—*GLORIA STEINEM*

I am larger, better than I thought.
I did not know I held so much greatness.

—*WALT WHITMAN*

I believe that we're all born with enough personal self-esteem messages to last us a lifetime. But when these messages don't get nurtured when we are children, they become almost nonexistent when we are adults. Just as our infant and childhood bodies need care, nurturing, and stimulation in order to help us grow into healthy adults, our self-esteem needs the same type of care in order to remain a healthy part of our lives.

—*JULIA BOYD*

High self-esteem comes from coming to terms with yourself somewhere between your ambitions and your limitations.

—*LEE SAUL DUSHOFF*

SELFISHNESS

Heaven's gate is shut
To him who comes alone,
Save thou a soul
And it will save thine own.

—*JOHN GREENLEAF WHITTIER*

Selfishness is not doing what you want to do for yourself. It is expecting other people to do what you want them to do all the time.

—*OSCAR WILDE*

A person wrapped up in oneself makes a very small package.

—*ANONYMOUS*

Doing nothing for others is the undoing of one's self. We must be purposely kind and generous, or we miss the best part of existence. The heart that goes out of itself, gets large and full of joy. This is the great secret of the inner life. We do ourselves the most good doing something for others.

—*HORACE MANN*

Selfishness is the only real atheism; aspiration, unselfishness, the only real religion.

—*ISRAEL ZANGWILL*

SELF-FULFILLING PROPHECY

The one who says it can't be done should not interrupt the one who is doing it.

—CHINESE PROVERB

It's a funny thing about life. If you refuse to accept anything but the best, you very often get it.

—W. SOMERSET MAUGHM

Whatever you can do, or dream you can do, begin it. Boldness has genius, power and magic in it. Begin it now.

—JOHANN VON GOETHE

Perhaps the most important single cause of a person's success or failure ... has to do with the question of what he believes about himself.

—ARTHUR W. COMBS

Argue for your limitations, and sure enough, they're yours.

—RICHARD BACH

They can conquer who believe they can.

—JOHN DRYDEN

SELF-RELIANCE

According to Moshe of Kobryn, even God lets the flame of fervor go out, once it is kindled, so that the person who has been awakened to holiness "may act for himself and of himself attain to the state of perfect awakening." ... In contrast to those zaddikim who prayed that those in need of help might come to them and find help through their prayers, Rabbi Naftali of Ropshitz prayed that those in need of help might find it in their own homes and not have to go to Ropshitz and be deluded into thinking that the rabbi had helped them.

—MAURICE FRIEDMAN

Whosoever shall be a lamp unto themselves, and a refuge unto themselves, holding fast to the Truth as their lamp, shall not look for refuge to any one besides themselves—it is they who shall reach the very topmost height.

—BUDDHA

SELF-RESPECT

The first principle of nonviolent action is that of noncooperation with everything humiliating.

—*MAHATMA GANDHI*

Uniqueness is the essential good of humans that is given to them to unfold.

—*MARTIN BUBER*

The more faithfully you listen to the voice within you, the better you will hear what is sounding outside.

—*DAG HAMMERSKJOLD*

The trouble with you, my friend, is that you sweat too much blood for the whole world. Sweat some for yourself first. You cannot bring the Kingdom of God into the universe unless you first bring it into your heart.

—*LEO TOLSTOY*

In one of the most poignant and direct declarations in all of literature, God begins His message to the prophet Ezekiel by declaring: "Son of man, stand upon your feet that I may speak to you" (2:1). Ezekiel must rise, swell to the height of his human dignity. When human beings are prepared to stand upon their own two feet, to present themselves in the plenitude of their abilities and integrity, God will speak.

—*RABBI DAVID J. WOLPE*

It is not always necessary to prove to others that one is right; it is sometimes enough to know it ourselves.

—*CHAIM GRADE*

There are those who think they can, and those who think they can't. They are both right.

—*HENRY FORD*

The full development of each individual is not only a right, but a duty to society.

—*JUSTICE LOUIS D. BRANDEIS*

One who does not love oneself, does not love well.

—*ARTHUR KOESTLER*

I took a train today, to see
If I could get away from Me.
Though swift and far the engine sped,
My Self went hurrying on ahead.
I went into a room to hide.
My Self already was inside.
I hastened through a secret door....
My Self had entered there before.
However fast and far I flee,
I cannot get away from Me!

—JAMIE SEXTON HOLME

From a transpersonal perspective, one might say that to heal the self is to transcend the self. Wholeness lies in recognizing the illusory nature of all self-concepts and holding them all in healing awareness. Improving self-concept, then may be considered an expedient teaching in which one illusion is exchanged for another, judged to be better, or more "realistic." However, since all self-concepts are misperceptions of reality and hence some form of delusion, they all tend to perpetuate suffering. As long as one remains attached to a separate self-sense, dualistic polarities that generate conflict remain an integral part of experience. Only in complete disidentification and transcendence can the psyche be wholly or fully healed.

—FRANCES VAUGHAN

Yet before we can surrender ourselves we must become ourselves. For no one can give up that he does not possess.

—THOMAS MERTON

If I were asked to give what I consider to be the single most useful bit of advice for all humanity, it would be this:

Expect trouble as an inevitable part of life and, when it comes, hold your head high, look it squarely in the eye, and say, "I will be BIGGER than you. You cannot defeat me."

Then repeat to yourself the most comforting of all words, "This too shall pass."

Maintaining self-respect in the face of a devastating experience is of prime importance.

—ANN LANDERS

We are all born originals. Why die as a copy?

—ANONYMOUS

You are amazing grace
You are a precious jewel
You—special miraculous
Unrepeatable, fragile, fearful, tender,
Lost
Sparkling ruby emerald
Jewel rainbow splendor
Person

—*JOAN BAEZ*

I perceive that, when an acorn and a chestnut fall side by side, the one does not remain inert to make way for the other, but both obey their own laws, and spring up and grow and flourish as best they can, till one perhaps overshadows and destroys the other. If a plant cannot live according to its nature, it dies; and so a man.

—*HENRY DAVID THOREAU*

The soothing feeling of peace and plentitude that I experienced in that mysterious place aroused some deeply buried emotions in me. I began to talk about my life. I confessed that I never respected or liked anybody, not even myself, and that I had always felt I was inherently evil, and thus my attitude towards others was always veiled with a certain bravado and daring.

"True," don Juan said. "You don't like yourself at all."

He crackled and told me that he had been "seeing" while I talked. His recommendation was that I should not have remorse for anything I had done, because to isolate one's being mean, or ugly, or evil was to place an unwarranted importance on the self.

—*CARLOS CASTANEDA*

The worst thing the Evil Urge can achieve is to make one forget one's royal descent.

—*RABBI SHLOMO OF KARLIN*

Father to son: What do you want to be?
Little boy: I want to be myself. All the other parts are taken.

—*ANONYMOUS*

Let man ever esteem himself as though the Holy One dwells within him.

—*RABBI ELAZAR*

If a person could be persuaded that we are all originally descended from God, and that He is the Father of gods and men, I conceive he never would think meanly or degenerately concerning himself.

—EPICTETUS

This above all: To thine own self be true;
And it must follow, as the night the day,
Thou canst not then be false to any man.

—SHAKESPEARE

May I be no man's enemy, and may I be the friend of that which is eternal and abides. May I love, seek, and attain only that which is good. May I wish for all men's happiness and envy none. May I never rejoice in the ill-fortune of one who has wronged me. When I have done or said what is wrong, may I never wait for the rebuke of others, but always rebuke myself until I make amends.... May I win no victory that harms either me or my opponent.... May I respect myself.... May I always keep tame that which rages within me.... May I accustom myself to be gentle, and never be angry with people because of circumstances. May I never discuss who is wicked and what wicked things they have done, but know good men and follow in their footsteps.

—EUSEBIUS

A little criticism makes me angry and a little rejection makes me depressed. A little praise raises my spirits and a little success excites me. It takes very little to raise me up or thrust me down. Often I am like a small boat on the ocean, completely at the mercy of its waves. All the time and energy I spend in keeping some kind of balance and preventing myself from being tipped over and drowning shows my life is mostly a struggle for survival. Not a holy struggle, but an anxious struggle resulting from the mistaken idea that it is the world that defines me.

—HENRY J. M. NOUWEN

You can never enslave somebody who knows who he is.

—ALEX HALEY

If I am not for myself, who will be for me?
If I am only for myself, who am I?
If not now, when?

—HILLEL

Self-respect and self-love do not mean denigrating or hating other people.

—JAMES CONE

SERVICE

I slept and dreamt that life was joy
I woke and saw that life was service
I acted and behold! Service was joy.

—RABINDRANATH TAGORE

It is within my power either to serve God or not to serve. Serving God, I add to my own good and the good of the whole world. Not serving God, I forfeit my own good and deprive the world of that good, which was in my power to create.

—LEO TOLSTOY

You asked me to give you a motto. Here it is: SERVICE.

Let this word accompany each of you throughout your life. Let it be before you as you seek your way and your duty in the world. May it be recalled to your minds if ever you are tempted to forget it or set it aside. It will not always be a comfortable companion but it will always be a faithful one. And it will be able to lead you to happiness, no matter what the experiences of your lives are.

—ALBERT SCHWEITZER

You cannot live a perfect day without doing something for someone who will never be able to repay you.

—SAM RUTIGLIANO

I inherited a belief that no life was more satisfactory than one of selfless service to your country—or humanity. This service required a sacrifice of all personal interests, but likewise the courage to stand up unflinchingly for your convictions concerning what was right and good for the community, whatever were the views in fashion.

—DAG HAMMARSKJOLD

I believe that every human mind feels pleasure in doing good to another.

—THOMAS JEFFERSON

It is one of the beautiful compensations of this life that no one can sincerely try to help another without helping himself.

—RALPH WALDO EMERSON

There is no joy for the self within the self. Joy is found in giving rather than in acquiring; in serving rather than in taking.

—RABBI ABRAHAM JOSHUA HESCHEL

We may wonder whom can I love and serve?

Where is the face of God to whom I can pray?

The answer is simple. That naked one. That lonely one.

That unwanted one is my brother and my sister.

If we have no peace, it is because we have forgotten that we belong to each other.

—MOTHER TERESA

There is no greater satisfaction for a just and well-meaning person than the knowledge that he has devoted his better energies to the service of the good.

—ALBERT EINSTEIN

The essence of selfless service to God is to desire, whether in public or private, to serve for the sake of God rather than for the sake of winning approval by others.

—RABBI BAHYA IBN PAKUDA

SEX

I find it significant that human beings are the only species who face each other during sexual contact, because we are the only species to whom it matters with whom we are sharing the sexual act.

—HAROLD KUSHNER

The problems that get in the way of expressing and enjoying sexuality are rarely specifically sexual—they're all the problems with expressing feelings.... If you feel good about yourself as a person, if you're open and free with your feelings, you should have little difficulty enjoying a full sexual life. Problems in technique are generally minor. Few things improve your sexual performance and ability to enjoy sex as much as improving the way you feel about yourself.

—DAVID VISCOTT

Three things afford a foretaste in miniature of the world to come: the Sabbath, sexual intercourse and a sunny day.

—TALMUD

Remember when air was clean and sex was dirty?

—BUMPER STICKER

The most important sexual organ you have is your heart.

—ANONYMOUS

To use the word "sex" intelligently, means to connote by it more than a specific sensory excitement. It involves the whole affectional life of man, and a major part of his motive power in every realm of creativity.

—REV. HARRY EMERSON FOSDICK

There are people who want to keep our sex instinct inflamed in order to make money out of us. Because, of course, a man with an obsession is a man who has very little sales-resistance.

—C.S. LEWIS

Because of the fact of human freedom, sex is certainly an aspect of the doctrine of sin. But if we understand its nature, and attempt to have it include the sacramental, the romantic, and the interpersonal, it can also be a vital aspect of the doctrine of salvation.

—SEWARD HILTNER

To reduce cohabitation and the conjugal act to a simple organic function for the transmission of seed would be converting the home, the sanctuary of family, into a mere biological laboratory.

—POPE PIUS XII

SILENCE

All our miseries derive from not being able to sit quietly in a room alone.

—BLAISE PASCAL

Silence wears well on the wise and even better on fools.

—TALMUD

Learn to be silent.
Let your
Quiet mind
Listen and absorb.

—PYTHAGORAS

Just as silence is the footprint of God, so chatter, noise, and the business of the world are the footprints of the ego.

—GERALD JAMPOLSKY

One of the most encompassing miseries of all spiritual understanding is that language, a most useful human tool, is also limiting; we can experience and know more than we can say. Awareness of this limitation is essential to all communication about spiritual matters. Our words and ideas may point to a truth, but they are not in themselves the Truth. This is what Lao-Tzu, the traditional founder of Taoism, meant when he warned, "Those who know do not speak; those who speak do not know."

—WILLIAM H. HOUFF

May my lot be with you, ye meek and speechless,
Who wove your lines in secret, modest in word and deed.
Hidden deep within is the loveliness of your spirit,
Like a pearl in the sands of the seas....
Your hearts—a holy temple, your lips—its locked gates....
Artists of exquisite silence, and priests of the silence of God....
You are the faithful guardians of the image of God in the world!

—HAYYIM NAHMAN BIALIK

Silence is the loudest of all voices.

—THE KOTZKER RABBI

What a strange power there is in silence.

—RALPH WALDO EMERSON

For thus said the Lord God, the Holy One of Israel:
In sitting still and rest shall you be saved,
In quietness and trust shall be your strength.

—BIBLE (ISAIAH 30:15)

Minds are like TV sets: When they go blank, it's best to turn off the sound.

—ANONYMOUS

A word is worth one coin; silence is worth two.

—TALMUD

Since birth I have grown up in the company of sages and have concluded that here is nothing in the world more pleasurable than silence.

—RABBI SHIMON BEN GAMLIEL

Silence is the greatest persecution.

—BLAISE PASCAL

The cruelest lies are often told in silence.

—ROBERT LOUIS STEVENSON

It is as necessary as it is hard to practice a regular discipline of silence, solitude, or prayer. I have not fully succeeded but I cannot survive long without my moments. A few minutes every hour, a half hour or hour every day, a day a month, a week a year—in dedicated silence—is a goal to pursue. Even better is the attainment of an internal quiet space within yourself amidst never-ceasing external bedlam. It's tempting to hide behind a too-busy life as an excuse to avoid solitude, and in this I am guiltier than most. But each of us can do what we really want to do.

—MARIAN WRIGHT EDELMAN

A silent tongue does not betray its owner.

—AFRICAN PROVERB

SIMPLICITY

Live simply so that others may simply live.

—BUMPER STICKER

For simplicity that lies on this side of complexity I wouldn't give a fig. For the simplicity that lies on the other side of complexity, I'd give my life.

—OLIVER WENDELL HOLMES, SR.

The wiser and more skillful a teacher is, the more simply and with less artifice he achieves his ends.

—MEISTER ECKHARDT

I will try not to panic, to keep my standard of living modest and to work steadily, even shyly, in the spirit of those medieval carvers who so fondly sculpted the undersides of choir seats.

—JOHN UPDIKE

Anything meaningful must really be simple. Too simple for the sophisticated and the cynical.

—ANONYMOUS

It is no good asking for a simple religion. After all, real things aren't simple. They look simple, but they're not.

—C. S. LEWIS

SIN

Many of the insights of the saint stem from his experience as a sinner.

—ERIC HOFFER

Saints should always be judged guilty till they are proved innocent.

—GEORGE ORWELL

A sin well hidden is a sin half-forgiven.

—BOCCACCIO

I do not want my students to avoid sin merely because they have controlled the urge to sin. I want them to avoid sin because they have no time for sin!

—HASIDIC

Sin is the failure to live up to the highest moral potentialities in one's self in any given situation.

—ABBA HILLEL SILVER

There is a sin of omission, not only one of commission.

—MARCUS AURELIUS

Fight thine own sins, not the sins of others.

—CONFUCIUS

Other's sins are before our eyes; our own are behind our back.

—SENECA

But however much you may advance in the love of God and of your neighbor, and in true piety, do not imagine as long as you are in this life, that you are without sin.

—*ST. AUGUSTINE*

You are asked to get rid of your sins, not to show that others have committed the like.

—*ST. JOHN CHRYSOSTOM*

Whoever does not attempt to prevent sin is answerable for the sin.

—*TALMUD*

The soul accustomed to light transgressions has no horror of more serious ones.

—*POPE ST. GREGORY THE GREAT*

Think not of the smallness of your sin, but of the greatness of Him against whom you have sinned!

—*BAHYA BEN YOSEPH IBN PAKUDA*

Thy merry sins, thy laughing sins, shall grow to be crying sins even in the ears of God.

—*JOHN DONNE*

SINCERITY

What counts is sincerity and honesty. If you can fake these, you've got it made.

—*GEORGE BURNS*

I do not see how a man without sincerity can be good for anything. How can a cart or carriage be made to go without yoke or crossbar?

—*CONFUCIUS*

Sincerity is the way to Heaven.

—*MENCIUS*

SOCIAL RESPONSIBILITY

Activism pays the rent of being alive and being here on the planet.... If I weren't active politically, I would feel as if I were sitting back eating at the banquet without washing the dishes or preparing the food. It wouldn't feel right.

—*ALICE WALKER*

How wonderful it is that no one need wait a single moment to start to improve the world.

—*ANNE FRANK*

What begins as the inequality of some, inevitably ends as the inequality of all.

—*RABBI ABRAHAM JOSHUA HESCHEL*

It has been said that you judge a society by the way it treats the weakest in the dawn of life as children, a nation by the way it deals with the eldest and the weakest, and you judge America by how it concerns itself with the homeless, hungry and disabled.

—*RABBI SEYMOUR COHEN*

The question is not, "If I stop to help this man in need, what will happen to me?" "If I do not stop to help the sanitation workers what will happen to them?" That's the question.

—*MARTIN LUTHER KING, JR.*

When will there be justice in the world?
When the people who are not wronged feel just as indignant as those who are.

—*PLATO*

In the beginning I thought I could change man. Today I know I cannot. If I still shout today, if I still scream, it is to prevent man from ultimately changing me.

—*ELIE WIESEL*

If we are able to be involved, but remain indifferent, we are responsible for the consequences.

—*MIDRASH*

Humanity's sole salvation lies in everyone making everything his business.

—*ALEXANDER SOLZHENITSYN*

As life is action and passion, it is required of a man that he should share the passion and action of his time at peril of being judged not to have lived.

—OLIVER WENDELL HOLMES

If you are neutral in a situation of injustice, you have chosen the side of the oppressor. If an elephant has his foot on the tail of a mouse, and you say you are neutral, the mouse will not appreciate your neutrality.

—BISHOP DESMOND TUTU

Is this not what I require of you as a fast: to loose the fetters of injustice, to untie the cords of lawlessness, to snap every yoke and set free those who have been crushed.

—BIBLE (ISAIAH 58:6)

Any religion that professes to be concerned with the souls of people and is not concerned with the slums that damn them and the social conditions that cripple them, is a dry-as-dust religion.

—MARTIN LUTHER KING, JR.

I cannot imagine better worship of God than that in His name I should labor for the poor.

—MAHATMA GANDHI

It is only in assuming full responsibility for our world, for our lives and for ourselves, that we can be said to live really for God.

—THOMAS MERTON

If you see what needs to be repaired and how to repair it, then you have found a piece of the world that God has left for you to complete. But if you only see what is wrong and how ugly it is, then it is yourself that needs repair.

—RABBI TZVI FREEMAN

Come, my friends, it is not too late, to seek a better world.

—ALFRED LORD TENNYSON

And do not think that you have to make big waves in order to contribute. My role model, Sojourner Truth, slave woman, could neither read nor write but could not stand slavery and second-class treatment of women. One day during an anti-slavery speech she was heckled by an old man. "Old woman, do you think that your talk about slavery does any good? Why I don't care any more for your talk than I do for the bite of a flea." "Perhaps not, but the Lord willing, I'll keep you scratching," she replied.

—MARIAN WRIGHT EDELMAN

I would unite with anybody to do right and with nobody to do wrong.

—*FREDERICK DOUGLASS*

SOLITUDE

Loneliness is small, solitude is large. Loneliness closes in around you; solitude expands toward the infinite. Loneliness has its roots in words, in an internal conversation that nobody answers; solitude has its roots in the great silence of eternity.

—*KENT NERBURN*

One who is not alone has not discovered his identity.

—*THOMAS MERTON*

One who has tasted the sweetness of solitude and tranquility, is free from fear and free from sin.

—*DHAMMAPADA*

Come now.... Flee for a while from your tasks, hide yourself for a little space from the turmoil of your thoughts. Come, cast aside your burdensome cares, and put aside your laborious pursuits. For a little while give your time to God, and rest the Lord for a little while. Enter into the inner chamber of your mind, shut out all things save God and whatever may aid you in seeking God; and having barred the door of your chamber, seek God.

—*SAINT ANSELM*

What I must do is all that concerns me, not what the people may think. This rule, equally arduous in actual and intellectual life, may serve for the whole distinction between greatness and meanness. It is the harder because you will always find those who think they know what is your duty better than you know it. It is easy in the world to live after man's opinion; it is easy in solitude to live after your own; but the great man is he who in the midst of the crowd keeps with perfect sweetness the independence of solitude.

—*RALPH WALDO EMERSON*

The cultivation of individual solitude is a first step to the solution of our social problems.

—*RALPH W. SOCKMAN*

But little do men perceive what solitude is, and how far it extendeth. For a crowd is not company; and faces are but a gallery of pictures; and talk but a tinkling cymbal, where there is no love.

—*SIR FRANCIS BACON*

One who lives in solitude and no longer communicates with others, is either a beast or a god.

—*ARISTOTLE*

I never found the companion that was so companionable as solitude.

—*HENRY DAVID THOREAU*

SOUL

The final mystery is oneself. When one has weighed the sun in the balance, and measured the steps of the moon, and mapped out the seven heavens star by star, there still remains oneself. Who can calculate the orbit of his own soul?

—*OSCAR WILDE*

The bounds of the soul you shall not find, though you travel every path.

—*HERACLITUS*

Great truths are portions of the soul of man;
Great souls are portions of Eternity.

—*JAMES RUSSELL LOWELL*

Out of the night that covers me,
Black as the pit from pole to pole,
I thank whatever gods may be
For my unconquerable soul!

—*W. E. HENLEY*

Of all things which a man has, next to the gods, his soul is the most divine and most truly his own.

—*PLATO*

O Lord, who can comprehend Thy power?
For Thou hast created for the splendor of Thy glory a pure radiance
"Hewn from the rocks and digged from the bottom of the pit."
Thou hast imparted to it the spirit of wisdom
And called it the Soul.
And of flames of intellectual fire hast Thou wrought its form,
And like a burning fire hast Thou wafted it,
And sent it to the body to serve and guard it,
And it is as fire in the midst thereof yet doth not consume it,
For it is from the fire of the soul that the body hath been created,
And goeth from Nothingness to Being,
"Because the Lord descended on him in fire."

—SOLOMON IBN-GABIROL

It is difficult for us to find the soul within ourselves. The soul in us is like God in the world, paradoxically hidden but present. The Talmud contains a hymn that describes the soul as analogous to God: "As God fills the entire world, so the soul fills the body. As God sees but is not seen, so the soul sees but is not seen. As God is pure, so the soul is pure. As God is deeply hidden, so the soul is deeply hidden." The infinite soul fills us, gives us life, and is the most authentic part of who we are. But we cannot grasp it, we cannot identify it, we cannot find the words adequate to express it. In Hebrew, we call the soul the neshamah, the breath.

—DAVID S. ARIEL

SPIRIT

We are not human beings having a spiritual experience. We are spiritual beings having a human experience.

—TEILHARD DE CHARDIN

I [the Lord] shall pour out My spirit on all flesh, and your sons and daughters shall prophesy, your old shall dream dreams, and your young shall see visions.

—BIBLE (JOEL 3:1)

Great men are they who see that the spiritual is stronger than any material force, that thoughts rule the world.

—*RALPH WALDO EMERSON*

The main problem facing us is not, as Freud said, sexual repression, but spiritual repression.

—*CARL JUNG*

True spirituality is not a removal or escape from life. It is an opening, a seeing of the world with a deeper vision that is less self-centered, a vision that sees through dualistic views to the underlying interconnectedness of all life. Liberation is the discovery of freedom in the very midst of our bodies and minds.

—*JOSEPH GOLDSTEIN and JACK KORNFIELD*

For this is the journey that men make: to find themselves. If they fail in this, it doesn't matter what else they find. Money, position, fame, many loves, revenge are all of little consequence, and when the tickets are collected at the end of the ride, they are tossed into a bin marked FAILURE. But if a man happens to find himself ... then he has found a mansion which he can inhabit with dignity all the days of his life.

—*JAMES MICHENER*

The longest journey is the journey inward.

—*DAG HAMMARSKJOLD*

Each one has to find his peace from within, and peace to be real must be unaffected by outside circumstances.

—*MAHATMA GANDHI*

Till now man has been up against nature; from now on he will be up against his own nature.

—*DENNIS GABOR*

The real voyage of discovery consists not in seeking new landscapes, but in having new eyes.

—*MARCEL PROUST*

A pleasant and happy life does not come from external things; one draws from within, as from a spring, pleasure and joy.

—*PLUTARCH*

There is worse than oppression—there is inward stagnation of the spiritual life.

—*ISRAEL ZANGWILL*

As for me, I think a relationship of trust, worth, and love between people is the highest and most satisfying way of experiencing one's humanity. I think this is where real spirituality takes place. Without it, humans become shriveled, destructive, and desolate.

—VIRGINIA SATIR

The spirit is a still, small voice, but the masters of vulgarity use loud-speakers.

—RABBI ABRAHAM JOSHUA HESCHEL

What lies behind us and what lies before us are small matters compared to what lies within us.

—RALPH WALDO EMERSON

The most spiritual people are the most human people. They are natural and easy in manner; they give themselves no airs; they interest themselves in ordinary everyday matters, and are not forever talking and thinking about religion. For them there is no difference between spirituality and usual life, and to their awakened insight the lives of the most humdrum and earth-bound people are as much in harmony with the infinite as their own.

—ALAN WATTS

After man masters the winds and the tides, he may harness the energy that can be generated by the capacity of human beings to love one another and, when he does this, he will once again discover fire.

—TEILHARD DE CHARDIN

If we work upon marble, it will perish. If we work on brass, time will efface it. But if we work upon men's immortal minds, if we imbue them with high principles, with the just fear of God and love of their fellow men, we engrave on those tablets something which no time can efface, and which will brighten and brighten to all eternity.

—DANIEL WEBSTER

Know, beloved, that we cannot understand the future world until we know what death is: and we cannot know what death is until we know what life is; nor can we understand what life is until we know what the spirit is— the seat of the knowledge of God.

—AL-GHAZZALI

The life of the spirit is not our life, but the life of God within us.

—ST. THERESA OF ÁVILA

STUDY

As there is always a fruit when the tree is searched, so is there always a pleasant surprise when Torah is searched.

—*RABBI YOHANAN BEN NAPPAHA*

SUCCESS

Don't confuse fame with success. Madonna is one. Helen Keller is the other.

—*ERMA BOMBECK*

Try not to become a man of success but rather become a man of value.

—*ALBERT EINSTEIN*

To laugh often and much; to win the respect of intelligent people and affection of children; to earn the appreciation of honest critics and endure the betrayal of false friends; to appreciate beauty, to find the best in others; to leave the world a bit better, whether by a healthy child, a garden patch or a redeemed social condition; to know even one life has breathed easier because you have lived. This is to have succeeded.

—*RALPH WALDO EMERSON*

The secret of success is this: there is no secret of success.

—*ANONYMOUS*

Why should we be in such desperate haste to succeed, and in such desperate enterprises? If a man does not keep pace with his companions, perhaps it is because he hears a different drummer.

—*HENRY DAVID THOREAU*

There's only one success—to be able to spend your life in your own way.

—*CHRISTOPHER MORLEY*

A successful person is one who can build a firm foundation with the bricks that others throw at them.

—*DAVID BRINKLEY*

SUFFERING

Although the world is full of suffering, it is full also of the overcoming of it.

—HELEN KELLER

What does not destroy me makes me stronger.

—FRIEDRICH NIETZSCHE

Pain is the breaking of the shell that encloses your understanding.

—KAHLIL GIBRAN

There is only one thing that I dread: not to be worthy of my sufferings.

—FYODOR DOSTOEVSKI

We bereaved are not alone. We belong to the largest company in the world, the company of those who have known suffering. When it seems that our sorrow is too great to be borne, let us think of the great family of the heavy-hearted into which our grief has given us entrance, and inevitably we will feel about us their arms, their sympathy, their understanding.

—HELEN KELLER

Let us be thankful that our sorrow lives in us as an indestructible force, only changing in form, as forces do, and passing from pain to sympathy. To have suffered much is like knowing many languages. Thou hast learned to understand all.

—GEORGE ELIOT

If you desire life, expect pain.

—RABBI AZARIAH

He has seen but half of the universe who has not been shown the house of pain.

—RALPH WALDO EMERSON

My dear, if you would recognize that life is hard, things would be so much easier for you.

—JUSTICE LOUIS D. BRANDEIS, TO HIS DAUGHTER

Adversity makes the man, prosperity makes the monster.

—VICTOR HUGO

Sweet are the uses of adversity;
Which, like the toad, ugly and venomous,
Wears yet a precious jewel in his head,
And this our life, exempt from public haunt,
Finds tongues in trees, books in the running brooks,
Sermons in stones, and good in everything.

—SHAKESPEARE

He who has a why to live for can bear almost any how.

—FRIEDRICH NIETZSCHE

No suffering befalls the man who calls nothing his own.

—DHAMMAPADA

The best prayers have often more groans than words.

—JOHN BUNYAN

It is in suffering that we are withdrawn from the bright superficial film of existence, from the sway of time and mere things, and find ourselves in the presence of a profounder truth.

—YVES M. CONGAR

The gem cannot be polished without friction, nor people perfected without trials.

—CONFUCIUS

TEACHING

No man can reveal to you aught of that which already lies half asleep in the dawning of your knowledge.

The teacher who walks in the shadow of the temple, among his followers, gives not of his wisdom, but rather of his faith and his lovingness.

If he is indeed wise he does not bid you enter the house of wisdom, but rather leads you to the threshold of your own mind.

—KAHLIL GIBRAN

A teacher affects eternity; he can never tell where his influence stops.

—HENRY ADAMS

A teacher can never truly teach unless he is still learning himself. A lamp can never light another lamp unless it continues to burn its own flame. The teacher who has come to the end of his subject, who has no living traffic with his students can only lead their minds, he cannot quicken them. Truth not only must inform, it must inspire; if the inspiration dies out and the information only accumulates, then truth loses its infinity. The greater part of our learning in the schools has been wasted because for most of our teachers their subjects are like dead specimens of once living things with which they have learned acquaintance but no communication of life and love.

—RABINDRANATH TAGORE

No printed word nor spoken plea
Can teach young minds what men should be,
Not all the books on all the shelves
But what the teachers are themselves.

—ANONYMOUS

In seeking knowledge, the first step is silence, the second is listening, the third remembering, the fourth practicing, and the fifth teaching others.

—SOLOMON IBN GABIROL

There are only three ways to teach children: example, example and example.

—ALBERT SCHWEITZER

TECHNOLOGY

One machine can do the work of fifty ordinary men. No machine can do the work of one extraordinary man.

—ELBERT HUBBARD

When I wrote Brave New World in 1932, I had no idea how soon so much of it would come true. I had no idea—I don't think anyone did—how swiftly science would develop.... Our power for controlling—or devastating—the outside world already has proceeded beyond what I could have foreseen.

—ALDOUS HUXLEY (JUNE, 1962)

We continually amaze ourselves with what we can do, and in the process God seems less and less impressive. When Samuel F.B. Morse invented the telegraph almost one hundred years ago, the first words he sent by wire were "What has God wrought!" When Neil Armstrong stepped onto the surface of the moon in 1969, his first words were "That's one small step for man, one giant leap for mankind." Notice who gets the credit, and who gets left out, when it comes to twentieth-century marvels.

Technology is the enemy of reverence.

—HAROLD KUSHNER

Being an old and old-fashioned animal, I am no enthusiast for the TV age, in which I fear mass thought and action will be taken too much in charge of by machinery, both destructive and distracting.

—WINSTON CHURCHILL

Our mastery over nature and our control of physical power have so far outstripped our self-control that we have become very dangerous animals.

—WINSTON CHURCHILL

Having mastered the atom we must, under threat of annihilation, concentrate on mastering the Adam [Hebrew for "man"].

—RABBI SIDNEY GREENBERG

The path to hell is paved with good inventions.

—ANONYMOUS

The hope that technology will save us or will miraculously effect our moral improvement is a kind of modern idolatry.

—RUDOLF DIESEL

Modern technology unfolds before contemporary humans a vision so vast as to be confused by many with the infinite itself. As a consequence, one attributes to it an impossible autonomy, which in turn is transformed in the minds of some into an erroneous conception of life and of the world.

—POPE PIUS XII

The technological society has relegated religion, the arts and all other elements of high culture to a limbo from which they may still return to revenge themselves.

—PHILIP RIEFF

TOLERANCE

Consider these distinctions:

Tolerance—you can believe what you will even though it is wrong and of no value.

Pluralism—you can believe differently than I do and not only will I recognize your right to do so, but recognize that there is a measure of truth and value in your beliefs.

Openness—you have a right to believe as you do. I recognize that there is truth and value in your belief, and I can learn from you and be enriched thereby.

—AVI RAVITZKY

There would never be a moment, in war or in peace, when I wouldn't trade all the patriots in the country for one tolerant man. Or when I wouldn't swap the vitamins in a child's lunchbox for a jelly glass of magnanimity.

—E. B. WHITE

If there be any among us who would wish to dissolve this Union or to change its republican form, let them stand undisturbed as monuments of the safety with which error of opinion may be tolerated where reason is left free to combat it.

—THOMAS JEFFERSON

If err we must, let us err on the side of tolerance.

—FELIX FRANKFURTER

Like the bee gathering honey from different flowers, the wise person accepts the essence of different Scriptures and sees only the good in all religions.

—SRIMAD BHAGAVATAM

I have seen gross intolerance shown in support of toleration.

—SAMUEL TAYLOR COLERIDGE

In truth, each person has a unique opinion; everyone who is engaged in a dispute must acknowledge that his companion also has a unique point of view. One should not stay rigidly attached to his own idea, but search for truth. In this way, God will help their eyes see clearly, and peace will come from conflict.

—RABBI YEHUDAH LEIB ALTER

TOUCH

There is one temple in the universe—the human body. We touch heaven when we touch the human body.

—THOMAS CARLYLE

I, who cannot see, find hundreds of things to interest me through mere touch. I feel the delicate symmetry of a leaf. I pass my hands lovingly about the smooth skin of a silver birch, or the rough shaggy bark of a pine.... I feel the delightful, velvety texture of a flower, and discover its remarkable con-volutions; and something of the miracle Nature is revealed to me. Occasionally, if I am very fortunate, I place my hand gently on a small tree and feel the happy quiver of a bird in full song. At times my heart cries out with longing to see these things. If I can get so much pleasure from mere touch, how much more beauty must be revealed by sight. Yet, those who have eyes apparently see little. The panorama of color and action which fills the world is taken for granted.... It is a great pity that, in the world of light, the gift of sight is used only as a mere convenience rather than as a means of adding fullness to life.

—HELEN KELLER

TRADITION

Each of us is a bus in which our forbears travel with us.

—OLIVER WENDELL HOLMES

Progress might have been all right once, but it's gone on too long.

—OGDEN NASH

My enthusiasm glows the brighter and steadier for being kindled at a common flame and at an ancient and hallowed shrine.

—WILLIAM HAZLITT

We wish to preserve the fire of the past, not the ashes.

—WILLIAM JAMES

Life must be lived forward, but can only be understood backward.

—SÖREN KIERKEGAARD

Whoever controls the present controls the past; whoever controls the past controls the future.

—GEORGE ORWELL

Tradition does not allow contents and forms to be passed on unchanged from generation to generation. What is passed down is not a fixed content but a way of existing. Living tradition is change and renewal out of deep-seated spontaneity.

—MARTIN BUBER

There is something better than modernity, which is eternity.

—SOLOMON SCHECHTER

Stand by the roads, and look, and ask for the ancient paths, where the good way is; and walk in it, and find rest for your souls.

—BIBLE (JEREMIAH 6:16)

Though people may no longer realize it, the past is always alive as a major source of our basic interests and needs, our rights and duties, our hopes and fears. As a people, we can no more get along without some knowledge of it than an individual could without memory.

—HERBERT J. MULLER

What you have inherited from your fathers, earn over again for yourselves, or it will not be yours.

—GOETHE

Our past is our cradle, not our prison.

—ISRAEL ZANGWILL

Remove not the ancient landmark your ancestors have set.

—BIBLE (PROVERBS 22:28)

Those who do not look back to their ancestors cannot look forward to their progeny.

—EDMUND BURKE

One who looks constantly backward will fall on his face.

—ANONYMOUS

Pay your debt to the past by putting the future in debt to you.

—*ANONYMOUS*

TRANSLATION

Poetry is what gets lost in translation.

—*ROBERT FROST*

Anyone who translates a verse literally is a liar.

—*RABBI YEHUDAH, TALMUD*

Reading a translation is like kissing your girlfriend through a handkerchief.

—*HAYYIM NAHMAN BIALIK*

A translation is like a woman. She can be faithful OR beautiful – but not both.

—*ANONYMOUS*

Translations are like the black and white photograph of a colorful sunset. The form is reproduced, but the mood is lost.

—*MICHAEL GELBER*

Translators are matchmakers who extol the attractions of a half-veiled beauty; with all their exertions, they only kindle in us a longing for the original.

—*GOETHE*

TRUST

What has shaken me is not that you lied to me but that I no longer believe you.

—*FRIEDRICH NIETZSCHE*

The religious man has resources of trust that can break through, can meet the other, can build real community. But he must distinguish between genuine dialogue and mere togetherness, between the willingness to affirm the other even when opposing him and the shifting alliances formed on the basis of expediency.... Only a real listening—a listening witness—can plumb the abyss of that universal existential mistrust that stands in the way of genuine dialogue and peace.

—MAURICE FRIEDMAN

Delay not the health of thy soul through trust in friends or in neighbors; for men will forget sooner than thou thinkest; it is better to make some provision betimes and send before thee some good than to trust in other men's help.

—THOMAS Á KEMPIS

TRUTH

From the cowardice that shrinks from new truth
From the laziness that is content with half-truths
From the arrogance that thinks it knows all truth
O, God of truth, deliver us.

—RABBI MORDECAI M. KAPLAN

Seek the company of those who seek the truth.
Avoid the company of those who have found it.

—VACLAV HAVEL

There are two kinds of truth, small truth and great truth. You can recognize small truth because its opposite is a falsehood. The opposite of a great truth is another great truth.

—NIELS BOHR

I can always tell if a politician is lying. Here's the key: If he looks you straight in the eye, he's telling the truth. If he tugs his ear, he's telling you the truth. If he puts his hand on your arm, he's telling you the truth. If he opens his mouth, he's lying.

—JULES FEIFFER

If one tells the truth, one is sure sooner or later to be found out.

—OSCAR WILDE

One day, according to an Eastern story, the gods decided to create the universe. They created the stars, the sun, the moon. They created the seas, the mountains, the flowers, and the clouds. Then they created human beings. At the end, they created Truth.

At this point, however, a problem arose; where should they hide Truth so that human beings would not find it right away? They wanted to prolong the adventure of the search.

"Let's put Truth on top of the highest mountain," said one of the gods. "Certainly it will be hard to find there."

"Let's put it on the farthest star," said another.

"Let's hide it in the darkest and deepest of abysses."

"Let's conceal it on the secret side of the moon."

At the end, the wisest and most ancient god said, "No, we will hide Truth inside the very heart of human beings. In this way they will look for it all over the Universe, without being aware of having it inside themselves all the time.

—PIERO FERRUCCI

I don't say these men are liars, it's just that they have such respect for the truth that they use it sparingly.

—PAUL PORTER

When you stretch the truth, people usually see it through it.

—ANONYMOUS

You may fool all of the people some of the time; you can even fool some of the people all the time; but you can't fool all the people all the time.

—ABRAHAM LINCOLN

Beauty is truth, and truth beauty—
That is all ye know on earth,
And all ye need to know.

—JOHN KEATS

Oh what a tangled web we weave,
When first we practice to deceive.

—SHAKESPEARE

But such is the irresistible nature of truth, that all it asks, and all it wants, is the liberty of appearing.

—THOMAS PAINE

Feelings without honesty are defenses
The world without honesty is an illusion
Memory without honesty is only a fantasy
Time without honesty can never be now
Space without honesty can never he here
Love without honesty is possessiveness.

—DAVID VISCOTT

If all people would speak the truth, there would be no need to bring the Messiah; the Messiah would be here already. Just as the Messiah brings truth, truth brings the Messiah.

—RABBI PINHAS OF KORETZ

The most dangerous of all dilemmas: When we are obliged to conceal truth in order to help the truth to be victorious.

—DAG HAMMERSKJOLD

You must not tell a lie, but you don't have to give expression to every truth that comes to mind.

—YIDDISH PROVERB

Truth springs forth from the earth.

—BIBLE (PSALM 85:15)

Let us bend down, reach for truth, and spread it far and wide in order that our world be ruled not by falsehood but by truth, not by apathy and indifference, but by knowledge and commitment; not by hatred, but by love; not by war but by peace.

—LOUIS M. TUCHMAN

I am different from Washington; I have a higher, grander standard of principle. Washington could not lie. I can lie, but I won't.

—MARK TWAIN

Those who know the truth are not equal to those who love it.

—CONFUCIUS

The surest way to lose truth is to pretend that one already wholly possesses it.

—GORDON W. ALLPORT

God is seen as lying in order to make peace between Avraham and Sarah in Genesis (18:12-13). Sarah has just heard that she will give birth and laughs to herself saying "Now that I am withered, am I to have enjoyment, WITH MY HUSBAND SO OLD?" In the next verse, God says to Avraham, "Why did Sarah laugh, saying, "Shall I in truth bear a child, OLD AS I AM?"

One reference to this is the saying, "Great is peace, seeing that for its sake even God modified the truth."

—MIDRASH

The courtroom oath—"to tell the truth, the whole truth and nothing but the truth"—is applicable only to witnesses. Defense attorneys, prosecutors and judges don't take this oath – they couldn't. Indeed, it is fair to say the American justice system is built on a foundation of not telling the whole truth.

—ALAN DERSHOWITZ

Telling the truth is so much easier than lying, because it doesn't require a good memory.

—ANONYMOUS

I broke all my bones while working on myself to attain truth. This lasted twenty-one years: seven years to discover what truth is; another seven years to expel falsehood from my being; and the last seven years to receive truth and live it.

—RABBI PINHAS OF KORETZ

To be absolutely sure of the truth of matters concerning which there are many opinions is an attribute of God not given to man.

—PLATO

Truth is not only violated by falsehood; it may be equally outraged by silence.

—HENRI-FREDERIC AMIEL

If God were able to backslide from truth I would fain cling to truth and let God go.

—MEISTER ECKHART

The grave of one who dies for truth is holy ground.

—GERMAN PROVERB

If you shut your door to all errors truth will be shut out.

—RABINDRANATH TAGORE

If God had all truth shut in his right hand, and in his left nothing but the ever-restless search after truth, although with the condition of for ever and ever erring, and should say to me, "Choose!" I should bow humbly to his left hand and say, "Father, give! Pure truth is for Thee alone!"

—G. E. LESSING

Truth often suffers more by the heat of its defenders, than from the arguments of its opposers.

—WILLIAM PENN

Men often stumble over the truth, but most pick themselves up and walk on as if nothing had happened.

—WINSTON CHURCHILL

One falsehood spoils a thousand truths.

—ASHANTI PROVERB

Truth is proper and beautiful in all times and in all places.

—FREDERICK DOUGLASS

What this nation needs is a Renaissance of reverence for the truth.

—W.E. BE. DU BOIS

You must speak straight so that your words may go like sunlight to our hearts.

—APACHE CHIEF COCHISE

The eyes believe themselves; the ears believe others; and the heart believes the truth.

—IBO PROVERB

UNITY

All things by immortal power near or far,
Hiddenly to each other linked are
That thou canst not stir a flower
Without the troubling of a star.

—FRANCIS THOMPSON

When you pray say our, not mine or thine;
Our sins, our debts, our health and our dead.
When you commune with God in His holy shrine,
Or in your private solitude instead.
God will reign in all His might and power,
When all will pray not mine or thine but our.

—ANONYMOUS

It really boils down to this: that all life is interrelated. We are all caught in an inescapable network of mutuality, tied into a single garment of destiny. Whatever affects one directly, affects all indirectly.

—MARTIN LUTHER KING, JR..

All that humans have here externally in multiplicity is intrinsically One. Here all blades of grass, wood and stone, all things are One. This is the deepest depth.

—MEISTER ECKHART

O God, I never listen to the cry of the animals, or the quivering of the trees, or the murmuring of water, or the song of the birds, or the rustling wind, or the crashing thunder, without feeling them to be an evidence of Thy unity.

—RUMI

UNIVERSALITY

God gave all men all earth to love
But since our hearts are small
Ordained for each one spot should prove
Beloved over all.

—RUDYARD KIPLING

We are all members of one another and, thus, the heart must love the limbs and the limbs must love the heart.

—RABBI MEIR LEIBUSH BEN YEHIEL MICHEL (MALBIM)

The universe is the same for all of us, and different for each of us.

—MARCEL PROUST

It is through the very diversity of human culture that the universal in our humanness may be found.

—MARGARET MEAD

VALIDATION

Let people realize clearly that every time they threaten someone or humiliate or hurt unnecessarily or dominate or reject another human being, they become forces for the creation of psychopathology, even if these be small forces. Let them recognize that every man who is kind, helpful, decent, psychologically democratic, affectionate, and warm, is a psychotherapeutic force even though a small one.

—ABRAHAM H. MASLOW

Man wishes to be confirmed in his being by man, and wishes to have a presence in the being of the other ... secretly and bashfully he watches for a Yes which allows him to be and which can come to him only from one human person to another.

—MARTIN BUBER

How powerful are right words!

—BIBLE (JOB 6:25)

Ask the Hasidim: How could Moses sing? He was a stutterer. Answer: He could sing because his people now had faith in him. Thus he had faith in himself.

—ELIE WIESEL

VALUES

If you don't get what you want in life, perhaps you didn't want it badly enough, or you tried to bargain over the price.

—VICTOR HUGO

The state of being without a system of values is psycho-pathogenic. Human beings need a philosophy of life, religion, or a value system, just as they need sunlight, calcium and love.

—ABRAHAM H. MASLOW

The moral order is not something static, it is not something enshrined in historic documents, or stowed away like the family silver, or lodged in the minds of pious and somewhat elderly moralists. It is an attribute of a functioning social system. As such it is a living, changing thing, liable to decay and disintegration as well as to revitalization and reinforcement, and never any better than the generation that holds it in trust.

—JOHN GARDNER

Don't moralize unnecessarily or your children will turn you off like a record player with its needle stuck in a groove. Values clarification is the name of the process, not value inculcation. With the incredible future ahead of us all, we must affirm the idea that few of us can really know what our children should value. We can't be there all the time to value for them.

On the other hand, we as parents should make the clearest statements we can about where we stand. We should do it not punitively, not with flattery, not with manipulation. We need to be open and less uptight as we come in touch with alternatives for our family values which may be more creative than the ones we picked up during our own upbringing.

Finally, we must give dignity to the family's search for its meaning. It is only as we teach a process, a way of negotiating the as yet unfathomable future, that we leave our children with an estate more valuable than stocks, bonds, jewels, or gold. We leave a way of making sense out of the confusion and conflict surrounding all of us.

—SIDNEY B. SIMON

Since no way can be found for deciding a difference in values, the conclusion is forced upon us that the difference is one of tastes, not one as to any objective truth.

—BERTRAND RUSSELL

Man's chief purpose ... is the creation and preservation of value; that is what gives meaning to our civilization, and the participation in this is what gives significance, ultimately to the individual and human life.

—LEWIS MUMFORD

VANITY

If you are blessed with a sympathetic disposition, don't waste it on yourself.

—BENJAMIN FRANKLIN

God hates those who praise themselves.

—ST. CLEMENT OF ROME

Vanity of vanities; all is vanity.

—BIBLE (ECCLESIASTES 1:2)

No sickness worse than imagining thyself to be perfect can afflict thy soul.

—RUMI

The ugliest vanity is the vanity of one who boasts of his humility.

—JACOB KLATZKIN

VIOLENCE

We should never forget that everything Adolf Hitler did in Germany was "legal" and everything the Hungarian freedom fighters did in Hungary was "illegal."

—MARTIN LUTHER KING, JR.

VISION

Some people look at things as they are, and say, Why? I look at things as they might be, and say, Why not?

—GEORGE BERNARD SHAW

According to the theory of aerodynamics, and as may be readily demonstrated through laboratory tests, the bumblebee is unable to fly. The size, weight and shape of its body in relation to the total wing spread, make flying impossible. But the bumblebee, being ignorant of these profound scientific truths, goes ahead and flies anyway—and manages to make a little honey as well.

—ANONYMOUS

Methinks we have hugely mistaken this matter of Life and Death. Methinks that what they call my shadow here on earth is my true substance. Methinks that in looking at things spiritual, we are too much like oysters observing the sun through the water, and thinking that thick water the thinnest of air.

—HERMAN MELVILLE

The fact of the religious vision, and its history of persistent expansion, is our one ground for optimism. Apart from it, human life is just a flash of occasional enjoyments lighting up a mass of pain and misery, a bagatelle of transient experience.

—ALFRED NORTH WHITEHEAD

The Vision of God is the greatest happiness to which one can attain. Our imprisonment in bodies of clay and water and entanglement in the things of sense constitute a veil which hides the Vision of God from us.

—AL-GHAZZALI

The astonishing thing about the human being is not so much his intellect and bodily structure, profoundly mysterious as they are. The astonishing and least comprehensible thing about him is his range of vision; his gaze into the infinite distance; his lonely passion for ideas and ideals.

—W. MacNEILLE DIXON

Vision looks inward and becomes duty. Vision looks outward and becomes aspiration. Vision looks upward and becomes faith.

—RABBI STEPHEN S. WISE

Some may be color-blind, but others see the bright hues of sunrise. Some may have no religious sense, but others live and move and have their being in the transcendent glory of God.

—WILLIAM CECIL DAMPIER

The prophet and the martyr do not see the hooting throng. Their eyes are fixed on the eternities.

—BENJAMIN N. CARDOZO

You can put two humans to sleep in the same bed, but you can't make them dream the same dream.

—CHINESE PROVERB

I have lived in the pursuit of a vision, both personal and social. Personal: to care for what is noble, for what is beautiful, for what is gentle; to allow moments of insight to give wisdom at more mundane times. Social: to see in imagination the society that is to be created, where individuals grow freely, and where hate and greed and envy die because there is nothing to nourish them.

—BERTRAND RUSSELL

No one regards what is before our feet; we all gaze at the stars.

—QUINTUS ENNIUS

VOLUNTEERISM

When an American asks for the cooperation of his fellow citizens, it is seldom refused; and I have often seen it afforded spontaneously and with great good will.

—ALEXIS DE TOCQUEVILLE

The highest office in a democracy is the office of citizen.

—JUSTICE LOUIS D. BRANDEIS

God has predestined ... great things from our race; and great things we feel in our souls.... We are the pioneers of the world ... sent on through the wilderness of untried things to break a new path in the New World that is ours.... And let us remember that, with ourselves, almost for the first time in history, national selfishness is unbounded philanthropy.

—HERMAN MELVILLE

WAR

Let not the atom bomb
Be the final sequel
In which all people
Are cremated equal.

—ANONYMOUS

But the word of the Lord came to me, saying: You have shed blood abundantly, and have made great wars; you shall not build a house to My name, because you have shed much blood upon the earth in My sight.

—BIBLE (I CHRONICLES 22:8)

The price of peace can never reach such dimensions as to equal the smallest fraction of war's deadly cost.

—ABBA EBAN

Attitudes toward war have been changing rapidly as the fundamental nature of war changed. Since World War II, war is no longer a contest between trained armies; it is the desolation of civilian populations. In World War I, approximately 15% of the casualties were civilian; in World War II, over 50%; in the Vietnam War, close to 90%. One can only imagine what the figure would be for a nuclear war. Serving one's country in war, which as recently as World War I was regarded as "glorious" and "heroic," has so lost its glamour that the veterans of Vietnam complain about being treated like pariahs. It is difficult to be enthusiastic about being a participant in the mass slaughter of innocent victims.

We have before us the example of progressive withdrawal of legitimacy from various forms of slavery, oppression, torture, and murder that were formerly condoned or even encouraged. Delegitimating war and preparation for war, seeking national and global security through other means, is the next logical step in the sequence.

—*WILLIS HARMAN*

All war is civil war and all killing is fratricide.

—*ADLAI STEVENSON*

> I beheld the earth,
> And, lo, it was waste and void;
> And the heavens, and they had no light.
> I beheld the mountains, and, lo, they trembled,
> And all the hills moved to and fro.
> I beheld, and, lo, there was no one,
> And all the birds of the heavens were fled.
> I beheld, and, lo, the fruitful field was a wilderness,
> And all the cities thereof were broken down
> At the presence of the Lord,
> And before God's fierce anger.

—*BIBLE (JEREMIAH 4:23-26)*

The fourth world war will be fought with sticks and stones, for if we continue heading in the direction we are heading, we shall revert to pre-historic times, to the days of the jungle.

—*ALBERT EINSTEIN*

In the next war, there will be no winners. The losers will be destroyed, and the winners will be committing suicide.

—*DWIGHT D. EISENHOWER*

And for our country, 'tis a bliss to die.

—HOMER

How sweet and how honorable it is to give one's life for one's country!

—HORACE

The spokesmen of each side say they know that war is obsolete as a means of any policy save mutual annihilation, yet they search for peace by military means and in doing so, they succeed in accumulating ever new perils. Moreover, they have obscured this fact by their dogmatic adherence to violence as the only way of doing away with violence.

—C. WRIGHT MILLS

A single death is a tragedy. A million deaths are a statistic.

—JOSEPH STALIN

Let necessity, and not your will, slay the enemy who fights against you.

—ST. AUGUSTINE

War some day will be abolished by the will of man. This assertion does not in any way invalidate the truth that war is fundamentally caused by impersonal, political, economic and social forces. But it is the destiny of man to master and control such force, even as it is his destiny to harness rivers, chain the lightning and ride the storm. It is human will, operating under social forces, that has abolished slavery, infanticide, dueling, and a score of other social enormities. Why should it not do the same for war?

—JOHN HAYNES HOLMES

There never was a good war or a bad peace.

—BENJAMIN FRANKLIN

O war! Thou son of Hell!

—SHAKESPEARE

As never before, the essence of war is fire, famine and pestilence. They contribute to its outbreak; they are among its weapons; they become its consequences.... After my experience, I have come to hate war. War settles nothing.

—DWIGHT D. EISENHOWER

War is death's feast.

—GEORGE HERBERT

What we now need to discover in the social realm is the moral equivalent of war: something heroic that will speak to men as universally as war does, and yet will be compatible with their spiritual selves as war has proved itself to be incompatible.

—WILLIAM JAMES

Oh, Lord Our Father, our young patriots, idols of our hearts, go forth to battle. Be Thou near them! With them—in spirit—we also go from the sweet peace of our beloved firesides to smite the foe.

Oh, Lord our God, help us to tear their soldiers to bloody shreds with our shells; help us cover their smiling fields with the pale forms of their patriot dead; help us to drown the thunder of the guns with the wounded, writhing in pain; help us to lay waste their humble homes with the hurricane of fire; help us to wring the hearts of their unoffending widows with unavailing grief; help us to turn them out roofless with their little children to wander unfriended over wastes of their desolated land in rags and hunger and thirst, sport of the sun-flames of summer and the icy winds of winter, broken in spirit, worn with travail, imploring Thee for the refuge of the grave and denied it—for our sakes, who adore Thee. Lord, blast their hopes, blight their lives, protract their bitter pilgrimage, make heavy their steps, water their way with tears, stain the white snow with the blood of their wounded feet! We ask of One who is the spirit of Love and Who is the ever-faithful refuge and friend of all that are sore beset, and seek His aid with humble and contrite hearts. Grant our prayer, Oh Lord, and thine shall be the praise and honor and glory, now and forever, Amen.

—MARK TWAIN

War must be for the sake of peace, business for the sake of leisure, the necessary and the utilitarian for noble things.

—ARISTOTLE

Every gun that is made, every warship launched, every rocket fired signifies a theft from those who hunger and are not fed, those who are cold and not clothed. This world in arms is not spending money alone. It is spending the sweat of its laborers, the genius of its scientists, the hope of its children.

—DWIGHT EISENHOWER

War begins where reason ends.

—FREDERICK DOUGLASS

Violence seldom accomplishes permanent and desired results. Herein lies the futility of war.

—A. PHILIP RANDOLPH

War with all its glorification of brute force is essentially a degrading thing. It demoralizes those who are trained for it. It brutalizes men of naturally gentle character. It outrages every beautiful canon of morality. Its path of glory is foul with the passions of lust, and red with the blood of murder.

—GANDHI

The cause of war is the preparation for war.

—W.E.B. DU BOIS

War knows no law, except that of might.

—GANDHI

War is a poor chisel to carve out tomorrows.

—MARTIN LUTHER KING, JR.

WILL

I know of no more encouraging fact than the unquestionable ability of man to elevate his life by conscious endeavor.

—HENRY DAVID THOREAU

Will ... is the foundation of all being; it is part and parcel of every creature, and the permanent element in everything.

—ARTHUR SCHOPENHAUER

In God's will lies our peace.

—DANTE

WISDOM

If you have wisdom, what do you lack?
And if you lack wisdom, what do you have?

—MIDRASH

By thoughtfulness, by restraint and self-control, the wise man may make for himself an island which no flood can overwhelm.

—DHAMMAPADA

The wise man could ask no more of Fate
Than to be simple, modest, manly, true,
Safe from the Many, honored by the Few;
To count as naught in the World, or Church, or State;
But inwardly in secret to be great.

—JAMES RUSSELL LOWELL

Wisdom is to the soul what health is to the body.

—LA ROCHEFOUCAULD

The virtue of wisdom more than anything else contains a divine element which always remains.

—PLATO

A knife of the keenest steel requires a whetstone and the wisest person needs advice.

—ZOROASTER

Knowledge is proud that he has learn'd so much;
Wisdom is humble that he knows no more.

—COWPER

The greatest good is wisdom.

—ST. AUGUSTINE

WOMEN

Woman was not taken from man's head to be ruled by him, nor from his feet to be trampled upon by him, but from his side to walk beside him, under his arm to be protected by him, and from his heart to be loved by him.

—MIDRASH

I would have woman lay aside all thought, such as she habitually cherishes, of being taught and led by men. I would have her free from compromise, from complaisance, from helplessness, because I would have her good enough and strong enough to love one and all beings, from the fullness, not the poverty of being.

—MARGARET FULLER

I long to hear that you have declared an independency. And, by the way, in the new code of laws which I suppose it will be necessary for you to make, I desire that would remember the ladies and be more generous to them than your ancestors. Do not put such unlimited powers into the hands of the husbands. Remember, all men would be tyrants if they could. If particular care and attention is not paid to the ladies, we are determined to foment a rebellion, and will not hold ourselves bound by any laws in which we have no voice or representation.

—*ABIGAIL ADAMS*

A hundred men can build an encampment, but it takes a woman to make a home.

—*CHINESE PROVERB*

Is it not women that ruin or uphold families, that regulate all the details of domestic life, and that decide, consequently, what touches most closely the whole human race?

—*FRANÇOIS FÉNELON*

There is no worse evil than a bad woman; and nothing has ever been produced better than a good one.

—*EURIPIDES*

Without woman the beginning of our life would be helpless, the middle without pleasure, and the end void of consolation.

—*VICTOR DE JOUY*

WORDS

Watch your thoughts: they become words.
Watch your words: they become actions.
Watch your actions: they become habits.
Watch your habits: they become character.
Watch your character: it becomes your destiny.

—*ANONYMOUS*

Without words poetry could not exist.
Neither could war.

—ANONYMOUS

To the man of our age, nothing is as familiar and nothing as trite as words. Of all things, they are the cheapest, most abused, and least regarded.... We all live in them, feel in them, think in them, but, failing to uphold their independent dignity, to respect their power and weight, they turn, elusive, a mouthful of dust.... There can be no prayer without a sense for the dignity of words, a degree of deference to what they stand for....

—RABBI ABRAHAM JOSHUA HESCHEL

WORK

The harder I work the luckier I get.

—ARNOLD PALMER

A man lamented to his rabbi: I am frustrated that my work leaves me no time for study or prayer. The rabbi replied: Perhaps your work is more pleasing to God than study or prayer.

—HASIDIC

When you work you are a flute through whose heart the whispering of the hours turns to music. To love life through labor is to be intimate with life's inmost secret. All work is empty save when there is love, for work is love made visible.

—KAHLIL GIBRAN

It's not work unless you'd rather be doing something else.

—RABBI SIDNEY GREENBERG

Your vocation should be a vacation.

—MARK TWAIN

If you aren't fired with enthusiasm, you'll be fired with enthusiasm.

—VINCE LOMBARDI

Thinking is the hardest work there is, which is the probable reason why so few engage in it.

—HENRY FORD

Big shots are only little shots who keep shooting.

—CHRISTOPHER MORLEY

The reason why worry kills more people than work is that more people worry than work.

—ROBERT FROST

It's easier to do a job right than to explain why you didn't.

—MARTIN VAN BUREN

If there is no struggle there is no progress. Those who profess to favor freedom, and yet deprecate agitation, are men who want crops without plowing up the ground. They want rain without thunder and lightning. They want the ocean without the awful roar of its waters.

—FREDERICK DOUGLASS

WORLD-TO-COME

Because the Hebrews of the type who wrote the psalms concentrated on the trustworthiness of God and not on the gift of afterlife, they did not ask for more living after death. They pleaded with God as the giver of life to endow the meaning of their seasons with value. Seldom do they stand in the divine marketplace and bargain for a life to come, though some do haggle for more years. God as the Lord of life matters more than their ego and their survival....

Rabbi Zalman, one of the great successors to Hasidism's founder, the Baal Shem Tov, was said to have interrupted his prayers to say of the Lord: "I do not want your paradise. I do not want your coming world. I want you, and you only." This was in the spirit of his predecessor, who said, "If I love God, what need have I of a coming world?"

—MARTIN E. MARTY

WRITING

It is with a certain wonder and curiosity that I look back on what was written above. I sometimes had feeling, while writing it, of an affinity with the proverbial old lady who is supposed to have said, on one occasion, "How do I know what I think until I hear what I say?" I comfort myself with the thought that I can scarcely have been the first writer who learned what he thought only when he had looked at what he had written. But such is the case; and I find it necessary to review what I have done before offering any comments on it.

—GEORGE F. KENNAN

The writer, perhaps more than any of his fellow artists, has access to the human subconscious. His words sink deep, shaping dreams, easing the pain of loneliness, banishing incantations and omens, keeping alive the memories of the race, providing intimations of immortality, nourishing great anticipations, sharpening the instinct for justice and imparting respect for the fragility of life. These functions are essential for human evolution. Without them, civilization becomes brittle and breaks easily.

Society must be measured, therefore, not just by its display of power but by its attention to the conditions of creativity and its acceptance of human sovereignty as the highest value.

—NORMAN COUSINS

The way to be boring is to say everything.

—VOLTAIRE

Spend words as you would dollars.

—DANIEL WEBSTER

Three steps to good writing:
Clarity, clarity, clarity.

—ANATOLE FRANCE

What is written without effort is in general read without pleasure.

—DR. SAMUEL JOHNSON

I continue to create because writing is a labor of love and also an act of defiance, a way to light a candle in a gale wind....

—ALICE CHILDRESS

If I could be cloned, I'd like to be three people. One would stay at the desk writing; one would be a public writer, the one who goes around making speeches and being personable; the third would be a normal human being. A writer cannot be all these things at one time.

—ALEX HALEY

YOUTH

In youth we want to change the world.
In old age we want to change youth.

—GARTH HENRICHS

Youths have exalted notions, because they have not yet been humbled by life or learned its necessary limitations; moreover their hopeful disposition makes them think themselves equal to great things—and that means exalted notions.... All their mistakes are in the direction of doing things excessively and vehemently.... They love too much, hate too much, and the same with everything else.

—ARISTOTLE

Could I climb to the highest place in Athens, I would lift my voice and proclaim, "Fellow citizens, why do you turn and scrape every stone to gather wealth, and take so little care of your children to whom one day you must relinquish it all?"

—SOCRATES

Let your left hand push away the child, and let your right hand draw him near.

—TRACTATE SANHEDRIN, TALMUD

Our youth now loves luxury. They have bad manners and show contempt for authority. They show disrespect for their elders, because they no longer rise when elders enter the room. Children are now tyrants—they contradict their parents and tyrannize their teachers.

—SOCRATES

There is a feeling of Eternity in Youth, which makes us amends for everything. To be young is to be as one of the Immortal Gods.

—WILLIAM HAZLITT

Youth, though it may lack knowledge, is certainly not devoid of intelligence; it sees through shams with sharp and terrible eyes.

—H. L. MENCKEN

Crabbed age and youth cannot live together:
Youth is full of pleasance, age is full of care;
Youth like summer morn, age like winter weather;
Youth like summer brave, age like winter bare.

—SHAKESPEARE

Young men have a passion for regarding their elders as senile.

—HENRY ADAMS

It is as natural and as right for a young man to be imprudent and exaggerated, to live in swoops and circles, and beat about his cage like any other wild thing newly captured, as it is for old men to turn grey, or mothers to love their offspring, or heroes to die for something worthier than their lives.

—ROBERT LOUIS STEVENSON

The deepest definition of youth is life as yet untouched by tragedy.

—ALFRED NORTH WHITEHEAD

When I shall be divorced, some ten years hence,
From this poor present self which I am now;
When youth has done its tedious vain expense
Of passions that forever ebb and flow;
Shall I not joy youth's heats are left behind,
And breathe more happy in an even clime?
Ah no! for then I shall begin to find
A thousand virtues in this hated time.
Then I shall wish its agitations back,
And all its thwarting currents of desire;
Then I shall praise the heat which then I lack,
And call this hurrying fever, generous fire,
And sigh that one thing only has been lent
To youth and age in common—discontent.

—MATTHEW ARNOLD

Bliss was it in that dawn to be alive,
But to be young was very Heaven!

—*WILLIAM WORDSWORTH*

Youth is a wonderful thing. What a crime to waste it on children.

—*GEORGE BERNARD SHAW*

ZEAL

Zeal is a great ease to a malicious man, by making him believe he does God's service, whilst he is gratifying the bent of a perverse revengeful temper.

—*JOSEPH ADDISON*

I do not love a man who is zealous for nothing.

—*OLIVER GOLDSMITH*

Violent zeal for truth hath an hundred to one odds to be either petulancy, ambition, or pride.

—*JONATHAN SWIFT*

Not too much zeal!

—*TALLEYRAND*

Zeal is fit only for wise men, but is found mostly in fools.

—*THOMAS FULLER*

Zeal, not rightly directed, is pernicious; for as it makes a good cause better, so it makes a bad cause worse.

—*OLD FARMER'S ALMANAC, 1860*

If we have learned anything at all in the two thousand years of Christian history, we should have learned that few things are more dangerous than zeal without knowledge.

—*CHARLES W. KEGLEY*

About Dov Peretz Elkins

Dov Peretz Elkins was born in Philadelphia. He is a graduate of Gratz College for Hebrew Teachers, received his BA in literature from Temple University, and his M.H.L. and rabbinic ordination from the Jewish Theological Seminary. He received his doctorate in counseling and humanistic education in 1976 at Colgate Rochester Divinity School. In 1989 he was given an honorary Doctor of Divinity degree for distinguished rabbinic service by his alma mater, the Jewish Theological Seminary.

After 2 years as military chaplain at Fort Gordon, Georgia, Rabbi Elkins became Associate Rabbi of Har Zion Temple of Philadelphia. From 1970 to 1972, he served as spiritual leader of the Jacksonville Jewish Center in Florida. From 1972 to 1976, he occupied the pulpit of Temple Beth El, Rochester, New York, one of America's largest and most prestigious congregations. From 1976 to 1985, he maintained a private practice in Pastoral Counseling, and was consultant to synagogues and many national Jewish and non-Jewish organizations, as well as in the corporate world, such as Xerox, Kodak, IBM, etc.

From 1985 to 1987, Rabbi Elkins was spiritual leader at Beth El Temple, Norfolk, Virginia. From 1987-1992, he was Senior Rabbi at The Park Synagogue, Cleveland, Ohio, and now is Rabbi at The Jewish Center, Princeton, NJ.

A nationally known lecturer, educator, workshop leader, human relations trainer, organizational consultant, author, and book critic, he has written widely for the Jewish and general press, including such journals as *Reader's Digest, New Woman, The Christian Century, Judaism, Hadassah Magazine, Religious Education, Conservative Judaism, The Reconstructionist*, and many others. He is a regular book reviewer for several Anglo-Jewish weeklies throughout the country.

Dr. Elkins is the author of over thirty books, including *Humanizing Jewish Life: Judaism and the Human Potential Movement*, and a series of handbooks for Jewish group leaders called *Series in Experiential Education (S.E.E.)*. These include, to date, *Clarifying Jewish Values, Jewish Consciousness Raising, Experiential Programs for Jewish Groups, Loving My Jewishness*, and *Prescription For A Long and Happy Life: Age-Old Wisdom for the New Age* (1993). He has published a two-volume collection of inspirational readings on the High Holidays, *Moments of Transcendence* (Jason Aronson, 1992), a softcover re-issue of *Shepherd of Jerusalem: A Biography of Rabbi Abraham, Isaac Kook* (Jason Aronson, 1995), a calligraphed collection of Hasidic sayings, *Melodies From My Father's House—Hasidic Wisdom For the Heart and Soul,* and an innovative handbook called *Jewish Guided Imagery—A How-To Book For Rabbis, Educators, and Group Leaders* (Growth Associates, 1996).

Other recent books include *Hasidic Wisdom: Sayings of the Jewish Masters,* compiled by Simcha Raz, translated by Dov Peretz Elkins and Jonathan Elkins (Jason Aronson, 1997), and *A Shabbat Reader: The Universe of Cosmic Joy* (UAHC Press, 1998). In 1999 he published *Forty Days of Transformation: Daily Reflections of Spiritual Growth from Rosh Hodesh Elul to Yom Kippur,* and *Meditations for the Days of Awe.* In October, 2000 his first children's book was published, *Seven Delightful Stories for Every Day* (Pitspopany Press).

His latest book is *Chicken Soup For The Jewish Soul*®, co-edited with Jack Canfield and Mark Victor Hansen (Health Communications, September, 2001). This book was on the *NY Times* best-seller list two weeks after publication, and has already been acclaimed as one of the best in the 50-volume *Chicken Soup* series.

Dr. Elkins has been trained in group dynamics, human development, and humanistic education at leading growth centers throughout North America, including Esalen Institute, at Big Sur, California, NTL (National Training Labs) at Bethel, Maine, and the Gestalt Institute of Cleveland. He is a certified instructor of Parent Effectiveness Training (P.E.T.) and Teacher Effectiveness Training (T.E.T.).

Dov Peretz Elkins is a member of the Rabbinical Assembly, the Council for Jewish Education, the Jewish Educators Assembly, the Coalition for the Advancement of Jewish Education (CAJE), the Conference of Jewish Communal Service, and the Association for Humanistic Psychology. He was honored by Gratz College in 1996 with the "Distinguished Alumnus Award."

Rabbi Elkins and his wife, Maxine reside in Princeton, New Jersey. Their children and grandchildren live in Los Angeles, Tel Aviv, Cleveland, and Philadelphia.

Personal favorite quotes and notes

Personal favorite quotes and notes

<u>Personal favorite quotes and notes</u>

Personal favorite quotes and notes

Personal favorite quotes and notes

Personal favorite quotes and notes

Personal favorite quotes and notes

COMMENTS ON

JEWISH GUIDED IMAGERY:
A HOW-TO BOOK FOR RABBIS, EDUCATORS AND GROUP LEADERS
Rabbi Dov Peretz Elkins

Dov Peretz Elkins is one of the most spiritual people I know. His creative work in education and nourishing human beings is known throughout the world. He has made another useful contribution through this book. His work continues to be chicken soup for my soul."

—Jack Canfield,
Co-author, *Chicken Soup For the Soul*

Rabbi Elkins has written another creative, useful, and user-friendly book that will help teachers, groups workers and Rabbis enrich their teaching of Jewish subject matter.

—Audrey Friedman Marcus,
Executive Vice-President, A.R.E. Publishing, Inc.

A most creative application of guided imagery techniques to Jewish education. If my Hebrew school teachers had used these tools to involve me personally and emotionally in my Jewish heritage, I would not have had to reach my thirties before coming to accept and prize my Jewishness. These activities are interesting, enjoyable, practical and useful with young people and adults of all ages.

—Howard Kirschenbaum,
co-author, *Values Clarification*

What a treat! Dov Elkins has compiled a rich collection of guided imagery scripts, with invaluable suggestions for implementation.

—Dr. Mel Silberman,
Professor of Organizational Development, Temple University,
and author of *Active Learning*

Imagining, visualization, and meditation have been part of Jewish prayer and life for the longest time. In the Talmud we read that the early hasidim would spend an hour before prayer in order to direct their minds to God. In his book on guided imagery, Dov Peretz Elkins helps the Jewish community recapture this grand tradition and practice. This guidebook will assist all who dare experience a new way of Jewish growth and development.

—Rabbi Samuel K. Joseph, Ph.D.,
Professor of Jewish Education, Hebrew Union College
Jewish Institute of Religion

Dr. Elkins has masterfully compiled a crystal clear, step-by-step introduction to the much misunderstood technique of guided imagery, which will undoubtedly make an invaluable contribution to the field. As a frequent user of this educational and personal growth approach, I appreciate the care, understanding and skill that went into its preparation.

—Murray Wilkow,
Ed.D., Adjunct Professor of Counselor Education, Hofstra University

WHAT PEOPLE ARE SAYING ABOUT

The *New York Times* bestseller
Chicken Soup for the Jewish Soul™
Edited by
Jack Canfield, Mark Victor Hansen
and Rabbi Dov Peretz Elkins

My family reads these stories out loud to each other. We laugh. We cry. We hug. A family that eats chicken soup together will remain culinary Jews. A family that reads *Chicken Soup* together will remain part of an enduring tradition that has transformed the world with its humor, passion and generosity of spirit.

—Alan M. Dershowitz,
Felix Frankfurter Professor of Law, Harvard Law School, and author,
Supreme Injustice:How the High Court Hijacked Election 2000

The people who made chicken soup a synonym for healing love now have a heartwarming book of their own. Read it and kvell!

—Rabbi Harold Kushner,
author, *Living A Life That Matters*

I defy anyone to read this book and not be moved to tears, several times. This is a stunning collection of stories that will make you want to be a blessing in the lives of all the people you encounter. What more could one ask for, a book that actually makes one want to be a better person?

—Rabbi Joseph Telushkin,
author, The Book of Jewish Values: A Day-by-Day Guide to Ethical Living

If Jewish humor and wisdom need nourishing, *Chicken Soup for the Jewish Soul* will feed it. It is the traditional food for the soul and for the mind, whether served in a bowl or in a book.

—Bonnie Lipton,
National President, Hadassah, Women's Zionist Organization of America

Chicken Soup for the Jewish Soul serves wisdom for and from the ages, informed by horror and by humor, by lessons of the battlefield and of the kitchen table. It will nourish anyone's faith.

—U.S. Senator Joseph R. Biden, Jr.

Wisdom, intelligence and resourcefulness, but above all, a particular sort of gentle humor, have enabled the Jewish people to survive thousands of years of adversity. These are wonderful stories, reflecting joy and sorrow and warmth, and the authors have compiled them with great sensitivity, affection and thoughtfulness.

—Ronald S. Lauder,
Chairman, Conference of Presidents of Major American Jewish Organizations

This serving of Jewish soul food is a collection of poignant and touching anecdotes, true life accounts of *hashgacha pratit*—God's intervention in one's personal history. The editors are to be congratulated for their efforts in amassing these delicious morsels for the mind, tidbits of Jewish life.

—Limor Livnat,
Minister of Education, The State of Israel

When the world's miseries and sheer ugliness threaten to overwhelm—as they too often do—our best defense is to recall the kindness of which we are capable. This lovely book, a collection of examples of humanity and humaneness at their most basic levels, is a valuable—and inspiring— refutation to those who think our condition hopeless. One story a day— especially on a gray day—and your spirit will be lifted.

—Leonard Fein,
Founder, "Mazon: A Jewish Response to Hunger," author, *Against the Dying of the Light*

This book is a masterpiece. I laughed and cried and wished for more. May it warm the hearts of many and serve as a living legacy for our people. Were my grown sons still small, I would read them a story from this precious book every night, over and over again. It would be a complete education in life—its joys and sorrows—and how an unseen hand with a great sense of humor works magic in our lives through our love of one another.

—Joan Borysenko,
author, *Inner Peace for Busy People*

I had never thought of that Greco-Roman term of "soul" as being "Jewish," but *Chicken Soup for the Jewish Soul* gives it the materiality it needs! These are great stories for people of every culture.

—The Reverend Dr. Ross H. Trower,
Former Chief of Chaplains, U.S. Navy (ret.)

These personal stories from every corner of the world inspire us with their tales of the small, everyday miracles that have nourished Jews since time immemorial. They speak to the nobility of Jewish ethics, the Jewish passion for life, and the universal dignity of the human soul.

—Rabbi Irving Greenberg,
President of Jewish Life Network, author of *The Jewish Way* (Summit Books, 1988) and *Living in the Image of God* (Jason Aronson, 1998).

With all the turmoil and violence in contemporary culture, here is a book that provides rest and nourishment for our souls.

—Susannah Heschel,
Eli Black Professor of Jewish Studies, Dartmouth College

Chicken Soup for the Jewish Soul not only nourishes and warms the soul, as a good bowl of chicken soup should (not too much salt please), but I found that it both inspired me and filled me with pride for the legacy given me by my fellow Jews.

—Rudy Boschwitz,
United States Senator,1978-1991

The Jewish Soul has nourished us Christians for 2000 years. Now we get the chicken soup version. It is life-giving, edifying and graceful. All people will be enriched by these words that so beautifully capture the essence and the joy of what it means to be a Jew.

—Bishop John Shelby Spong,
author, *Liberating the Gospel: Reading the Bible with Jewish Eyes*

Chicken Soup for the Jewish Soul covers so many aspects of the Jewish experience, it touches us deeply. What a wonderful read for Jew and non-Jew alike.

—Abraham H. Foxman,
National Director, Anti-Defamation League

A heart-warming and edifying work; guaranteed to make you feel better.

—Gideon Patt,
President and CEO, Israel Bonds; former Minister of Science and Minister
of Tourism, State of Israel

These stories are like a steaming bowl of chicken soup on a cold, rainy
day—they make you feel warm inside and you want to come back for
more!

—Linda Gradstein,
NPR Correspondent in Jerusalem

Chicken Soup for the Jewish Soul is a book that you need to own. In the
wisely chosen stories we meet no less than ourselves at our best. It will
inspire, excite and transform you. What more can a person ask for?

—Rabbi Marc Gafni,
author, *Soul Prints*

A great collection. Inspiring tales, uplifting stories and great jokes. They
make us cry, they make us laugh. And if laughter is the best medicine,
this book is a cure for the common cold. It's truly delightful.

—Bernie Marcus,
Chairman of the Board, The Home Depot

Chicken Soup for the Jewish Soul offers a wellspring of inspiration to
help us celebrate in our moments of joy and fortify us in our moments of
deep despair. There are moments when the experiences of the stories are
as powerful as a prayer, there are times that it feels as though heaven
and earth have met and are living together on the same plane, and there
are moments when we feel we have been enveloped by the angels and
we are dancing with them, one word to the next, across the pages and
into the soul and from every page into every soul there is healing.

—Debbie Friedman,
composer, singer

ORDER FORM

GROWTH ASSOCIATES PUBLISHERS
212 STUART ROAD EAST
PRINCETON, NJ 08540
(609) 497-7375 • Fax (609) 497-0325
E-mail: GrowthAssociates@earthlink.net • web site: www.DPElkins.com

PLEASE PRINT OR TYPE

NAME _____ DATE _____

ADDRESS _____

_____

CITY _____ STATE _____ ZIP _____

E-MAIL _____ PHONE _____

Qty.	Titles Available	Cost	Total
	Spiritual Awakenings: Illuminations on Shabbat and the Holidays, Rabbi Yehoshua Rubin ISBN 965-7108-41-1	$22	
	Torah Guidelines for Living Like a Mensch, Rabbi Sidney Greenberg ISBN 0-918834-22-8	$24	
	A Treasury of Stories and Wisdom for Living at our Best, Rabbi Sidney Greenberg ISBN 0-918834-48-1	$30	
	EDUCATIONAL MATERIALS BY DR. DOV PERETZ ELKINS		
	New York Times Bestseller Chicken Soup for the Jewish Soul: 101 Stories to Open the Heart and Rekindle the Spirit Trade paper ISBN 1-55874-898-9 Hardcover ISBN 1-55874-899-7	$12.95 $24	
	Moments of the Spirit: Quotations to Inspire, Inform and Involve **NEW** ISBN 0-918834-24-4	$30	
	Seven Delightful Stories for Every Day (For ages 3 to 6) Illustrated by Zely Smekhov Hardcover ISBN 1-930143-02-8 Paper ISBN 1-930143-03-6	$16.95 $ 9.95	
	A Shabbat Reader: Universe of Cosmic Joy ISBN 0-8074-0631-7	$15	
	Hasidic Wisdom: Sayings From the Jewish Sages by Simcha Raz ISBN 0-7657-9972-3	$35	
	Jewish Guided Imagery: A How-To Book for Rabbis, Educators and Group Leaders ISBN 0-918834-16-3	$35	
	New and Old Prayers and Readings for the High Holidays, Shabbat & Festive Occasions (Inquire about quantity prices for congregational use.) ISBN 0-918834-21-X	$12	
	Forty Days of Transformation: Daily Reflections of Teshuvah for Spiritual Growth — From Rosh Hodesh Elul to Yom Kippur ISBN 0-918834-201-1	$15	
	Meditations for the Days of Awe: Reflections, Guided Imagery and Other Creative Exercises to Enrich Your Spiritual Life ISBN 0-918834-19-8	$20	
	Moments of Transcendence: Inspirational Readings for Rosh Hashanah Hardcover ISBN 0-87668-506-8	$40	
	Moments of Transcendence: Inspirational Readings for Yom Kippur Hardcover ISBN 0-87668-504	$40	
	Moments of Transcendence: 1992, 1993, 1994, 1995, 1996, 1997 Annual Supplements, each (CIRCLE THE YEAR/S YOU WANT TO ORDER.)	$20	
	Moments of Transcendence: 1998, 1999, 2000, 2001, 2002, 2003 Annual Supplements, each	$30	
	Computer disk and Annual Supplement $50 each set. (CIRCLE THE YEAR/S YOU WANT TO ORDER.)	$50	
	Melodies From My Father's House: Hasidic Wisdom for the Heart and Soul ISBN 0-918834-15-5	$12	
	Shepherd of Jerusalem: A Biography of Rabbi Abraham Isaac Kook ISBN 1-56821-597-5	$20	
	Prescription for a Long and Happy Life: Age-Old Wisdom for the New Age ISBN 0-918834-14-7	$20	

OVER

EDUCATIONAL MATERIALS BY DR. DOV PERETZ ELKINS (cont'd.)

Qty.	Titles Available	Cost	Total
	My Seventy-Two Friends: Encounters With Refuseniks In the USSR ISBN 0-918834-11-2	$10	
	God's Warriors: Dramatic Adventures of Rabbis In Uniform	$10	
	Rejoice With Jerusalem: Prayers, Readings and Songs for Israel Observances	$ 6	
	Organization Development for Jewish Institutions	$7.50	
	A Treasury of Israel and Zionism: A Source Book for Speakers, Writers and Teachers ISBN 0-918834-17-1 Includes computer disk of entire text.	$50	
	Four Questions On the Weekly Sidrah — formatted for distribution to congregations and schools	$45	
	Sidrah Sparks and Questions for Discussion — formatted for distribution to congregations and schools	$45	
	More Sidrah Sparks and Questions for Discussion — formatted for distribution to congregations and schools	$45	
	Loving My Jewishness: Jewish Self-Pride and Self-Esteem ISBN 0-918834-04-X	$10	
	Experiential Programs for Jewish Groups: Thirty Full-Length Programs ISBN 0-918834-05-8	$10	
	Clarifying Jewish Values: Values Clarification Strategies for Jewish Groups ISBN 0-918834-02-3	$10	
	Jewish Consciousness Raising: A Handbook of 50 Experiential Exercises ISBN 0-918834-03-1	$10	
	The Ideal Jew: Values Clarification Program	$10	
	Why Did Susan Cohen Desert Judaism? A Values Clarification Program On Intermarriage and Assimilation	$10	
	Teaching People To Love Themselves: A Leader's Handbook of Theory and Technique for Self-Esteem Training ISBN 0-918834-06-6	$22	
	Self-Concept Sourcebook — Ideas and Activities for Building Self-Esteem ISBN 0-918834-09-0	$19	
	Glad To Be Me: Building Self-Esteem In Yourself and Others ISBN 0-918834-10-4	$12	
	Twelve Pathways To Feeling Better About Yourself ISBN 0-918834-08-2	$7.50	

SHIPPING & HANDLING:
   USA: 15% of order (10% of orders over $100. 5% for orders over $200.)
   Canada: 20% of order
   Foreign: 30% of order

Subtotal:_____
Shipping & Handling:_____
TOTAL:_____

All orders must be prepaid by credit card or check. _Minimum S&H on all orders: $3_

❑ My check is enclosed.
   Please make checks payable to Dov Peretz Elkins (US Funds only).

❑ Charge my: ❑ VISA   ❑ MasterCard

Account Number: Expiration Date:_____

Name on card: _____

Signature:_____

___ Check here if interested in inviting Dr. Elkins to give lectures, workshops,
     retreats, and/or other training events for group, board, staff or faculty, etc.